Poetics of Listening

Poetics of Listening

Inner Life, Social Transformation, Planetary Practices

Brandon LaBelle

BLOOMSBURY ACADEMIC
NEW YORK • LONDON • OXFORD • NEW DELHI • SYDNEY

BLOOMSBURY ACADEMIC
Bloomsbury Publishing Inc
1385 Broadway, New York, NY 10018, USA
50 Bedford Square, London, WC1B 3DP, UK
29 Earlsfort Terrace, Dublin 2, Ireland

BLOOMSBURY, BLOOMSBURY ACADEMIC and the Diana logo are trademarks of
Bloomsbury Publishing Plc

First published in the United States of America 2025

Copyright © Brandon LaBelle, 2025

For legal purposes the Acknowledgments on pp. ix–x constitute an extension
of this copyright page.

Cover design by fliegende Teilchen, Berlin and Louise Dugdale

Cover photo: Hana Lee Erdman, performing as part of Monument to
the Wild Imagination, 2014, a project by Brandon LaBelle (originally developed
for Part of the Game, ngbk, Berlin, curated by Berit Fischer). Photo: Brandon LaBelle.

All rights reserved. No part of this publication may be reproduced or transmitted
in any form or by any means, electronic or mechanical, including photocopying,
recording, or any information storage or retrieval system, without prior
permission in writing from the publishers.

Bloomsbury Publishing Inc does not have any control over, or responsibility for, any
third-party websites referred to or in this book. All internet addresses given in this
book were correct at the time of going to press. The author and publisher regret any
inconvenience caused if addresses have changed or sites have ceased to exist, but can
accept no responsibility for any such changes.

A catalog record for this book is available from the Library of Congress

ISBN: HB: 979-8-7651-2580-9
PB: 979-8-7651-2581-6
ePDF: 979-8-7651-2583-0
eBook: 979-8-7651-2582-3

Typeset by Newgen KnowledgeWorks Pvt. Ltd., Chennai, India

To find out more about our authors and books visit www.bloomsbury.com
and sign up for our newsletters.

for steve roden, a friend to listening
& katy marsh, sister of the stars

Contents

Acknowledgments	ix
Note on Text	xi

Introduction: An Apprentice to Listening		1
1	Listening-into: Inner Life, Consciousness-Raising, and the Care of the Self	15
2	Listening-toward: Recognition, Thirdness, and Compassionate Action	51
3	Listening-with: Sympathy, Bodily Life, and Healing Justice	91
4	Listening-against: Power, Negative Method, and the Diplomatic Arts	129
5	Listening-across: Ecological Thinking, Biopoetics, and Planetary Practices	169
Postface: The Will to Listen		209

Bibliography	213
Index	221

So many stars are twinkling above me that I can hear them. I listen to their hum, countless voices whispering in my ear. I can imagine what they're saying to me. I'm carrying the whole universe on my shoulders. We all do, all of us.

—Nona Fernández, Voyager

In my experience, healing happens when a place of trauma or pain is given full attention, really listened to.

—adrienne maree brown, Emergent Strategy

Acknowledgments

Poetics of Listening has been greatly influenced by the experiences I've had in directing The Listening Biennial and related Listening Academy, which were launched in 2021. In particular, The Listening Academy has provided an extremely dynamic framework through which diverse ideas and practices related to listening have been encountered and explored. As an educational, learning initiative, the Academy takes place in different cities, inviting participants and contributors to share practices and knowledges, and to engage in an extended co-learning process. I am extremely thankful for all the shared conversations, experimental testings, participatory offerings, collective listenings and speculative imaginings, as well as new friendships, that have emerged across the different Academy sessions, all of which has expanded my own thinking and approach to listening. In particular, I want to extend my warmest thanks to Lucia Farinati, Anastasia (A) Khodyreva, Sara Hamdy, Luísa Santos, Margarida Mendes, Alecia Neo, Jill J. Tan, Giuliano Obici, Camila Proto, Anna Papaeti, Budhaditya Chattopadhyay, Yang Yeung, Katía Truijen, Anna Orlikowska, Thiago Granato, Miriam Jakob and Lisa Densem, Nicole Michalla, Lukas Lund, Arendse Krabbe, Carla J. Maier, Verica Kovacevska, Danijela and Andreja Dugandžić, Lala Raščić, Golnoosh Heshmati, Giada Dalla Bontà, and Suvani Suri for their incredible support in helping to realize The Listening Academy over the years, keeping it grounded in experimentation and generosity. These have been deeply edifying as well as personally enriching experiences and collaborations. With that in mind, I want to also thank all the contributors and participants whose support, curiosity, expertise, and warmth can be felt as currents throughout *Poetics of Listening*. Many times I have been moved by the spirit of care and conviviality filling the days spent together immersed in a shared listening journey.

I want to also express my gratitude to Víctor Aguado Machuca and Ramón del Buey Canas, as well as Alberto García Aznar and María del Buey Canas, from la Asociación de Música Electroacústica y Arte Sonoro de España, Madrid, for their collaborative engagement over the recent years. Through our research into party studies, I've grown to understand more fully the value of festivity. Also, I'm grateful for the opportunities I've had to present my research regularly at the Rewire Festival taking place in The Hague. Thanks to the ongoing support and warmth extended by Katía Truijen, these annual presentations have afforded an important time and space for sharing ideas and testing out emerging perspectives. I would also like to thank Piersandra Di Matteo, a friend and colleague whose support over the years I'm truly grateful for, and which has contributed to shaping these pages. I'm also grateful for the opportunities to work with Dayang Yraola, Luisa Santos, Lucia Udvardyova, Florencia Curci, Hardi Kurda, Rayya Badran, Guely Morato, and Alexandre St-Onge, whose deeply committed work has contributed greatly to the activities of The Listening Biennial. Finally, working with Budhaditya Chattopadhyay, Yang Yeung, and Israel Martínez as collaborators on The Listening Biennial has been an ongoing source of nourishment, keeping me connected to the diversity of listening experiences and issues, not to mention the importance of auditory thinking: my deepest thanks.

And extending across and under all these and other conversations, collaborations, and activities is the more personal, intimate support given by family, and especially by A. le Fort, whose love and care fill me. This also contains, as deep threads of memory, those first friendships that taught me of the poetics of listening—and which I often return to, with their music and long nights, their lonely walks and enthusiastic loves, I'm eternally under your tender influence.

Note on Text

Throughout *Poetics of Listening* I have incorporated a loose structure of breaks. Marked by a graphic symbol, the breaks are invitations to pause, to look up from the page, or even to put the book down, letting the mind wander or attend to other things. They are there to suggest a listening approach, where breaks in the text may complement the ongoingness of language and voice with their silences. Throughout my process I have also found in writing a form of listening, not only in terms of following the unfolding of thoughts and ideas, but also recognizing the book itself as a holding environment, a listening space. Books are such special objects—they are deeply quiet and yet full of voice, full of rhythm and tone, melody and movement; they hold all this energy and spirit, holding while threading connections: the book is a type of ecosystem, one that awakens under listening's participation. Is not reading a form of listening as well? One that participates in the cultivation of inner life, self-awareness, and knowledge of others, and that gives to the life of imagination as well as community? I hope the integration of pauses throughout *Poetics of Listening* can enhance the experience of reading, where having room for reflection, for breathing more deeply, for taking time, and for being open to distraction are important factors.

Introduction: An Apprentice to Listening

As poetry is often that which gives rescue when falling, emerging as a language, a voice, a song when faced with the passion of love, the tearing of grief, the rupture and repair informing our deepest moments, it can be appreciated as what supports one to speak the unspeakable, to break or hold the silence, to find ways of narrating when identity and language and the body are undone, as well as listening out for directions and new partnerships, ways of mending and healing.

It is early morning, the studio is quiet. I hear the hushed murmur of the streets outside the closed window. There are the emerging melodies of birds and the sudden thud of a neighbor; the sounds of myself as well, as I reach for things on the desk or shuffle to the kitchen, aware of the possibility of disturbing others as they sleep. Toward the morning quiet I bring my attention, listening to all that is there. By listening the quiet is made something else; it materializes, it becomes a figure, however vague or diffuse. Listening points at the morning quiet, surrounds it with its own quiet fingers. How does it feel, the silence of the early hour? What are its qualities, its colors and reverberations? How does it sit within the room, already informing the day that waits for animation? Listening not only observes and notes, it raises questions as well. Listening *listens out* for things, for signs and signals—it lies in wait, and it also beckons forward: it says, *come with me!* Even if we go nowhere, remaining still, listening affects. Listening involves itself with things—it goes places, it scouts and seeks, it partners with others, from the morning quiet that floats under these words to the memories that fill the heart. Listening holds, and it also rests—it is always oscillating between intention and nonintention, being direct or indirect. While I may listen to something, listening also strays, giving way to drift, reverie, letting go.

It is in this way that listening is a broader form of sensing; it gathers the senses together, compiling them into ways of noticing, and also ways of thinking and relating. Importantly, it draws the imagination forward in terms of feeling beyond the senses, giving way to unique forms of knowing and intuiting. Listening is *radically receptive*, becoming key to sensitivity and the cultivation of attention. From the material facticity of the immediate to the stirrings of what lies out there, or deep within, listening names that attentional reach that is never purely actual but is equally evocative, generative. It affects, as it is affected.

I have been led to write about listening, feeling the pull of its deeply transformative influence, its patient and caring presence, which seems increasingly needed within today's environments marked by political violence and crisis. Throughout *Poetics of Listening*, listening is emphasized as crucial for working at forms of collaborative living as well as for challenging systems of abuse. Such views are elaborated by engaging specific practices and discourses, showing listening's influence upon personal, interpersonal, social, political, and ecological contexts: from inner life, self-awareness, and the emancipatory work of consciousness-raising, to the urgencies and processes defining social and political change, in which hearing and being heard, listening to and listening out for others, underpin the responsiveness of dominant power, and further, to the living, sacred worlds of planetary coexistence and how it is systems founded on mastering nature can be altered, made more livable and just. Each of these perspectives reveals listening as fundamental in terms of building ethical practices, cultivating shared responsibility, and enacting care for oneself and others. As I work at demonstrating, listening is a language of connection, one that lends definition to a paradigm of life.

I'm also concerned with the ways in which listening may go missing in terms of discussing it as a topic, manifesting it as a practice, understanding it as a politics, and giving value to it across social and institutional settings, so as to learn of its importance and to experience its effects, as well as recognize its absence. While listening may seem rather weak in the face of pressing concerns and urgent realities, it is my view that it is essential. As I emphasize, listening is the basis for radical care. From being a caring individual to building caring communities and systems, listening is deeply formative.

〜

As *Poetics of Listening* works at showing, listening is not only an act, it is a sensibility, a subject position, an ethics, and furthermore, a worldview, one that gives challenge to dominant systems that emphasize individualism, human exceptionalism, visibilization, and even vocality, not to mention assertiveness and progress, at the expense of more collaborative, attentive, liminal, and quiet work. Listening is deeply influential and yet so hard

Introduction

to notice—*in what ways is listening expressive?* It is easily overlooked, undervalued, disregarded. Yet, without it we would feel extremely alone, and we would certainly lose a great deal. Importantly, listening underpins the life of intimacy, community, democracy, justice, love, the devotional— it is foundational to human flourishing as well as connections with the more-than-human and the sacred. It is an essential personal, interpersonal, social, political, and ecological anchor. While it's important to recognize that listening does not solve all problems, or is always beneficial, I'm led to find in it a means for working at relations in ways that create possibilities, that open and sustain paths of connection, where learning from and caring for each other become transformative.

Following these affirmative views, it seems vitally important to give greater attention to listening, to build a discourse on and for listening, and to explore ways of listening so as to understand, appreciate, and enhance its place across society. This includes being critical as to how listening is positioned within social and political systems. Listening can be both empowering and controlling—it names a vulnerability that is enriching and easily exploited, it can heal as well as hurt, mend as well as break. As many scholars demonstrate, it is important to remain engaged in how listening is instrumentalized in mechanisms of control and violence, however intentional or unintentional.[1] At times, it may also be

---

[1] Mhamad Safa emphasizes the importance of recognizing what he calls "collateral listening" in states of war and zones of conflict, in which whole populations are subjected to harsh sounds that result in deep traumas. The notion of collateral listening helps in elaborating not only legal frameworks to address the effects of the sounds of war, but equally the complexities of listening itself and how it can be instrumentalized in states of war. This speaks toward the larger question of the weaponization of sound as well as music. As the scholar Anna Papaeti details in her research into the use of music in enactments of torture during the dictatorship in Greece, former prisoners continue to carry traumas related to the hearing of particular songs during detention and torture. See Anna Papaeti, "On Music, Torture and Detention: Reflections on Issues of Research and Discipline," *Transposition*, Hors-série 2 (2020): 1–18. Questions of sonic trauma, as well as ear-witnessing, are given attention in the important work of J. Martin Daughtry, see: J. Martin Daughtry, *Listening to War: Sound, Music, Trauma and Survival in Wartime Iraq* (Oxford: Oxford University Press, 2015. An additional critical perspective is found in the work of Dylan Robinson, a xwélmexw scholar and artist who calls for a "critical listening positionality," as a way to highlight how listening can also wield a colonizing effect through its appropriation of Indigenous cultures. I highlight these examples, out of many others, to consider the ways in which listening can wield its own form of violence, or result in pain. See Mhamad Safa, "Reverberations and Post-War Trauma: The Sustained Aftermath of Aerial Strikes on Lebanon in 2006," *Sound Studies*, vol. 8, no. 1 (2022): 73–99; and "Collateral Listening: Towards an Acoustemology of Shockwaves," in *The Listening Biennial Reader*, vol. 2, edited by Rebecca Collins and Brandon LaBelle (Berlin: Errant Bodies Press, forthcoming). Also, Dylan Robinson, *Hungry Listening: Resonant Theory for Indigenous Sound Studies* (Minneapolis: University of Minnesota Press, 2020).

necessary not to listen, to shut down or turn away. In this way, listening carries risk and responsibility. As it is important to care for what we say and how we speak, it is equally so with listening.

The morning is more awake now, as the sun fills the window and the sounds outside intensify—the neighbors are also active, and I sense the quiet in new ways. Its colors are changing, moving from a soft blue to a bright yellow; I listen with its slow progression and sudden punctuations—in what ways does it listen to me I wonder.

〜

In writing about listening, I have also followed it as a method of research, one that is about gathering, collecting, holding, that is about attending to what is there, and in doing so, shifting the dynamic from the argumentative to the explorative, from the strictly logical to the analogical and associative. I follow Gemma Corradi Fiumara in this regard; as she writes in *The Other Side of Language: A Philosophy of Listening*, "There is a whole world yet to be discovered, not of unsolved issues but of relationships among things we know, of ways in which they might fit together."[2] As a caring act or sensibility, listening finds ways in which things might fit together.

Following this perspective, it is my view that listening is less performative, in terms of the staging of identity or asserting a social position; rather, I'm interested to underscore listening as *conductive*. While listening is clearly implicated in processes of subjectivation—in the social construction of identity—I'm concerned to explore listening less as a production. Rather, I follow it in terms of enabling reproductive, dialogical, and liminal work. Conductivity is aligned with maintenance, with care and compassion; it gives support to the ongoingness of things, the living; it participates in keeping the conversation going, in fostering a greater whole; it is receptive rather than actionist, enabling things to pass through, gain momentum, even rest and dream. Listening does not necessarily intervene in the traditional sense, but it certainly influences and impacts, touches and pulls, holds and nurtures; it can be deeply restorative, lending to ways of repairing. As such, it conducts what is there, rather than performing itself; it gathers, lends support, affords

---

[2] Gemma Corradi Fiumara, *The Other Side of Language: A Philosophy of Listening* (London: Routledge, 1990), 17.

movement—finding ways for things to fit together. This is not to say that listening is without intensity, force, politics; as I work at showing, listening underscores the political itself. In posing conductivity over performativity, I'm concerned to open a discursive and practical view, to suggest that while listening may performatively wield power and politics, it also gives traction to less articulated dimensions. Listening is enacting *otherwise*, keeping one close to the vulnerability of oneself and others, to feeling interdependency as defining of embodied life and experience. This can be appreciated by considering how listening aligns easily with the diffuse, the ephemeral, the weak, and gentle. It is less possessive, in terms of self-containment, and more distributive; it is less a position and more a disposition, less a spectacle and more a sensitivity, giving to ways of bridging mind and body, self and other, people and places, and that connects physical and spiritual worlds.

As such, listening often stretches binary thinking. Listening holds and gives room for others. In holding, it allows for the coexistence of differences; in gathering, it opens onto things fitting together, often solving problems in ways that are hard to quantify—because we are often looking for the calculable logic of a given action, the effects and its identifiable cause, the object of a given articulation, the agency of standing up and out. Instead, listening eases in to mediate impasse, to resolve conflict, to aid in overcoming disagreement, or finding compromise—to conduct a reproductive, dialogical, and liminal work, helping to synchronize people and places. These are qualities that make of listening a means for building trust, for creating a space outside of judgment, where things can be said and feelings acknowledged. And where the rigidity of a binary construct gains flexibility, is put on hold, or allowed to move in unexpected ways. In this regard, listening offers a framework, a form of subjectivity, a paradigm aligned with an ecological perspective. By way of listening, a deeper feeling of interdependency is nurtured, a gathering together by which to approach the world less in terms of the foreign and more in terms of the domestic, where the planet is felt as a *home*. These are paths that shape an approach to feeling, to living, to thinking, and that make of us "apprentices of listening rather than masters of discourse."[3]

It is along these lines that the poetic is drawn in.

---

[3] Fiumara, *The Other Side of Language*, 57.

On Poetics

Poetics of Listening works at elaborating a view onto listening as a caring act, which impacts onto states of embodiment, subjectivity, and social and political worlds. As I explore, listening to oneself and to others are essential forms of care that give greatly to supporting human flourishing. This extends to the capacity for empathy and bodily awareness, and for moving the defining limits of certain regimes of intelligibility so as to support others, especially those at risk. Listening is a responsibility and it shapes our capacity for responsiveness, where listening contributes to a *meaningful life*: these are the feelings of being listened to by others, of being recognized and appreciated, valued and protected, and that give intensely to personal well-being; they are also the feelings of joy and fulfillment found in being there for others, in attending to the life experiences of friends and strangers, and which give to nurturing community and social connection; and they are the feelings of hurt and injustice experienced when confronting certain social, political realities, giving way to calls for change and where listening contributes an ethics, a sensitivity, a critical diplomatic art. And furthermore, they are the feelings of connection with the web of life, where listening enables learning the languages of place, of the land and the trees, the waters and the wind, lending to practices of reciprocity. By way of such processes and experiences, listening is generative of meaningfulness, which extends from the immediate, the present, to the deeper stories of community, family, nation. To listen is to acknowledge these stories; it is to appreciate the lives of others as stories as well, whose meanings are carried and held by way of listening.

As I elaborate, listening's ability to foster connection is suggestive for a poetic view: to recognize listening as a poetic figure, and how it traverses material, affective, social, and spiritual dimensions. *Listening is literal as well as metaphoric—it is always on the way to poetry.* It not only brings meaning to life and experience, it opens onto a *poeticization* of them—because listening is a carrier of imagination and feeling, of memory and spirit. While it may aid in attending to the actual reality of people and places, of issues and debates, it does so in ways that become *transformative*, resonant. From deepening self-awareness to anchoring social worlds, from healing original wounds to attuning us to the sacred gifts of a living planet, listening wields a poetic force. "Poetry is the language of the body,"[4] and listening is how we learn that language. This

---

[4] Willa Blythe Baker, *The Wakeful Body: Somatic Mindfulness as a Path to Freedom* (Boulder, CO: Shambhala Publications, 2021), 14.

Introduction

includes appreciating how listening brings attention to the details of things while recognizing these as part of a greater whole. As Johanne Thingnes Leira, a nurse working in Norway, suggests, listening is about knowing the whole person through a sensitivity for detail.[5] Listening is, in fact, the cultivation of sensitivity. And it brings sensitivity into the open, onto people and places, minds and bodies. In doing so, listening aligns with poetics in that poetics is a *sympathetic* form of knowing—what James S. Taylor highlights as *knowing by way of the inside*. Poetics is derived from its tendency to *incline* toward the object in a sympathetic manner, bringing us inside the experience of reality.[6] This finds echo in Theodor Reik's reflections on listening by way of "the third ear" within the context of psychoanalytic work. For Reik, one must cultivate a sensitivity for silence as a carrier of meaning: "The psychoanalyst has to learn how one mind speaks to another beyond words and in silence."[7] The capacity for listening beyond words, finding in silence a "thousand little signs" by which to deepen understanding of others, speaks toward a poetics of listening and its sympathetic, transformative manner.

〜

As the articulation of a sympathetic way of knowing, poetics moves across what counts as reason and unreason, sense and nonsense, within a prevailing regime of intelligibility. It does not sit still, rather, it inclines toward an intensity of feeling, a freedom of thought, manifesting the pulse of bodily experience and imagination, and it draws from the materiality of ideas as well as that of dreams, the unconscious, *the silences that speak*. It is grounded in the generative work of metaphor, as the birthing of new meaning, the play of language, and how it is we may hold a relation to the not-yet. As Luce Irigaray suggests, poetics gives guidance to an ethics of intersubjectivity and what she terms "the sharing of speech."[8] This is a speaking aligned with radical hospitality, a *thirdness*, which requires a form of poetic labor: where speech must be invented, relations *poeticized*. "Poetry is how things get together," Fred Moten notes.[9] It

---

[5] Johanne Thingnes Leira, in conversation with the author, 2023.

[6] James S. Taylor, *Poetic Knowledge: The Recovery of Education* (Albany: State University of New York Press, 1998), 62.

[7] Theodor Reik, *Listening with the Third Ear: The Inner Experience of a Psychoanalyst* (New York: Farrar, Straus, 1949), 144.

[8] Luce Irigaray, *The Way of Love* (London: Continuum, 2004), 8.

[9] Fred Moten, from a lecture, "Hesitant Sociology: Blackness and Poetry," held at the University of Chicago, spring 2016. Found online: https://www.youtube.com/watch?v=J5Zwuq898AY (accessed July 2024).

gives onto ways of feeling with others, and which engenders a deeply relational approach—a *poethics*. Poetics is not an abstract, analytical form of knowing, rather, it is immersed in the vibrant matter of things, aligned with wonder and curiosity. "Poetry discovers, science proves."[10] A *poetics of listening* is therefore a poetics of noticing, an art of feeling and of nurturing things getting together. And which lends to a poetic way of knowing, as the capacity to "see the life within the object."[11] This is a view aimed at recovering a sympathetic position, one that knows by way of the inside, and gives way to what Robin Wall Kimmerer terms a "grammar of animacy."[12] A poetics of listening is cast here as expressive of a grammar of animacy, and the language of the body, enabling feeling with others and seeing the life within the object as well as across all things. It is along these lines that I understand a poetics of listening as a contribution to the social movements that work on behalf of a paradigm of life, that resist the ongoing systems of political violence which not only fail to see the life within the object, but all the shared vitality that supports us with its gifts.

Into, toward, with, against, across—Modalities of Listening

Poetics of Listening is structured around five chapters, each of which elaborates a particular modality of listening. These modalities are frameworks for deepening an understanding of listening as a particular act and capacity, a way of leaning into things, relations, power. I also follow these modalities as ways of telling the story of listening, giving detail to its many sides, spanning theoretical study, somatic practice, field work, creative methodology, and personal reflection. I have tried to observe listening from a distance, identifying its attributes, its discursive implications, its histories, while also coming close, feeling what listening does, how it affects people's lives. These are aspects that I also feel are inherent to listening itself, how it specifically bridges mind and body, intellect and emotion, human and more-than-human, providing us with a holistic language, a language of connection. Overall, I have tried to listen to listening, using it as a guide, a

---

[10] Taylor, *Poetic Knowledge,* 64.
[11] Robin Wall Kimmerer, *Braiding Sweetgrass: Indigenous Wisdom, Scientific Knowledge and the Teachings of Plants* (London: Penguin Books, 2020), 155.
[12] Ibid., 49.

Introduction 9

partner, a method, holding onto its presence as well as absence, to discover its power, which is simple and complex at the same time.

Importantly, I emphasize listening as distinct from hearing and the experience of sound. While listening is clearly connected to hearing, it is also profoundly unique. Listening, instead, names a much broader form or quality of attention, one that compiles all the senses together, enhancing receptivity, feeling, care as well as reflection, knowing, intuiting. Listening is a way of attending to things, a way of caring, that extends far outside the sense of hearing. As such, listening is positioned as being available to all persons regardless of ability or disability; listening takes many forms, it is itself shaped by a spectrum of unique embodiments and sensorial configurations, contributing as well to the expression of diverse forms of life. This is carried throughout *Poetics of Listening*, and is generally implied across the range of perspectives and analyses I offer.

Poetics of Listening is also a series of journeys, where each modality is unfolded as a narrative, a movement, a lyric. Starting with *listening-into*, Chapter 1 considers the ways in which listening actively supports inner life. This includes examining the significance of inner voicing. As Michel Foucault poses, inner voice is key to a care of the self, supporting the cultivation of *logos* and reasoning.[13] In effect, inner voice manifests the ways in which the self is shaped by an exterior world, for inner voice is constituted by all the input received from an outside and how it is one speaks back. Importantly, this entails a process of negotiating one's place within constructs of power: inner voicing is an "emancipatory work," affording self-awareness and the cultivation of an inner truth. I follow these perspectives, identifying *inner listening* as an equally important mechanism, which lends greatly to a care of the self. Yet, inner listening is not only about engaging with the external systems of a societal order. By way of reflecting upon the autobiography of Marcellus "Bear Heart" Williams, a Native American shaman of the Muscogee Nation, listening-into is also about learning lessons from the natural world, where voices of the environment act as fundamental guides.[14] Listening to oneself is a vital process for finding inner truth, and how such truth contributes to ways of addressing and acting upon a surrounding world. At times, *raising consciousness* confronts systems of discrimination and

---

[13] Michel Foucault, "The Hermeneutic of the Subject," in *Ethics: Subjectivity and Truth*, ed. Paul Rabinow (London: Penguin, 2000).

[14] Bear Heart with Molly Larkin, *The Wind Is My Mother: The Life and Teachings of a Native American Shaman*(New York: Berkley Books, 1996).

oppression, giving way to inner struggles. Through following the writings of Clarice Lispector, Gloria Anzaldúa, and Theresa Hak Kyung Cha, I develop an elaborated view onto the emancipatory work of listening-into, which may move from an intensely personal labor to ways of building community. I speak to this understanding by considering feminist practices of consciousness-raising, which, from the late 1960s onward, has been foundational to the fight for gender equality and more. As Lucia Farinati and Claudia Firth highlight, the "force of listening" is one that contributes to political action bound to the personal.[15]

Moving from a focus on inner life, and the reverberant complexities of the self, Chapter 2 considers listening's participation in the work of social recognition, which I highlight through the modality of *listening-toward*. Recognition is underscored as important to social and political participation, and which supports self-esteem as well as community bonds. To be recognized by others, and to recognize others in return, forms a general ground for community and individual agency. Such views are guided by appreciating how urgent it is to experience being heard within one's environments and institutions, not to mention as part of more intimate relationships. Identifying listening's influential role in experiences of recognition is supported through notions of "thirdness" following the work of Luce Irigaray and Jessica Benjamin, whose theories on intersubjectivity are discussed.[16] Thirdness underscores an ethics of difference, where persons are viewed as participating in a shared process of mutual engagement and coordinated collaboration, of speaking-with and listening-toward. Recognition is thus emphasized as a process rather than a status, one that requires a deeply ethical approach as well as critical questioning. I reflect upon such views, conceptualizing "third listening" as a means for addressing a politics and ethics of recognition, which can also be found in the macropolitical arenas of national debate. Through considering the Uluru Statement from the Heart, and the referendum calling for constitutional recognition of First Nations Peoples in Australia (2023), I follow how listening is mobilized in projects of cultural and political self-determination.[17]

Extending from the previous chapters on inner voice and social recognition, Chapter 3 delves into questions and enactments of embodiment. Importantly,

---

[15] Lucia Farinati and Claudia Firth, *The Force of Listening* (Berlin: Errant Bodies Press, 2017).
[16] Luce Irigaray, *The Way of Love* (London: Continuum, 2004); Jessica Benjamin, *Beyond Doer and Done To: Recognition Theory, Intersubjectivity and the Third* (New York: Routledge, 2018).
[17] For more on the Uluru Statement from the Heart, and to access the Statement itself, see https://ulurustatement.org/ (accessed July 2024).

Introduction

the chapter seeks to follow the understanding found within care practices of listening's role in cultivating a sensitivity for bodily hurt and need. Through research into somatic therapies, nursing and healing work, the chapter unpacks an active listening culture found within these areas, in which listening affords ways of attending to the body, if not reclaiming its vitality against systems of exploitation. This includes engaging with the issue of colonialism and the perpetuation of slow violence across generations, especially against Black, Indigenous, and People of Color.[18] Establishing a link between listening and somatic health, I strive to elaborate what it means to *listen-with* the body by examining a number of theoretical and practical references, including the writings of Silvia Federici (and her understanding of bodily power), the work of craniosacral therapist Susan Raffo (and her concept of healing justice), meditation practitioner Willa Blythe Baker (on deep listening as healing), philosophers Jane Bennett and Catherine Clément (on theories of sympathy and delirium), and ethnomusicologist Judith Becker (on trance ritual and experience). These provide a transdisciplinary framework for elaborating listening as a practice of embodiment, especially in terms of working at healing justice—or what Rupa Marya and Raj Patel term "deep medicine."[19] Reclaiming the body as a natural power is grounded in the ability to *listen to its languages*.

Following questions of bodily hurt and healing, Chapter 4 focuses on the topic of power. How is listening instrumentalized by systems of control, surveillance, extraction? And in what ways can listening be understood as a counter-force, enabling acts of peace-building within today's environments? I bring into consideration debates on artificial intelligence and the emergence of algorithmic power, reflecting upon the realities of machine listening. This includes questions of bias and racial profiling, and how current technologies reinforce listening's instrumentalization as part of mechanisms of control and profit. Shifting focus, the chapter brings attention to a range of nongovernmental organizations and social initiatives that work at building more affirmative listening cultures, institutions, and strategies, such as the Center for Peace and Conflict Studies and the Center for Feminist Foreign Policy. In particular, I'm concerned with how listening—or what I term *listening-against*—operates

---

[18] See Linda Villarosa, *Under the Skin: The Hidden Toll of Racism on Health in America* (New York: Anchor Books, 2022).

[19] Rupa Marya and Raj Patel, *Inflamed: Deep Medicine and the Anatomy of Injustice* (London: Penguin Books, 2022), 20.

in nurturing restorative justice and deep democracy models that may counter dominant power structures. Subsequently, listening is elaborated as a power in itself, which supports processes of negotiation, group healing, and the working through of what Krista Ratcliffe and Kyle Jensen term "rhetorical problems."[20] This includes bringing into discussion a politics of listening, and the importance of finding ways to listen to that which one truly disagrees with. Central to the chapter is an engagement with the ruins of political violence: in what ways can listening enable ways of attending to the remains of unfinished history? By following Yael Navaro's concept of "negative methodology,"[21] along with the writings of M. NourbeSe Philip and Saidiya Hartman, I posit the idea of "negative listening," which is cast as a means for giving agency to the missing and the lost as well as enhancing the diplomatic arts.

Concluding the book, Chapter 5 focuses on listening as a power that can enable greater environmental understanding and connection. Following from Anna Lowenhaupt Tsing, listening is highlighted as a vital means for upsetting human exceptionalism, affording contact and connection with planetary others—what Tsing highlights as an "art of noticing."[22] This includes establishing critical discourse on dominant knowledge practices and epistemic injustice, emphasizing the importance of decolonizing Western knowledge paradigms built upon settler-colonialism and the exploitation of the planet and people. Such work and discourse are given traction in relation to the urgencies around climate crisis and environmental collapse, the emergent shift toward non-Western cultures, Indigenous thinking and practices, along with the proliferation of self-organized educational initiatives in support of more holistic methods. Throughout the chapter I draw from these current discussions and work, emphasizing listening's contribution to nurturing the art of noticing. As Tsing argues, such an art challenges human exceptionalism so as to better attune to the planetary rhythms and polyphonies constituting a deeply shared world. Expanding on the art of noticing, the chapter calls for a listening culture which can act as a foundation for a pluriversal conceptualization of knowledge practices. Drawing from

---

[20] Krista Ratcliffe and Kyle Jensen, *Rhetorical Listening in Action: A Concept-Tactic Approach* (Anderson, SC: Parlor Press, 2022).

[21] Yael Navaro, "The Aftermath of Mass Violence: A Negative Methodology," *Annual Review of Anthropology*, vol. 49 (2020): 161–73.

[22] Anna Lowenhaupt Tsing, *The Mushroom at the End of the World: On the Possibility of Life in Capitalist Ruins* (Princeton: Princeton University Press, 2015).

Mario Blaser, Marisol de la Cadena, and Lorraine Code, ecological and planetary thinking are positioned as ways that challenge legacies of settler-colonialism, to foster an *ecological poetics*, and where *listening-across* worlds and cultures is supportive of what Andreas Weber terms "policies of life."[23] This is exemplified in the Spectral Listening research group, whose approach to field work and situated knowledge practices lends to defining routes toward a planetary way of being.[24]

A Vitalist Position

Moving from inner life, and the emancipatory work of inner voicing, to acknowledgment of others and an ethics of mutual recognition; from listening's attendance to bodily hurt and healing, mending its breaks and reclaiming its power, to political processes and how listening contributes to working through conflict. And finally, to engaging questions of epistemic justice, finding in listening a planetary way of being that can nurture practices of receptivity, reciprocity, and situated co-learning. It is my intention to map the ways in which listening contributes across individual lives, communities, and societies, aiding in maintaining a care of self and of others, as well as lending to transformative processes and experiences. As such, *Poetics of Listening* invites a fuller understanding of listening's important influence. While listening is a caring, it is equally something to care for.

It is my view that listening is a language of connection—it greatly affords ways of nurturing and sustaining connection, and as such, it is positioned as a challenge to systems that operate by way of disconnection. These are the systems, the ideologies, the practices that interrupt and break the web of life. And which a great many individuals, communities, institutions, and initiatives are currently fighting against. As Rupa Marya and Raj Patel convincingly outline, by way of a situated or deep diagnosis, "the inflammatory diseases we are seeing today are not the cause of the body's dysfunctional relations. They are the body's correct

---

[23] Andreas Weber, *Enlivenment: Toward a Poetics for the Anthropocene* (Cambridge, MA: MIT Press, 2019).

[24] Anastasia (A) Khodyreva with Taru Elfving, Yvonne Billimore, Jaana Laakkonen, Anu Pasanen, Nina Vurdelja, and Kari Yli-Annala, "Attempts at Spectral Listening," published on *The Listening Biennial* website. See https://listeningbiennial.net/discourses/attempts-in-spectral-listening (accessed July 2024).

responses to a pathological world."[25] For the authors, it's imperative that we come to terms with colonialism's ongoing shaping of the world, which continues to drive inequalities and injustices, perpetuating an abusive approach to the planet and people. This finds echo in Andreas Weber's call for a return to a paradigm of life, where the "beauty of living things" needs to be centered within political and economic policy.[26] These are radical propositions—calling for economies of enlivenment, for deep medicine—against today's catastrophic realities, and they boldly and tenderly speak toward a *vitalist* position, a vitalist politics. *Poetics of Listening* is written as a contribution to wielding such a vitalist position and politics, one that aims at restoring connection, to ourselves and others, and to the thick relationality defining planetary coexistence and imagination.

From listening-into to listening-toward, from listening-with to listening-against, and finally, listening-across, these are envisioned as ways of listening that are equally ways of living, thinking, feeling, ways of knowing and relating, of carrying a knowledge of oneself and others that remains open, curious, sympathetic, guided by a poetic view, a poetic sensitivity. And above all, that is aligned with wisdom. To listen, might be, to remain a student of the world.

---

[25] Marya and Patel, *Inflamed*, 13.
[26] Weber, *Enlivenment*, 102.

1

Listening-into: Inner Life, Consciousness-Raising, and the Care of the Self

Understandings of inner life carry a pronounced connection to listening, where listening enables forms of personal orientation. In fact, the configuration of a private self can be seen to gain traction by way of a *listening imaginary*. From acts of self-reflection to moral deliberation, from critical thinking to processes of psychological work and remembering, the self is cast as an inner dimension to which listening gives critical and creative access. A poetics of listening may begin here, as a listening that turns inward, to open a path to understanding and taking care of oneself.

In what way is it possible to listen inwardly, making of oneself *another*—a partner, a friend, a story? Turning inward is to attend to the home that is the self, one that is carried as we go and, at the same time, carries us. This inner dimension, this primary home, is cast as a base for truth-seeking and the moral ground by which human behavior takes guidance—the gesture of going inward often emerges when faced with a social or spiritual dilemma, when bearing the weight of an external challenge. At the same time, it is extremely personal, this inner dimension or world—to go inward is to work through what counts as oneself, what we may hold as private, as one's own. It is, in this sense, that inner life is a noisy, reverberant dimension, where desire and need, memory and dream, thought and feeling, are all jumbled up. To search for meaning and balance within this mix of inner matter is made possible by way of listening—it might be said that it is listening's role to make sense of such matters, ordering them as a central part of one's life story.

Although notions of the self as an original ground of experience are open to critical questioning, as well as different cultural understandings, it is my interest to follow the ways in which listening is understood to turn inward, affording personal orientation as well as the cultivation of thought and feeling. By way of listening, or *listening-into*, inner life is brought forward, animated, placing listening as fundamental to the realization of the self. Listening is a calling forth, drawing toward itself all that is often hidden, suppressed or unclear, and in need of direction. As Jean-Luc Nancy suggests, "to listen is to be straining toward a possible meaning and consequently, one that is not immediately accessible."[1] While listening aids in the search for guidance, found within the chambers of an inner world, it is through being *another* for oneself—to speak to oneself, to carry the voices of others, to hear all the humming within—that inner life is made approachable. Listening, as Nancy proposes, evokes the self to itself, making of it an "omnidimension"—to be at the same time outside and inside.[2]

A poetics of listening, from my perspective, emerges as central to conceptualizing the self as omnidimensional, as full of things that call out for attention, understanding, narrative, care. I want to suggest that to turn inward is a poetic act—it is to figure this body, this self as a carrier, a chamber, as metaphoric, capable of invention and ongoing discovery: turning inward is imaginative, where insights or *inheards* are grasped from out of the nebulous scene within. As a poetics, turning inward locates the self as a process, a never-ending story full of multiple voices. The possibility and experience of listening-into evokes a sense of wonder and mystery—*Who am I? What am I?*—as well as anxiety and restlessness; it is a listening that hovers around itself, that waits for messages, signs and signals, as to where to go and what to do. Pulling through the jumble of an inner world, which is always piled high with things, the richness and vitality of living, the turbulence and tearing of being involved, all the memories, worries, wishes, criticisms and ideas—all this that needs to be heard, made meaningful—listening wields a poetic force that supports ways of understanding, of finding meaning and of conversing or negotiating with all the external forces that locate one within particular forms of socialization. This includes recognition as to the cultural logics and languages that greatly shape one's listening. To listen inwardly is to cultivate critical reflection and self-awareness, a care of the self that fosters ways of listening thoughtfully, responsibly, poetically.

In listening inwardly we become witness to ourselves, a partner to the ongoingness of the life we lead, and that takes us, with all its joy and hardship, as well as day-to-day maintenance. Poetics comes to support inner listening, which is performative, or rather, *conductive*, making of oneself one's own audience—to

---

[1] Jean-Luc Nancy, *Listening* (New York: Fordham University Press, 2007), 6.
[2] Ibid., 13–14.

figure what Steven Connor terms the "inner auditorium" of the self.[3] One comes to audition for oneself; it is a small staging, this inner listening, for it brings a much-needed light onto oneself. Such a form of listening illuminates, it is aligned with epiphany, thoughtfulness, realization, and transformation. And yet, it is also ordinary, it keeps things going through a ceaseless activity, as what works at caring for the world within.

⌒

Emphasizing inner life as a reverberant dimension, I'm concerned with how listening is positioned as the primary means for a care of the self—for making sense of the multiple voices within. I follow this concern through readings into psychoanalytic and sociological theories and the ways in which the self is understood as an inner dimension full of voices, from positive to negative. And which also functions as a link with the outer world. There is always so much passing between inside and outside, suggesting that what we may know as the self is less singular, less individuated or autonomous. Finding ways of shaping connections across inner and outer worlds is part of the work of the self. From the inner voice of a reasoning self to the reception of sacred stories and gifts, listening is positioned as a form of radical receptivity that aids in finding balance between inner and outer—to cultivate a truth for oneself. This includes the deep necessity at times to find within oneself the courage to work against systems of oppression; inner life can emerge as both a world of struggle, riddled with a range of burdens, as well as the very means for combatting oppression. As I consider, to find and keep hold of one's truth, one's voice, and all the voices it gains support from, can be transformative to situations of struggle.

In what way can I even talk of myself? What makes it possible to recognize an I as part of the material configuration of things? To know of myself as a name which others call and from which I come to think myself as a self? I'm tracing these rather existential questions in order to recognize the degree to which listening is influential onto the cultivation and care of the self. In bringing attention to the issue of the self, I'm not claiming it as sovereign or universal, as the ground of metaphysical truth; rather, I see and hear the self as a deeply enduring thread within what we come to know as the human story. A story that is one's own—the story we tell ourselves, but that others may also tell, and

---

[3] Steven Connor, "Writing the White Voice," a talk given at the Sound, Silence and the Arts symposium, Nanyang Technological University, Singapore, February 28, 2009. See http://stevenconnor.com/whitevoice.html (accessed July 2024).

that we come to carry, and that in being carried is constantly shifting, becoming broken, rebuilt, staged, and remembered. A story that is also stitched through others' stories, which is but one stitch in a never-ending quilt of life and history, love and community. And which we may work at remaking, accenting particular meanings, perspectives, experiences. How to make sense of things, to enact ways of tending and telling, caring and resisting, giving critical attention to the complex arenas of shared life? Listening names that attentional power, and poetics that storying.

Inner Voicing, Impossible Listening

To speak of listening inwardly is to also encounter an inner voice—the two go hand in hand, where the inner voice sounds within, making of the self a depth, a chamber, an omnidimensional world. Inner voice resounds across the unseen and immeasurable geography of the self, calling one to attend to all that may emerge, in the reverberations and realizations, the discoveries and confirmations, making of oneself a subject, a person, a living body. Inner voicing percusses into place a sense of identity, giving substance to thought and feeling, to the nebulous swirl of human emotion and consciousness. While the voice is often understood as an external event, as what participates in social life, in what way does the inner voice operate? What is the relationship between speech as it performs among friends or peers and the private speaking taking place under the breath, in the humming of thoughts? The inner voice is such a special voice, for it is a voice that remains obscured, unsounded, and yet its effects are profound. How important is the inner voice in terms of personal experience and orientation? And how can it be heard to influence social relations and one's sense of participation and belonging?

In his work on the care of the self, Michel Foucault underscores the importance of inner voice as what enables a *processing* of external systems and discourses that define and influence the self.[4] For Foucault, inner voice is vital to the cultivation of *logos* and a reasoning self, in that it assists in managing all the input arriving from outside, from the social environments and cultural languages that shape much of subjectivity. As Foucault argues, the self is fundamentally defined by

---

[4] Michel Foucault, "The Hermeneutic of the Subject," in *Ethics: Subjectivity and Truth*, ed. Paul Rabinow (London: Penguin, 2000), 100.

way of a social exterior and the (linguistic, moral, social, medical, legal) orders that bring one into being. While voices from outside are indispensable to the cultivation of *logos*, teaching and enabling individual thought and practice, inner voice is necessary in steering as well as defending the self.[5]

Importantly, for Foucault, inner voice, as key to the cultivation of reason, is politically significant, in that it "allows for the resistance of authority and orders, of different attempts to govern us."[6] Speaking to oneself—through an inner voicing that carries the lessons and learnings, the influences and experiences of worldly contact—is a process that works at fostering an inner truth by which to critically engage with modes of power that attempt to capture subjectivity through persuasion and the manipulation of meaning. Inner voice thus emerges as important to the crafting of one's singularity, to figure an inner truth that aids in defining oneself as a social subject.

Inner voicing is, at the same time, an "art of listening," which functions as an essential condition for "acquiring truth."[7] Listening is positioned as a "technology of the self," one whose inward reach is enabling for the cultivation of *logos*. The art of listening becomes, on some level, a critical listening that helps negotiate the influencing directives that come from outside, whether from family or educational environments, for example, and that informs the movements and directions of an inner voice. Consequently, inner voice is the result of an ongoing process, a labor of self-reflection and inner listening that works through all that is ceaselessly taken in. While the inner voice might be said to emerge under the influence of an external social process, always already contoured by the cultural logics and languages of a given society, it also becomes the very means by which to work at forms of criticality, self-awareness and understanding, to find and care for the truth of oneself. This inner work radically underpins the care of the self and the articulation of a "style of existence."[8]

---

[5] Lauri Siisiäinen, *Foucault and the Politics of Hearing* (London: Routledge, 2013), 92.

[6] Ibid., 93.

[7] Michel Foucault, "Technologies of the Self," in *Ethics: Subjectivity and Truth*, ed. Paul Rabinow (London: Penguin, 2000), 236.

[8] Michel Foucault, *Politics, Philosophy, Culture: Interviews and Other Writings of Michel Foucault* (New York: Routledge, 1990), 49. In his work on a care of the self, Foucault is interested in the ways in which the self may fashion itself, taking itself as a project, or as raw material to be crafted into a particular "style" or "ethics." Inner voice and the art of listening are always positioned in relation to an outside world, as "technologies of the self" that aid in acquiring truth. I'm following Foucault's formulations, yet, for this chapter, I'm more interested to stay with the inside. Through the modality of listening-into, the art of listening is explored as what deepens an inner work, one that may certainly be tied to styles of existence, but which equally contributes to fashioning an inner world.

20 *Poetics of Listening*

↜

As part of the dynamic of inner voice, it is important to recognize the ways in which an inner voice can also be self-destructive; by taking in the presence, the voices and languages of others, those that surround and that may support as well as dominate, internalization may also integrate *negative others* and related experiences of rejection and criticism. Subsequently, the inner voice may replicate the shaming, the scolding, the destructiveness placed upon oneself by others, giving way to an inner voice that is difficult to challenge, and that may wield its obstructive influence over one's life and actions. In fact, inner voicing is difficult to escape or turn down altogether; there is a constant murmuring or internal commentary occupying inner life, where thoughts and statements flow across the arena of consciousness, provoking an array of images, words, feelings, actions. It may be necessary to conceive the inner voice as an arena in which self and others, interior and exterior, are brought together to incite a labor that works at defining a personal world: that navigates the continuous interweaving of social encounter and private reflection, the positive and negative experiences shaping how one feels about oneself, not to mention the ongoingness of memory. The negative other can be positioned as part of a larger ensemble of voices that populate inner life; the inner auditorium Connor describes contains a plethora of voices and viewpoints. There are negative and positive, hopeful and despondent, lazy and feverish voices, as well as instructive and destructive, soft and hard. And at times, inner voicing becomes garbled, tired, hoarse; it loses itself. Are these all independent voices, under different conditions? Or are they dimensions or sides of a single voice, one that also changes as it ages, as it undergoes all the world offers or forces upon it? As inner voicing matures, multiplies or softens, so does inner listening. These are living things whose ceaseless activity comes to shape an inner truth, one held in the reverberant arena within, as fundamental to the story of oneself.

↜

In focusing on listening as what enables a care of the self, in terms of attending to thoughts and feelings, and the cultivation of a personal truth or story, there emerges an emphasis on interior and exterior as a dichotomy. Such an emphasis comes to reinforce the idea of a "split subject" (articulated in the works of Sigmund Freud, and further, through a broader existential view onto modern subjectivity[9]). This finds elaboration in the psychoanalytic theories of

---

[9] The fundamental understanding of the self as divided emerges through Freud's theories of the unconscious. By posing the self as constituted by conscious thought and unconscious drives, the

Jacques Lacan. I want to follow these perspectives, as a way to further open a view onto the issues of inner voicing and listening-into; yet, my ultimate aim in this chapter, and throughout *Poetics of Listening*, is to pose listening as what works at overcoming or diffusing often entrenched configurations of binary thinking. While on some level listening inwardly can be seen to follow from a conceptualization of the self as divided, as held between inner and outer, I'm interested to pursue an alternative perspective, where listening, instead, *bridges* and even *mends*. It can be appreciated to enable holding a space of complexity in which oppositional terms take on more nuanced meanings.

↪

To continue elaborating listening's role in a care of the self, I'll first offer some reflections on Lacan's theorizations of subjectivity, which can help in following listening's unique inward reach. Lacan's model of subjectivity, and the organization of the unconscious, is defined around three key areas: that of the symbolic, the imaginary, and the real.[10] For Lacan, these name the fundamental axes around which the subject turns, with the symbolic functioning as the order of language and the realm of the signifier, the imaginary as the arena of (mis)identification and projection, even intuition, and finally, the real which is understood as presymbolic and prelinguistic. Importantly, the real has no representation, no image, therefore it is opposed to the imaginary; it is, in fact, impossible to image. Furthermore, the real resists the symbolic, as it is outside language, harnessing instead all that evades knowability, transparency, and signification. Interestingly, Lacan highlights the emergence and persistence of the real as founded upon the *split* or separation with "the mother" (understood as a plenitude or primary unity); the real relates precisely to what we can no longer have, this presymbolic, prelinguistic cohesion or unity experienced in the first months or years of childhood.

I'm particularly interested in Lacan's formulation of the real, as this is underscored as that which is beyond graspability and yet shapes a great deal of one's sense of self. Moreover, Lacan furthers an understanding of the real as

---

notion of the "split subject" emerges. This further plays out in ideas of the id, ego, and superego as constituting the self, which Freud would further develop, for instance, seeing how modern society itself is influenced by this fundamental split. See, for example, Sigmund Freud, "A Note on the Unconscious in Psychoanalysis," in *The Complete Psychological Works of Sigmund Freud*, vol. 12 (London: Penguin Books, 2001), and Sigmund Freud, *Civilization and Its Discontents* (London: Penguin Classics, 2002).

[10] For an introductory overview of Lacan's theories, see Jacques Lacan, *Écrits: The First Complete Edition in English* (New York: W. W. Norton, 2007).

being resistant to representation, yet importantly, it shows itself nonetheless. This is what Lacan enigmatically calls the Thing.[11] The Thing can be thought as a "remainder" that falls away from that moment of separation, of seeing oneself and realizing oneself as an I (described in what Lacan terms "the mirror stage"[12]). As (mis)identification takes place, as I see myself *over there*, there is an experience of alienation: I am only myself through a kind of estrangement, a cut (to see myself as distinct from "the mother," as a break from unity), leading one to feel that there is something "not-me" about "me." The Thing comes to designate the not-me of myself. There is an excess, something that is cut off and irretrievable, Lacan suggests, and yet it remains central, at the core of subjectivity. This something is the real, the Thing. The Thing emerges as a type of "empty center," a nothing or void at the core of subjectivity. This empty center, this not-me, is therefore always uncanny, unsettling the primary home of the self with its strange familiarity: the not-me that is of me and yet remains fully other. The Thing takes on the role of something foreign within myself, what Lacan emphasizes as the "first outside," which comes to haunt or unsettle the subject. Finally, the Thing comes to manifest the real by taking shape through fantasy: as he argues, following the cut, the separation and subsequent entry into language, the symbolic, we turn back, seeing the real as what needs to be symbolized. As there is no returning, no going back, the real spins into fantasy: it figures itself as an impossible object. As Mario Vrbančić outlines in his account of the Lacanian Thing, "the Thing unfolds as an object of desirable fullness only in its absence."[13]

ↄ

Lacan's formulation of subjectivity, and the organization of the unconscious, can lend input into approaching the self as an inner dimension, and furthermore, how listening gives critical and creative access. It is my view that the empty center, the void that figures dramatically at the core of subjectivity, can be cast as an *acoustic dimension*, one that reverberates with all this that is not-me. While Lacan emphasizes the real as prelinguistic, I'm more interested in the ways in which it *nonetheless speaks*, and whose influence is one that participates, however uncannily, in what we come to know as the self. The Thing, may in

---

[11] For an insightful reading and elaboration of Lacan's theory of The Thing, see Mario Vrbančić, *The Lacanian Thing: Psychoanalysis, Postmodern Culture, and Cinema* (Amherst, NY: Cambria Press 2011).

[12] Lacan, *Écrits*.

[13] Vrbančić, *The Lacanian Thing*, 7.

fact, refuse to keep its place—as the first outside it may cast its shadows; as the empty center it may reverberate in ways that become *listenable*. What kind of language is this, the speech of the Thing? How might I understand it, attend to it, respond to this thing that is no-thing? Is there a way in which inner voicing acts as a channel, a medium for corresponding with the irretrievable harmony or unity once experienced? In what ways is inner voice the Thing itself, as the real forever lost but which never goes away? And is inner listening, as an impossible form of listening, specifically attending to the impossible objects by which the Thing manifests, speaks, affects, and guides? As the irretrievable experience of unity, the Thing might be heard to speak in whispers, in grunts, or murmurings; it is a language of intensities, drives; it is *fantastical*, spinning into all sorts of imaginings, voicings, tendencies, hearings. A voice that is me and not-me at the same time, that is uncannily familiar (perhaps the voices overheard as a child, or those that resound within dreams, that are reassuring and also terrifying …). As the Thing never quite shows itself, but is nonetheless ever-present, such is its voice as well—it might be heard to utter a language *before* or *after* language, one that figures in fragments, interruptions, silences, songs, and which never stops. In doing so, it requests the work of listening, one that can especially follow all that the empty center offers.

⌣

If the Thing names a part of inner voicing that is deeply influential, a voicing that sits under or within all other voicing, it can be heard to incite a particular form of listening, one that proceeds *poetically*. To know oneself is to not only know the facts of oneself, those things that can be spoken about; rather, it is also to know oneself as fundamentally *multiple*, as not-me, an empty center, and yet which can be sensed and made approachable by way of a poetics of listening: a listening-into that may attend to the whispers and grunts, the rather unpronounceable vibration of an inner world, what the author Clarice Lispector mysteriously names X. As she writes in her deeply experimental work *Água Viva*: "I must interrupt to say that 'X' is what exists inside me. 'X'—I bathe in that this. It's unpronounceable. All I do not know is in 'X.'"[14] Turning inward, Lispector arrives at X, for X marks *something*; it points at the empty center, this unpronounceable thing. X designates the Lacanian real, as what is before or after language, a type of impossible language standing in for all that "exists inside me"

---

[14] Clarice Lispector, *Água Viva* (New York: New Directions, 2012), 72.

and yet which "I do not know." X speaks by way of a certain pressure or energy, what the author describes as a music "without melody."[15] A vibration.

Água Viva is a shimmering, unstable text driven by an inner listening, one that gives access to the empty center, figuring it as a labyrinth of unknowability and yet which is all there is; it is somehow unavoidable, appearing as the fundament, a bass-note, a material chamber from which meaning unfolds. And that is followed by way of an inner listening attuned to or prodded into being by the music within. "What beautiful music I can hear in the depths of me. It is made of geometric lines crisscrossing in the air. It is chamber music. Chamber music has no melody. It is a way of expressing the silence. I'm sending you chamber writing."[16] Such are the poetic listenings driven by the Thing, the unpronounceable X, and which are essential enactments of a care of the self.

↪

To arrive at *logos*, it seems, is done by way of a poetic journey, a *poeticization* by which to know of the empty center, the inner silences and all they carry. Here, what comes to pass as a reasoning self emerges under the influence of poetics— the hearing of voices that sound their impossible music. It is by way of poetics that access may be found precisely to what cannot be fully named and which listening helps address. Listening-into figures much-needed paths of attention and awareness that explicitly shift the borders between reason and unreason, rational and irrational, inside and outside, that knows of the empty center as multiple and reverberant. Consequently, inner voicing can be heard as the Thing around which other things circulate, the languages and viewpoints, the wishes and desires, the doings and makings that one may work at or is susceptible to. In fact, the Thing names the very drive of creativity. It points toward all that one may do as a means for recovering the primary unity, the first harmony of a stable identity, a place of belonging, giving this new forms through stories of the self, the crafting of material expressions, the making of families. The Thing is always closer than imagined, sounding routes toward the reordering of the symbolic and the imaginary, law and identity. Listening-into is a listening that poses or evokes a path toward partnering with the not-me of myself, to figure a type of sympathetic relation with the Thing (and all those things it contains or contributes to creating).

↪

---

[15]   Ibid.

[16]   Ibid., 40.

In moving from Foucault's understanding of inner voice, as what engages or negotiates an external world with all its discourses and social structures, to Lacan's mapping of the unconscious, as a deep influence onto what we come to know as the self, I'm interested in how listening traffics across inside and outside: the care of the self is a practice that works at *logos*, at the making of discourses in dialogue with a knowable world, and it is also a practice that confronts the unknowability of an inner dimension. Inner listening and inner voicing are stretched across the articulations that make of one a social subject and the unpronounceable mysteries that continuously resound at the center of the self.

Following Foucault's reflections on inner voice, and its place within the care of the self, and Lacan's formulations of the subject, how might we think further about this inner process, this voicing that appears as me and not-me? In what ways does the inner voice entail a form of listening adept at cultivating an inner truth, to sustaining and protecting what counts as self-determination? And that aids in relating to others, to navigating the structures of society, or for maintaining the bonds that support or hold us? If inner voice is central to being a reasoning self, able to negotiate the impingement of an external world, it strikes as crucial to deepen a view onto inner listening. For inner voice is only ever meaningful in so far as one listens—as Nancy suggests, listening evokes the self to itself. Furthermore, I'm tempted to position the strange figure of the Thing—as the inner vibration around which one is centered—as what guides us into listening. If the real is that which resounds within, that in effect has no name, this X, it is by way of listening that it becomes approachable, and as such, listening itself becomes tied to reclaiming a possible unity or connectedness.

The capacity to listen inwardly must be understood to depend upon experiences of listening outwardly as well; by attuning to exterior voices, to the lessons and learnings of worldly contact, not to mention the diverse and tumultuous noises that constitute a social world, listening outwardly is shaped. How such experiences and lessons are made available to an inner process of critical consciousness and self-reflection seems dependent on the ability to listen toward others, and toward the joys and challenges arising in daily life. In other words, I'm concerned to consider how the urgencies of inner voice are affected by the ways in which outward listening performs and is supported in daily environments. As a great deal of attention is given to developing language skills at an early age, to the cultivation of one's own voice within a social world, not to mention the ability to articulate oneself across all types of institutional situations—voice as what will take us further in our careers and relationships—in what ways is listening afforded equal attention? Greater appreciation for listening's role in nurturing self-reflection and awareness, as well as ways of orienting within the social worlds that surround, seems vital. If the inner voice is the means by which to care and protect the self, it is equally that voice by which to cultivate an ethics of care and concern for others.

A care of the self, and the cultivation of inner voice, is bound to questions of health, to processes of caregiving and recovery, healing and repair—to an overall attention to the body. This finds expression in the general understanding that the body *speaks*. Listening inwardly is not only to attune to mental, moral, and ethical deliberations, to reflect to oneself about given challenges or decisions needing to be made; it is also to stay in touch with the vitality of the body, the metabolism of somatic life, even the unknowable, empty center (reverberant with all that I am/not) affecting physical well-being. While inner voice contributes to the cultivation of *logos*, it is intimately bound to feeling and the rather unreasonable drives of the unconscious. The omnidimensional nature of the self that Nancy speaks of must include a sense of the self as a physical vitality—an emotional, psychological world. This is the X that Lispector circulates around in *Água Viva*, and which gives way to a writing that *listens-into*, that works at following the mystery within—and as such, can only proceed by way of fragments. Paradoxically, or uncannily, this is a writing done while the author sleeps: "I work while I sleep because that is when I move inside the mystery."[17] Her sleep-work emerges as the means by which to correspond with X, to open an unconscious channel by which to encounter what the author further terms "Pure it."[18] Is not *Pure it* the Thing at the center of the self and which can be heard to pull at *logos*, refiguring the constructs of language, law, the symbolic, by making of dissonance the basis of existence, the basis of writing? Lispector proclaims—"dissonance is harmonious to me."[19] It emerges as the very ground of meaning, as the inner music of the self and that vibrates across the chambers of the body. Guided by a sleep-work, the art of listening establishes not only the capacity for self-reflection, in terms of the cultivation of reason; it equally opens the self as a poetic ground of intuitive knowledge, where dissonance is

---

[17] Ibid., 59.
[18] Ibid.
[19] Ibid.

harmonious and where sleeping gives way to an inner truth—the X at the center of the self.

↩

Understandings of the self as multiple, as being outside and inside at the same time, are echoed in the notion of the "I" and the "Me" developed by social psychologist George Mead in the late nineteenth century.[20] Mead's early emphasis on a form of social constructivism leads him to conceive of the self as divided, constituted by a dynamic interplay between the I and the Me. In Mead's formulation, the Me is that part of the self which takes on the attitudes of others, the leanings and values encountered within a social environment, whereas the I becomes a form of response—the I as articulated expressions of an individuated self. The I and the Me thus form a process, even a dialogue, that constitutes the self and which acts as a model of what it means to be an individual immersed in the ongoingness of a social world.

What comes to bind these two sides of the self? In what ways do they know of each, working side by side or in tandem? Mead suggests an answer through an idea of consciousness—a becoming-conscious of the self. In fact, Mead would argue early on that the self only emerges and becomes apparent to itself *through* others; that is, selfhood is made possible through developing the capacity to speak of oneself as others might do—to make of oneself an object, a reference, a story. For Mead, language contributes greatly to this process, and to which I would add voice in general. The voices of others are never simply bound to language, rather, knowing of oneself by way of others is influenced by the tonalities and textures, the volumes and rhythms, intensities and emotionalities those voices carry. Environments may be social, as Mead suggests, but such sociality is deeply affective, acoustic, textured, dynamic; voices are never only linguistically or semantically meaningful, but constitute an ecology of force, a material-emotional world, a sounded reality. Accordingly, to speak of oneself as others might do finds guidance by way of the tonalities of others, and the care and sensitivity, the aggression and intensity with which others speak. This may be akin to Mead's concept of *gestures*, as those things that indicate the attitude of others—gestures within conversation for example, but equally found in any number of social encounters and experiences.[21] Gestures are never only directed

---

[20] For more on George Mead's theories of the self, see the collected lectures published as George Herbert Mead, *Mind, Self and Society: The Definitive Edition* (Chicago: University of Chicago Press, 2015).

[21] Ibid., 178.

at me, for instance, but come to constitute an environment in general, through the arrangements of material things, the lawful order of a social world, the humdrum and rhythms of surroundings, all of which indicate and promote a general attitude, a form of social composition.

⌒

Returning to understandings of listening inwardly, I'm interested in the formulation of I and Me, and how this speaks toward a split between mind and body. From the I as the articulated response to a given exterior, to the Me as what takes in, is susceptible and impressionable, the concept of the self emerges as an ongoing oscillation across these two arenas or positions. Yet, I'm also concerned to think how the self is not only in dialogue with an exterior; inner voicing is not only constituted by the voices of others, it is also shaped by the *voice* of one's body. To listen inwardly is not only attuned to the social encounters we have of a world, but it is greatly fostered by way of embodied experience—the body speaks, and in doing so, listening turns inward. This might be part of the foundational basis for listening inwardly, found not only in the separation from a parent, as a cut from the unity of this primary togetherness that prompts us to speak to ourselves, but also in that moment when a child turns and says, *my tummy hurts.* Knowing of the body as something that speaks, that tells things to oneself, that is me and not-me at the same time, is deeply influential in how one comes to listening, as that which enables feeling what the body needs, what it enjoys and how it may navigate through all types of dilemmas and desires. To be responsive to one's body participates in figuring the self as omnidimensional, as multiple, as being simultaneously I and Me—and to find ways of communicating with oneself, a conversation passing between who I am and what the body is. To listen-into is to work at bringing these into a form of inner truth, to find ways of bridging I and Me.

⌒

Inner voicing, a care of the self, a listening inwardly so as to bridge I and Me, me and not-me, to attend to the Pure *it* and the X of all I am and yet which I do not know—all of this names a deeply poetic construct: a listening that works at attuning to oneself as constituted by and through a given world. There is a lot going on here—within this beautiful music, this dissonant harmony—and as such, a great working through is called for. A reasoning self is full of emotion, anxiety, unrest, as well as the things that speak without speaking. I carry all these experiences, memories, wishes, and pains as I go, and as others go with me. If the inner dimension of the self is conceived as an auditorium, it is certainly a busy one. It is hard at times to know: is this *my voice* I am hearing—what is *my voice?* And in what sense is inner voice edging toward the limits of reason? If the self is shaped and given meaning by way of a poetics of listening, as an impossible listening, it is a self touched by where poetics leads: toward an unsettling of the differences we may make between reason and unreason, rational and irrational, me and not-me. Poetics names that point in which it is not so clear who or what is speaking; to *hear voices* is often the basis for poetic imagination—this is the sleep-work by which Lispector communes with X, the Pure *it.* Are not the Muses conceptualized as divine voices separate from oneself, and yet whose inspirational presence directly influences the inner world of the self, bringing forth epiphany, insight, clarity, knowledge? Inner voice, as Foucault argues, may assist in cultivating a reasoning self, but it is a reasoning that is never so reasonable. In fact, inner voice announces the possibility of knowing *otherwise.* This is a defining aspect of inner truth, as a truth of one's own.

It is my perspective that listening-into, as that which attends to the complexity of the self, teaches one how to speak and listen in transformative ways. To be in dialogue with the Thing, and the body that endlessly speaks, to work at attuning to all those voices which constitute an inner world, supplies a deep education on listening and voicing. If I can approach myself as the multiplicity I am, as figured around an empty center—which is, in fact, a jumble of memories, desires, injuries, and loves, *a disharmony that I understand*—then I may find the means for approaching all that the world presents, the friends and enemies, the loves and losses, the greed and joy filling the human story. It is on this level that I sense an urgency to attend to the self in ever-poetic ways, so as to work at cultivating and caring for a culture of listening and voicing, especially attentive to that which continually unhomes the self: the terrors of separation, of disconnection. It is along these lines that listening-into does much to hold the differences we may make between I and Me, between inner and outer worlds, and which opens a path toward rethinking the often entrenched view of a divided or multiple self as a dissonance needing to be resolved. As Lispector suggests, listening assists in dwelling with the inherent disharmony at the center of the self, hearing it as *água viva*—a *living water.*

⌒

A poetics of listening may be appreciated as what assists in hearing the multiplicity of the self as a form of beautiful music, a dissonance that is meaningful. As Lispector intuits, the presymbolic, prelinguistic real carried within is full of poetic force. Emphasized as the basis of fantasy, the empty center is there precisely so as to *resound* with all that one may touch or be touched by; it is the source of a music that passes across inner and outer, acting as a vibrational conduit by which to know of oneself as full of others, as singular and plural at the same time, and which creatively engenders all sorts of passions and projects.

These are the resonances, the communions, the gestures that feel mine and not mine, that come from somewhere and find their way as they go, in the imaginative motions and material forms taking up residence around us, that speak without speaking, but that I may hear as meaningful, as an inner becoming outer—even now, in writing these lines, I am listening inwardly, to what? To whom? To find the direction, to evoke the momentum by which words follow words, and which equally pulls me along, in the making that reveals what it is that matters, that feels right.

It is by way of such inner work that I want to locate Lacan's formulation of the Thing within a greater environmental construct, where the empty center of the self, as an interior profoundly shaped by an exterior, articulates itself through all types of impossible objects, gestures, imaginings—as a music without melody constituted by multiplicity. As Foucault suggests, inner voice is the working through of all the exterior forms and forces one experiences; as such, inner voice is radically constituted by a multitude of others, finding guidance by way of exchange or impingement, not to mention the affective and emotional intensities of embodied encounter. In this way, voice may be emphasized as always already *inter-voice*, as well as *intra-voice*, where a range of voices and voicings co-constitute each other, figuring an ongoing assembly or polylogue. The inner auditorium that Connor envisages is more a diffracted world where self-reflection is never a closed affair; rather, *reflection* passes across self and others, self and self, I and Me, giving shape to what Connor also describes as the "auditory I."[22] Rather than conceive of the individual as a singularity or an object standing in space, Connor follows sound and audition as the basis for reconceptualizing the I, understanding it more as a "membrane" that resonates with all that passes over or through it.[23] Listening, in this way, helps anchor and orient as well as put into question what we know as the self through an active exposure. The model of the self that starts to emerge by way of listening, full of the inter- and intra-voicings constituting a self, and the resonances or

---

[22] Steven Connor, "The Modern 'Auditory I,'" in *Rewriting the Self: Histories from the Renaissance to the Present*, ed. Roy Porter (London: Routledge, 1997), 203.

[23] Ibid., 207.

dissonances that evoke an omnidimensionality, an outside and inside at the same time, is suggestive for conceptualizing an *environmental self*.

Listening as Cosmopoetical

The question of inner listening, as a listening that, as Jean-Luc Nancy suggests, evokes the self to itself, draws forward insight into the phenomenon of inner voicing by which one attends to the experiences of worldly contact. While inner voicing, and the work of *logos*, may align with an idea of a split subject, of carrying the cuts that make of one an individual, it may also be turned toward a more environmental understanding. Inner voicing and inner listening are equally intersubjective, as what carries and attunes not only to a social world, but also to an ecological, cosmological order in which the voices of ancestors, the spirit guides, the wind and the trees all come to participate. The real that is beyond knowing but which resides at the center of the self may be heard as the intergenerational stories, the traditions and social musics, the memories and communal ceremonies that one carries in the bone, the blood, the cells; the X that Clarice Lispector identifies to designate the unpronounceable interiority of the self may equally emerge as the minerals, the waters, the inexplicable breath and rhythms of the body, and which are never so singular, but are vital matters and energies that remind of one's inseparability. These, in fact, might be *the real* residing deep within and that gestures toward a planetary, cosmopoetical vision of connectedness.

Here I take guidance from the teachings of Marcellus "Bear Heart" Williams, a Native American shaman of the Muscogee Nation whose autobiographical writings remain a source of insight into Indigenous cultures and practices.[24] In particular, the constructs and traditions of sacred knowledge provide input into what we may understand as the *existential challenges* often shaping inner work. Inner voicing and inner listening are often acts that are truth-seeking, that aim for self-knowledge as well as clarity pertaining to social questions or spiritual concerns. This finds meaningful expression in Bear Heart's writings and his work in *doctoring*.

---

[24] Bear Heart with Molly Larkin, *The Wind Is My Mother: The Life and Teachings of a Native American Shaman* (New York: Berkley Books, 1996).

32   *Poetics of Listening*

The environment was our starting point in learning as much as we could from what was around us—the seasons, the things that grow, the animals, the birds, and various other life forms. Then we would begin the long process of trying to learn about that which is within ourselves. We didn't have any textbooks, we didn't have any great psychiatrists, who lived years ago and presented theories in this and that. We had to rely on something else, and that was our senses. Rather than through scientific investigation, we sensed those things within and around us.[25]

The fundamental relation to the senses, as the means by which to learn, echoes with James S. Taylor's understanding of "poetic knowledge" as a *first knowledge*,[26] as a knowledge grounded in the senses and which, as Bear Heart elaborates, is informed by nurturing the capacity to observe, to notice, to listen: "I want you to learn to be like that tree. If that tree could only talk, it would tell us many things. When you're learning something, don't be yakking away. Learn to listen. Listen to the wind."[27] The capacity for such learning and communicativeness is essential not only for absorbing lessons, but in the case of Bear Heart, for the work of doctoring. As a shaman whose medicinal work led to a lifetime of caring, learning to listen is equally about developing ways of healing, ways of "bringing people to a place of safety" through empathy and receptiveness. "It's a matter of becoming sensitive to the environment ..."[28] as well as to others, cultivating respect and responsiveness, and knowing of oneself as a receiver of the gifts of the earth and the Creator.

⤔

These are teachings and practices shaped by sacred knowledges, and that figure the self and others, planetary kin and environments, as fundamentally spiritual and housed within a greater cosmological order—the beliefs and the stories, myths and musics, songs and the ceremonies through which individuals and communities cohere as well as give thanks. And from which processes of healing take guidance, informed by lessons offered by the environment, the trees and the wind, and the voices that gift knowledges across generations. Such views contribute to a poetics of listening, as they further the work of listening as precisely what assists in sensing and grasping all that is greater than ourselves,

---

[25] Ibid., 65–6.

[26] James S. Taylor, *Poetic Knowledge: The Recovery of Education* (Albany: State University of New York Press, 1998), 61.

[27] Bear Heart, *The Wind Is My Mother*, 55.

[28] Ibid., 67.

even that which is within. And that, as Bear Heart affirms, lends to the languages which may help in recognizing "universal love" as "the caring and love that can generate from our hearts into the lives of others" and which "carries us forward," along the Spirit Road.[29] These are poetic journeys, songs of love and tribulation, that carry the hurt and the healing as one walks this road in search of harmony.[30]

〜

In supporting the ongoing work of self-determination, and the stories that emerge in the making of inner truths, it can be appreciated how a poetics of listening figures a *tensing* of established discourses and knowledge regimes, the codes by which reasoning and ordering are defined. Inner listening plunges itself into a negotiation with power, with the negative other, all those voices that may impede speaking-truth, for oneself and for others. And that always influence listening itself. It searches for signs, it leaves itself open to messages, guided by the lessons offered from trusted friends and community members, and in the case of Bear Heart, from planetary kin, the voices and songs of land and animal. These are carried in the reverberant arenas of thought and feeling and spirit, in the recesses of the body, and one finds them by way of inner listening, an attentiveness that, at times, expresses itself by way of *dreaming*. Dreams fill inner life with a swirl of images—they are the stuff of the Thing, the X that is unpronounceable and yet profoundly present, manifested in vibrations, as the first outside: this outside that is the not-me of me and that uncannily aids in finding one's way. Dreams contribute to the inner voice, giving way to a depth composed of innumerable frequencies and that pull at the defining limits of *logos*: to make sense of dreams is to remain exposed to their mysterious interruptions, their strange and prophetic influence; they are the gifts of inspiration, poetry, as well as the source of new paths in life and belief. Dreams may turn us upside down, and they may set us right; they may carry the songs of the time of creation, as articulated in Aboriginal concepts of Dreamtime, to act as the basis of one's life journey and the cosmologies of a people, and dreams may also shatter held beliefs, forcing one onto other paths. As Lispector suggests, it is only through sleep-work that

---

[29] Ibid., 16.

[30] Drawing together the discursive and epistemological worlds of Lacanian psychoanalysis and the wisdom traditions of Native American culture is suggestive for a listening methodology, as one that finds connection by thinking across communities, knowledges, and practices. This is not to overlook or underrepresent the political struggles around epistemic justice, and the need to remain sensitive as to one's own positionality or ways of positioning others. I am aiming to be careful about overreaching, and which I want to underscore here.

the mystery within becomes navigable. To speak of inner life and the listening such life requests is to open an affirmative relation to the reasoning of dreams.

The omnidimensionality of the self Nancy describes can be cast as conducive to multiplicity, whose reverberant movements give way to all types of creative connections, frictions, communions as well as metaphors, ways of listening and telling, fantasies. To search for guidance, for bringing me and not-me into balance, the doctoring founded on lessons grasped by way of the senses, these are centered on giving room to greater sympathies, to the spectrum of reasoning that passes across a multiplicity of logics, knowledges, practices. Such a perspective is helpful in understanding inner voice and listening as what diffuse the borders between inside and outside, as well as rational and irrational, reason and unreason, giving way to an *environmental self*. This is a configuration of selfhood replete with voice and wind, Things and fantasies, *logos* and dreams, brimming with X and all its unpronounceable languages, and which gives rise to a range of inventive gestures, rituals, creations, *listenings* by which doctoring, and a care of the self, is approached and worked at.

⤿

I have been putting into play a range of perspectives as to the question of listening and inner life. From inner voice as the basis for a care of the self to an inner listening that works at balancing relations, from negotiating the cut underpinning concepts of the self to learning from the environment and planetary kin, listening-into emerges as the means by which to sense the deep bonds embedding oneself in a world with others. Inner listening is an essential form of listening, one that sets the tone for other listenings; it emerges as the primary ground from which to know of oneself, as inner and outer, as subject and world, and through which one works at critical understanding. This includes the capacity to be receptive to the voices and messages from the environment, and the sacred stories that weave land and self, body and spirit, together. Subsequently, listening is poised between the physical and metaphysical, between social and cosmological orders, between bodily sensing and the dreaming that calls for an intuitive knowing. It is by following these perspectives that listening may be cast as a *cosmopoetical technique*, where locality and the specificities of immediate experience are grasped while simultaneously being understood globally, as related to a greater ecology of relations. This is a technique, a mattering that moves and unsettles binary oppositions, and the often fixed schema of self and other, even me and not-me, positioning listening as what specifically traffics across singularities, discourses, bodies, worlds. Listening wields its influence through conducting connection, empathy, encounter, for bridging mind and body, inside and outside, the reverberant arena of inner life with the surrounding living world. The cosmopoetical work of listening is one that helps anchor and orient individuality, affirming one's place among others, while opening paths onto dreaming and the recognition of other worlds.

These are the ongoing reverberations that follow me through the day, from sudden melodies that appear when waking up, the summer sun already stirring, through to the tired thoughts that fall quiet, that already feel draped in dream, all this listening going on all day, every day, and that mysteriously, chaotically gather into a type of form at times, or that flow across the living time of myself, disappearing, returning, telling me their secrets—the red scarves tied to chain link fences or the small pockets full of sand—compiling themselves as part of the ongoing stitching piece by piece.

〜

The notion of listening as a cosmopoetical technique finds support in the writings of the psychoanalyst Theodor Reik.[31] Through his clinical work, Reik developed the concept of "the third ear" as a way of describing a particular modality of listening key to psychoanalysis. To listen with the third ear for Reik is to work at noticing what is unsaid within the said, or rather, what is said by way of the unsaid. This includes the capacity to attune to the silences that paradoxically resound with meanings, that capture something of the unconscious drives that animate individual lives. "Psychoanalysis is in this sense not so much a heart-to-heart talk as a drive-to-drive talk, an inaudible but highly expressive dialogue. The psychoanalyst has to learn how one mind speaks to another beyond words and in silence."[32] Being able to listen by way of the third ear as an analyst is essential to the therapeutic process in which the communication of patients is given expression across a diversity of gestures—what Reik terms "a thousand little signs," including a range of paralinguistic utterances, body movements, *how* things are said or left unsaid.

Importantly, for Reik, the third ear includes turning toward oneself as an analyst, to be aware of the effects of all that transpires between oneself and a patient. To listen with the third ear is, for the analyst, to become sensitive to

---

[31] Theodor Reik, *Listening with the Third Ear: The Inner Experience of a Psychoanalyst* (New York: Farrar, Straus, 1949).

[32] Ibid., 144.

one's own unconscious processes, the things one hears from others but also within oneself, and how one may come to respond and interpret a patient's statements or silences.[33] Essential to Reik's understanding of the third ear is to encourage a shift from mastering the problems exposed within analysis, or wielding a certain totalizing interpretation, in which a thousand little signs are reduced to a fixed set of meanings; instead, Reik invites a communion of unconscious minds, highlighting the importance of "touching" over "grasping," of continually broadening one's sensitivity to a given patient. "The psychoanalyst who must look at all things immediately, scrutinize them, and subject them to logical examination has often lost the psychological moment for seizing the fleeting, elusive material."[34] Listening with the third ear is to recognize all that is "whispered between sentences and without sentences," and which too often go unnoticed or unremarked, that appear as so little but which carry a great deal.[35] Moreover, it is a listening through which the analyst becomes sensitive to the ways in which analysis is equally an unconscious process—that everything which goes on within the analyst participates. The third ear is that listening-into which "can hear voices from within the self that are otherwise not audible because they are drowned out by the noise of our conscious thought-processes."[36] To receive the messages, the signals, the whispers of the unconscious voice is to put "reason" to the side Reik suggests, to proceed as a wanderer within oneself, so as to discover the "secret meanings of this almost imperceptible, imponderable language."[37]

I follow Reik's concept or practice of the third ear, with its approach to the communion of unconscious minds and the ways in which it is touched by the secret meanings of whispered languages, as suggestive for a cosmopoetical technique. This is a form of listening that works at acknowledging the fullness and density of individual lives, affording ways to honor the complex reverberations passing across inside and outside, and to which reason must give way, allowing entry of the almost imponderable language of the real, the unpronounceable X. Such cosmopoetical moves are grounded in appreciating the degree to which listening is not necessarily a form of focused attention; rather, listening also *erratically floats* in a movement at one and the same time conscious and

[33] Ibid., 147.
[34] Ibid., 145.
[35] Ibid.
[36] Ibid., 147.
[37] Ibid.

unconscious, direct and indirect, and which enacts that form of touching Reik emphasizes as key by drawing forward as much as retreating back, that wanders and wonders. This is expressive of the *auditory I*, as that form of I configured as a membrane affording all types of impressions and feelings, that is receptive and responsive, that follows the whispered meanings, and that, importantly, knows of silence as deeply resonant.

The relation between listening and health, between inner voice and a care of the self, is prominently figured in psychoanalytic practice. As Reik notes, psychoanalytic process is never strictly tied to outspoken forms of articulation. What resides within, in terms of repressed or forgotten memories, shameful desires, and difficult dreams, or dilemmas in life, influence much of one's psychological and emotional state, not to mention physical well-being. This extends to the analyst as much as the patient. Listening, in this context, is fundamental for giving time and space for challenging things to be said, for confronting difficult feelings, and for working at processes of repair. As Fred Griffin argues, listening contributes to creating a much-needed *holding environment*, making room for things needing to be said as well as for protecting them with silence.[38]

Following from Lacan's concept of the Thing, as that empty center that *nonetheless speaks*, that figures a range of impossible objects by way of absence, I'm interested to understand how silence becomes listenable—is cast as meaningful and central to the self. Inner life itself is constituted by a paradoxical silence, for this is a silence through which subjectivity is defined (the Thing designates this arrangement, revealing the self as empty); it is a silence that constitutes the inner voice—this voice that is no-voice, that is founded on not-me and which is so much Me: a paradoxical figure, X. As a cosmopoetical technique, listening-into knows of silence as resonant, as meaningful, as what holds the hurt as well as gives way to its assuagement.

What particular forms might this silence take, and how is it one can be aware of its influence? In what ways does silence speak, contributing to processes of repair or interfering with their work? And in what sense is silence a defining feature of inner life, contouring the dynamics of inner listening? How is silence

---

[38] Fred L. Griffin, *Creative Listening and the Psychoanalytic Process: Sensibility, Engagement and Envisioning* (London: Routledge, 2016).

made listenable? In her work on relational psychoanalysis, Jessica Benjamin argues for the importance of play.[39] As is often the case, experiences of trauma or repression can lock oneself in, provoking a mental, emotional, and physical block tensed by pain, shame, fear, and the inability to find a way out. Encountering such debilitating obstacles, Benjamin recognizes in play the possibility of restoring "movement," which can greatly assist in "trying on" other feelings and other narratives.[40] Play allows one to regain a sense of movement and flexibility when confronting loss or feelings of having *no way out*. These perspectives take guidance from the theories of D. W. Winnicott whose clinical work with children in the 1960s led to deeper understandings as to the importance of play.[41] From the perspective of a poetics of listening, and the ways in which inner life resounds with voicings as well as silences, play is not only the joyful enactments of certain games or narratives; play is also at the heart of imagination. Poetics, in fact, can be appreciated as being grounded in wonder and the capacity to be curious as to the world around; the ability *to marvel* at things stands as the basis for poetic imagination and leads to creative expression—playing with things, inventing words, staging stories, trying on other voices. To bring play into the scene of therapy is to invite a new sense for the potentiality of words, things, bodies, and relations, all of which may ease the burden of an unbearable silence or shift the weight of particular obstacles, allowing for new ways of *knowing silence*, even *trying it on*.

Silence shifts across different registers. It figures as a state of repression, that something is being held or forced back—a traumatic experience, an unspeakable desire—and which often contributes to illness or challenges in life. At the same time, silence gives, supporting the holding needed at times; it is therapeutic in itself, providing protection, or allowing one to hear the music within and the almost imperceptible, imponderable language of the self. The arena of therapeutic process shows these multiple ways in which silence *speaks* and, in doing so, emerges as a language. Knowing this language, trying it on—*finding ways of listening-into silence*—is therefore an essential part of a care of the self. One may listen for the inner voice as constituting *logos*, but such a voice is nothing but silence. In this way, silence may emerge less as something to fear,

---

[39] Jessica Benjamin, *Beyond Doer and Done To: Recognition Theory, Intersubjectivity and the Third* (New York: Routledge, 2018), 144.
[40] Ibid.
[41] D. W. Winnicott, *Playing and Reality* (London: Routledge, 2005).

as unbearable, as an empty center to be avoided, and more as something to befriend, as something to listen to in itself.

Listening as a cosmopoetical technique knows of the importance of silence, knows its shadowy as well as supportive capacities. It recognizes its painful and poetic dimensions, and how silence is at the heart of the self. While the real that hovers as an empty center of the self may be founded on lack and a cut from unity—it may be the thing one wants to avoid, to repress, that unbearable memory of separation—it may also participate in sustaining us, helping to listen ever-more creatively to what the self needs, desires, contains, and carries.

Lost Voices, Consciousness-Raising, and the Courage to Listen

Moving from the inner voicing that supports ways of navigating a social world to the complex movements of silence and speech central to psychoanalytic processes, the question of inner life and its relation to listening reveals many fundamental understandings. This includes recognizing how listening is positioned as the means for sensing, knowing, and figuring oneself and the inner truth one may carry. By defining such capacities as poetic I hope to gain a deeper appreciation for the work of listening, as one that not only contributes to participating within a given system or relationship, but that engenders new meeting points, new ways of telling and speaking, and that lends to acts of self-determination. As Foucault argues, inner voice is engaged in a work of liberation. This can be said of listening as well, where to listen inwardly is to cultivate a care of the self, to equip one with needed truths and techniques. From attending to the silences that speak, so as to know of their ever-shifting meanings, to being radically receptive to the environment and its voices, such poetic affordances give way to the care as well as the re-creation of the self—to tell one's own story.

The poetic invention of the self is given profound articulation in the work of Gloria Anzaldúa. Her writings engage with the power of storying oneself, especially in terms of speaking from the *borderlands* of mixed identity. Such a power finds direction by attuning to a multiplicity of inner voices: "We relate by going inward and relating to the different parts of ourselves. If I can relate to the negative, depressive Gloria, the greedy, stingy, starving-for-affection Gloria—if I have a good relationship with my different parts, my different selves, I can carry this inner relationship outward and have good relationships

40   *Poetics of Listening*

with others."[42] Anzaldúa's work is marked by mixed identity, whether in terms of being Chicana, growing up on the Mexican-American border in Texas, or by way of living as a lesbian within a patriarchal, heteronormative society and community, or in speaking across Spanish and English, or in recognizing herself as multiple, as home to a range of sacred beings, female spirits, historical and archetypal figures, from La Llorona to La Malinche, from Virgen de Guadalupe to the Serpent Woman of the Earth—these all reside within Gloria. And they appear in her writings by way of what the author calls "her awakened dreaming" (echoing Gaston Bachelard's poetics of reverie, as that instant of *dreaming with the eyes open*, or Lispector's *sleep-work*)—this poetic power assists Anzaldúa in speaking as a borderland, as *mestiza*.

> My "awakened dreams" are about shifts. Thought shifts, reality shifts, gender shifts: one person metamorphoses into another in a world where people fly through the air, heal from mortal wounds. I am playing with my Self, I am playing with the world's soul. I am the dialogue between my Self and *el espíritu del mundo*, I change myself, I change the world.[43]

This is the poetic birthing by which to survive, to transform, to reappropriate oneself as a borderland populated by multiple selves, spirits, languages: to enact a form of inner work so as to speak, as Anzaldúa does, against the orders imposed from an outside and which demand singularity, Oneness.

〜

The mixed subjectivity Anzaldúa embodies is founded on the shaping of an inner voice, one which finds truth in all that one is—the social complexities, the sacred stories, the strange dreams, the inner demons. These are struggles that reveal something of the process Foucault describes, and which can also be found in Frantz Fanon's understanding of the psychology of the colonized.[44] As Fanon outlines, the subject position of the colonized is often one that grapples with a complex internalization of the dominant culture, and which gives way to a continual feeling of inadequacy. Anzaldúa captures this experience when she writes

> There are many defense strategies that the self uses to escape the agony of inadequacy and I have used all of them. I have split from and disowned those

---

[42] Gloria Anzaldúa, *Borderlands/La Frontera: The New Mestiza* (San Francisco: Aunt Lute Books, 2012), 195.

[43] Ibid., 92.

[44] Frantz Fanon, *Black Skin, White Masks* (New York: Grove Press, 2008).

parts of myself that others rejected. I have used rage to drive others away and to insulate myself against exposure. I have reciprocated with contempt for those who have roused shame in me. I have internalized rage and contempt, one part of the self (the accusatory, persecutory, judgmental) using defense strategies against another part of the self (the object of contempt). As a person, I, as a people, we, Chicanos, blame ourselves, hate ourselves, terrorize ourselves. Most of this goes on unconsciously; we only know that we are hurting, we suspect that there is something "wrong" with us, something fundamentally "wrong."[45]

Anzaldúa's descriptions of the social, psychological challenges of the colonized subject speak toward the urgencies and complexities of the emancipatory work of an inner voice. The voice of self-determination that Anzaldúa comes to embody, there upon the borderlands of mixed subjectivity, is one aligned with an idiosyncratic cosmology of the sacred and the profane; it is a voice rich in ancestral songs and myths pulled through the imperial structures binding her to systems of abuse and that attempt to *tame the wild tongue,* and which give way to a *mestiza consciousness.* This is a consciousness built upon a negotiation with the hurting, with the internal battle reflective of the colonized subject position, and that Anzaldúa works at inhabiting—speaking by way of all that comes to constitute this multiple self.

Such is the poetic voice Anzaldúa configures, "one capable of communicating the realities and values true to themselves."[46] This is a language, an inner truth, a writing that invents itself, weaving from the rough wool of broken Spanish and English a "patois, a forked tongue."[47] Anzaldúa's poetics is marked by this state of being-between, which is both politically charged and cosmopoetically creative, for it affords navigating across worlds and languages, to materialize a communicative act that also works at building solidarity and alliances. These are words that call for greater listening—"We have to listen to the Native people, we have to listen to the Indian and the Chicana … We have to listen to the indigenous part of ourselves."[48] Anzaldúa is a guide into awakened dreaming, as the inner work that incites all types of shifts. And that in using the pen "as a weapon and means of transformation"[49] gives challenge to dominant society.

---

[45] Anzaldúa, *Borderlands/La Frontera,* 67.
[46] Ibid., 77.
[47] Ibid.
[48] Gloria Anzaldúa, *Interviews/Entrevistas* (New York: Routledge, 2000), 187.
[49] Ibid., 189.

> *It murmurs inside. It murmurs. Inside is the pain of speech the pain to say. Larger still. Greater than is the pain not to say. To not say. Says nothing against the pain to speak. It festers inside. The wound, liquid, dust. Must break. Must void.*

I share the above quotation from the opening pages of *Dictée* by Theresa Hak Kyung Cha, as it captures the tensed nature of speech/silence often shaping inner life.[50] In parallel to Gloria Anzaldúa's work, Theresa Hak Kyung Cha provides a compelling view onto how one may grapple with experiences of an external world marked, in her case, by military occupation.

Dictée is a complex text that employs a multiplicity of voices, and in doing so opens a means for negotiating the violence of an exterior world, in this case defined by the occupation of Korea throughout the twentieth century, first by the Japanese and then later, by the United States and the Soviet Union. Cha, a Korean American (born in Korea during the Korean War) working as a filmmaker and artist throughout the 1970s until her death in 1982, chronicles her personal relation to histories of colonialism, occupation, and war, doing so with a particular focus on the poetics and politics of language and speech, including questions of translation and mistranslation. Structured by way of nine chapters, each titled following the nine Greek muses (including the "mistaken" insertion of invented ones), *Dictée* performatively immerses a reader in an act of dictation, a language game that results in a collage of writing, photographs and film stills, handwritten letters, historical and scientific documents, all of which moves across multiple languages, including Korean, Latin, English, French, and Chinese. Importantly, *Dictée* brings a reader into the complicated condition of a speech withheld, yet one that nonetheless pushes itself across *the wound, the void*—that develops strategies for negotiating the politics of language, especially as aligned with nationalism. It is a text that maps in detail the continually interrupted journey of vocalization, a "rarely audible" or "hardly audible at all" voice, one "reduced to a moan, a hum, staccato inhalation, and finally, a wail."[51] As with Anzaldúa, Theresa Hak Kyung Cha writes from a position of the border—a border-subjectivity—which comes to impact onto the very nature of words, the relation between signifier and signified, and how one may find the courage to speak against or in spite of the Japanese occupation that would outlaw the Korean language. "There is no future, only the onslaught of time,"

---

[50] Theresa Hak Kyung Cha, *Dictée* (Berkeley: Third Woman Press, 1995).
[51] Ibid., 139.

Listening-into

Cha writes. How to speak from within such a condition? To move from the moaning and humming of a voice withheld, suppressed, foreclosed, to that of an affirmative articulation, one that might carry the inner truth of oneself and the histories of one's collective world?

↜

Dictée is a work that strategically inhabits the "oblivion of the present" in which writing proceeds by way of fragments, mistakes, imperfect translations, where letters and syllables, documents and notations move across the page to create gaps, frictions, auto-ethnographic threads that resist history, nation, and language as one of singularity—a writing that never quite adds up. Rather, *Dictée* is multilingual, multifaceted, dispersed; it learns and unlearns at the same time; and it is a voice whose rarely audible, inner utterances show themselves somehow:

> *She says to herself if she were able to write she could continue to live. She says to herself if she would write without ceasing. To herself if by writing she could abolish real time. She would live. If she could display it before her and become its voyeur.*[52]

These are strangely private articulations put on display *for herself*, made accessible through a disjointed writing, an externalization that figures as uncannily within, a within/without movement by which life is held. *To speak to herself* emerges as a horizon by which to regain connection, to herself, to the possibility of a return to language. For Cha, these are inner words that, by way of writing, open themselves against the real time of the present, which is a time marked by what Jalal Toufic terms the "surpassing disaster"—a disaster that withdraws tradition.[53] For Cha, this wields its influence by way of extended forms of occupation, as well as her own immigration to the United States when she was twelve (returning to Korea for the first time seventeen years later). Negotiating the oppressiveness of the Japanese occupation, which included being forced to learn and speak Japanese, and the state of exile she and her family would experience, *Dictée* is deeply marked by fragmentation, by a multilingual subjectivity that is both broken and self-determined. As Toufic suggests, the surpassing disaster leaves its variegated and diffused marks, rendering language and voice partially mute. This is a disaster whose echoes continue across time to enforce their weight and

---

[52] Ibid., 141.
[53] Jalal Toufic, "The Withdrawal of Tradition Past a Surpassing Disaster," 2009. Found on the author's website: https://jalaltoufic.com/downloads/Jalal_Toufic,_The_Withdrawal_of_Tradition_Past_a_Surpassing_Disaster.pdf (accessed July 2024).

44 *Poetics of Listening*

gravity, pulling the voice back down onto itself. Consequently, such disasters perform their influence by way of withdrawals, absenting tradition from within particular communities. The "oblivion of the present" for Cha is precisely this withdrawal, where history gives no room for the violences it holds, for the lives that persevere under its brutality; the languages by which to bear witness are equally removed, marginalized, made absent.

> I heard the signs. Remnants. Missing.
>
> The mute signs. Never the same.
>
> Absent.[54]

The withdrawn tradition instigated by the surpassing disaster is equally the withdrawn tongue, the withheld speech provoked by language's removal; rather, one starts and stops, "to bite the tongue. / Swallow. / Deep. / Deeper." One is left only with the physical organs of tongue, mouth, and the subsequent starts and stops of sound: "One by one. / The sounds. / The sounds that move at a time / stops."[55]—making it impossible to distinguish the signs, the said, the memory. Language, instead, is to be found "in the rain" and "onslaught of time," whose mists and pressures unsettle the clarity of the spoken, withdrawing the voice into itself—back into the mouth, making of it a "Cracked tongue. / Broken tongue." that produces only a semblance of noise.[56] These are states that, for Cha, are reflective of experiences of occupation while emerging as the very means by which to speak—the cracked tongue is reappropriated as a subject position in itself, one that neither "imagines a 'true' home nor proposes to construct one."[57]

↬

From Gloria Anzaldúa, and the articulations of a *mestiza* consciousness, to Theresa Hak Kyung Cha and how it is one may speak by way of withdrawal, I'm concerned to further an understanding of inner life as deeply influenced by listening's resistant work. Listening-into is a listening that grapples with all that comes to be buried within, the imponderable languages, the internalized shame, the suppressed voice, the withdrawn tradition which, as Anzaldúa and Cha both show, are deeply formative. From a *mestiza* consciousness that

---

[54] Cha, *Dictée*, 69.
[55] Ibid., 75.
[56] Ibid.
[57] Juliana Spahr, *Everybody's Autonomy: Connective Reading and Collective Identity* (Tuscaloosa: University of Alabama Press, 2001), 152.

speaks with a forked tongue, a wild voice constituted by multiplicity, to the impossibility of making a sound against an oppressive silence, which breaks the tongue altogether, their works give way to inner voicings that find the courage to write themselves aloud. These are the complex movements passing across inside and outside, that listen-into the dissonant multiplicities constituting a colonized self, and that come to carry the struggles, the memories, the hurting shaped by domination. By way of an impossible listening, and the poetic acts of writing that resist the violences one bears within, freedom is fought for.

༼

Working against systems of discrimination, Anzaldúa's poetics is deeply aligned with the capacity to inhabit the borderlands, a poetics tethered to the project of self-determination—and which finds expression in what the author highlights as her *Shadow-Beast*, or the rebel within.[58] The Shadow-Beast emerges as the inexhaustible drive toward liberation, toward remaining free from the "orders from outside authorities" as well as the dictates of her own conscious will shaped by colonization. This is a shadowy poetics, a cosmopoetical technique, taking guidance from *awakened dreams* and the visions of a deeper truth—"I am possessed by a vision: that we Chicanas and Chicanos have taken back or uncovered our true faces, our dignity and self-respect."[59]—visions that help in deflecting all those voices that impose their oppressive force. By way of her Shadow-Beast, which is clearly a type of *Thing*, a Pure *it*, Anzaldúa fathoms the courage to embody a new consciousness of mixed ideas, mixed identities, mixed languages, conjuring a path, a linguistic, social and sacred path of emancipation.

The emancipatory project of Anzaldúa finds parallel expression in Theresa Hak Kyung Cha's *Dictée*. While employing different creative tactics, Cha is equally focused on struggles of liberation; these are grounded in struggles of language and voice, of history and colonialism. Cha is also a child of the borderland, situated in relation to the 38th parallel as the dividing line marking North and South Korea (instituted by the US military at the end of the Second World War). The artist's inner struggle is deeply tied to the trauma of military occupation, as well as that of exile and immigration, and the violences that force one to speak *otherwise. Dictée* is a book of self-realization and resilience; it works at bearing witness to the author herself—it is a masked autobiography, a fragmented auto-ethnography, one whose inability to articulate in plain view

---

[58] Anzaldúa, *Borderlands/La Frontera*, 38.
[59] Ibid., 109.

leads to a labyrinthine construct of fragments, each of which inhibits as well as liberates its maker.

Importantly, for both authors there is a profound relation to the issue of women's lives; their's are unquestionably projects connected to histories of women, and the greater work of women's liberation. As a queer, Chicana writer Anzaldúa's new *mestiza* is one marked by an identity politics in which gender, queerness, and female power are key factors; Cha's *Dictée* is a book defined by the voices of women, from Joan of Arc and Sappho to the Korean revolutionary Yu Gwan-sun along with her own mother Hyun Soon You. Each of the writers are also developing their thinking and practices in the context of the 1970s and early 1980s (*Dictée* was published in 1982 and is influenced by Cha's time spent at the University of Berkeley in the 1970s studying art and comparative literature, and Anzaldúa's early editorial work on *This Bridge Called My Back: Writings by Radical Women of Color* (1981) contributed to her semi-autobiographical *Borderlands/La Frontera: The New Mestiza* published in 1987). In this regard, their projects can lend to appreciating the women's movement, and feminist activism, as a culture shaped by questions and practices of consciousness-raising. That is, I'm led to read their works as liberatory acts founded on consciousness-raising, on working through inner struggles—to cultivate a care of the self so as to equip one with needed truths and techniques; and which finds echo in the broader culture of feminist consciousness-raising practices starting in the late 1960s. These are movements and practices which, in turn, give expression to the transformative power of listening.

The researchers Lucia Farinati and Claudia Firth highlight in *The Force of Listening* how feminist consciousness-raising is grounded in a performative politics of listening.[60] This manifested itself through the act of women coming together, to share and discuss personal experiences, and to say things normally unsaid. Consciousness-raising groups allowed for a process where women "learned to ask new questions about themselves, built self-esteem and a sense of entitlement to opportunity, gave names to their common experiences and discovered that they were not alone. Consciousness-raising was a foundation for change."[61] Importantly, creating a circle of talking and listening became

---

[60] Lucia Farinati and Claudia Firth, *The Force of Listening* (Berlin: Errant Bodies Press, 2017).
[61] Paula Kamen, quoted in Stacey K. Sowards and Valerie R. Renegar, "The Rhetorical Functions of Consciousness-Raising in Third Wave Feminism," *Communications Studies*, vol. 55, no. 4 (Winter 2004): 536.

extremely supportive as well as nurturing of a greater process of liberation: to feel that one's own experience and voice matter. These are gestures and acts that came to nurture a deep form of self- and collective-empowerment. Anna Sherbany, an artist and one of the interlocutors Farinati and Firth interview, captures the experience by noting how consciousness-raising groups "gave us a space to talk, it gave us a language to talk with, it gave me the confidence to talk in a space like that, also it encouraged me to talk about things that otherwise I would not have talked about."[62] Such encouragement, as Farinati and Firth highlight, was not only the basis for personal development, but furthermore, created the conditions for political activism. Feminist consciousness-raising groups "made us feel that we had the power to achieve things, to have the right to do that and taking the message to the people we were working with."[63] This was about challenging the system, giving women the strength and critical means for talking back, instigating change, organizing the women's movement. As Carol Hanisch argues in her seminal article, "The Personal Is Political," consciousness-raising groups were a form of political action. "It is at this point a political action to tell it like it is, to say what I really believe about my life instead of what I've always been told to say."[64]

In turning to the history of feminist consciousness-raising, I'm concerned to elaborate understandings of inner life and the ways in which listening-into contributes to a care of the self as an emancipatory work. From Gloria Anzaldúa and Theresa Hak Kyung Cha we learn how the inner voice, and the struggles around speaking up against systems of oppression, can mobilize poetic forms of resistance, contestation, self-determination—to find the means for keeping close to an inner truth, one that helps manage or deflect the difficult experiences one may go through or inherit by way of particular systems of abuse. And which entails a broader therapeutic work that can contribute to building community. Gloria Anzaldúa gives expression to this through her focus on alliance-making as acts of healing: "You're trying to heal a community or a culture while healing yourself. That's all alliance work is: you're trying to heal the wounds. You're trying to bring in justice, human rights, to people who have been wounded."[65]

---

[62] Farinati and Firth, *The Force of Listening*, 45.
[63] Ibid.
[64] Carol Hanisch, "The Personal Is Political," in *Notes from the Second Year: Radical Feminism*, ed. Shulamith Firestone and Anne Koedt (New York: Notes from the Second Year, 1970), 76.
[65] Anzaldúa, *Interviews/Entrevistas*, 199.

These are feminist acts of organizing, of self- and collective-empowerment, that give challenge to a dominant order of language, gender, politics—to find within oneself and through others the capacity for speaking one's own language, however forked or broken, wild or withdrawn. "We were being listened to, we were listening to each other, that was the whole idea, but in order to be listened to, we were also learning to talk, to articulate things, to find the language."[66]

Co-ownership of an Inner World

In considering the ways in which listening is positioned as a capacity for approaching and attending to the self, I've sought to engage a range of perspectives. Moving from an examination of inner voice as central to a care of the self, as what assists in negotiating the constant impingement of an external world with all its teachings (and potential harms), and toward an appreciation for the unconscious drives that give greatly to defining subjectivity, listening is positioned as what attends—if not *evokes*—the reverberant arena of inner life. And in doing so contributes to cultivating a language, a voice, a poetics of transformation—to find ways of inhabiting the empty center, as the first outside of oneself. This is the living water, as Clarice Lispector underscores, whose dissonant harmonies carry a plethora of meaningful voices.

The dynamics of inner life find additional expression by way of an engagement with Indigenous cultural practices and belief systems, as articulated through the writings of Bear Heart, whose doctoring practice allows for understanding listening-into as a means for attuning to the voices of planetary kin and the lessons to be found in nature. The inner dimension of the self emerges as a reverberant arena through which sacred messages pass and are held. And which comes to necessitate a sensitivity, a listening-into by which to undertake the work of healing. Such perspectives and experiences lend to shifting understandings of the self from that of a contained singularity toward a more environmental construct.

Engaging the reverberations of an inner world, I'm led to find in listening an act, a gesture, a capacity for consciousness-raising, for finding, defining, and expressing an inner truth—of oneself, of a collective-communal body, of

---

[66] Farinati and Firth, *The Force of Listening*, 45.

a cosmopoetical ethos or vision of connectedness. Such processes elaborate a care of the self that give onto ways of enacting change. In following the intensely charged and experimental writings of Clarice Lispector, Gloria Anzaldúa, and Therese Hak Kyung Cha, poetics emerges as a challenge to forms of oppression, colonization, and discrimination. What the three authors reveal, in their profoundly individual and courageous ways, are the poetic paths by which to chart emancipatory journeys—to give way to the living waters, the *mestiza* consciousness, the withdrawn voice that speaks *otherwise*. These are journeys that draw from the complex inner worlds of personal lives, to lend to the care as well as the re-creation of the self.

⌒

Returning to a poetics of listening, and the urgencies I sense in terms of giving greater attention to listening, questions of inner voice seem strikingly important. For inner voice, as Foucault suggests, works at *logos* as critical consciousness and the capacity to speak truth, and which, as I've tried to highlight, include a profound relation to the unconscious. To be *thought-full* is to foster the inner life as an omnidimensional auditorium reverberant with insights and *inheards*, the ponderable and imponderable languages by which the voices within resound. From the positive to negative, familiar to unfamiliar, from those that support and those that hurt, all such voicings contribute to shaping consciousness, giving traction to the ongoing work of *logos* and the urgency of finding and holding a vision—an inner truth, *of dignity and self-respect*. Consciousness-raising practices reveal the ways in which inner life is greatly influenced by external systems and structures, relationships and environments that surround, and where internal transformations can do much to support collective forms of action.

What is this inner voice precisely? Is it even a voice in the conventional sense? How to follow from the empty center of the self, as the unconscious foundation of inner voicing, to the making of a discourse, a reasoning, that can challenge those fixed logics often cutting against the fullness of lives? As wisdom traditions emphasize, planetary voices are vital to shaping an inner voice, where the ability to give attention to the environment guides the respect and the doctoring one may give to others. To listen needs to be appreciated as an act, a subject position adept at moving across physical and metaphysical, grounded and spiritual perspectives, suggesting a cosmopoetical technique. I understand such a technique as one that can aid in contending with the politics of subjectivation and the socialization of the self, that may help one persevere against colonizing systems and violences; to find one's inner truth from within the borderlands, or by way of the mysteries whose voices we may only hear in our dreams.

By following these perspectives, I'm led to emphasize a *co-ownership* of inner life, in which learning how to speak, how to listen, to be listened to, and how to voice what truly matters are worked through. From the strange dynamic between me and not-me, the I and the Me of the self, and the Thing that is always there and not there at the same time, lending its unvoiced voice, through to the personal struggles within, and the guiding spirits and winds that give support when one needs it most, all these inter- and intra-voicings passing within and across bodies and worlds, it may be said that what counts as inner life are the multiple ways in which one listens: to oneself, to others, to the past and the present. As with the multiplicity of voices defining inner life, so there must be multiple listenings as well. While an inner life may feel singularly one's own—and this may be part of its strength, its meaningfulness, its ever-present and enduring voice—such singularity is always already shaped and populated by others, even the other of oneself. This multiplicity, this co-ownership, sets in motion so many imaginings, reflections, creations, so many dreams, troubles, resistances. All of which resound noisily and beautifully, painfully and passionately, as that chamber music Clarice Lispector cannot ignore and which she can only poetically name X. Such a name leans toward that empty center brimming with the real, as all those voices that call one into listening, that open us onto listening, as a path to self-realization.

2

Listening-toward: Recognition, Thirdness, and Compassionate Action

The turning inward that listening conducts, as part of a care of the self, is never far from listening outwardly, toward others. Knowing by way of listening is profoundly *in* the world, intensifying an attentional concern. As with sensing in general, listening extends the capacity to participate as part of a living world. Yet, in following listening a critical and creative view begins to emerge, in terms of recognizing the ways in which listening is never strictly tethered to sound and auditory experience. Listening, rather, traverses the senses, figuring a broader, thicker form of attention onto the sights and sounds, tastes and smells, the tenacity and tenderness of things. As with the capacity to listen inwardly, to care for the emotional, psychological, and spiritual composition of oneself, not to mention the physical vitality and strain of bodily existence, listening names a greater form and force of attention—a gesture, a capacity, a *poetics*, by which to attend to the never-ending story of self and others, and especially of all things together. Part of this entails a relation to ethics, where listening-toward others invites and demands a critical sensitivity as to positionality, history, ability. While listening is extremely supportive in fostering empathy and understanding, allowing for the working through or holding of differences, it can also injure and harm; listening may wield a force of capture, compounding histories of discrimination by *othering* others.

Questions of positionality open important considerations as to listening's role in nurturing social bonds and the ways in which it participates and informs structural and systemic marginalizations of particular individuals and communities. To contend with these ethical concerns, I want to bring forward a consideration of the relation between listening and recognition. Recognition is underscored as a process by which individuals gain self-esteem and feelings of connection across social worlds; moreover, recognition contributes to the ongoing work of political representation and action, functioning as a primary mechanism for struggle.[1] Such views are guided by appreciating how urgent it is to experience *being heard* within given environments, social circles, and institutions, however intimate or extended, formal and informal. This gains greater traction by recognizing how hearing and being heard are central to the functioning of democratic societies in terms of securing forms of social and political representation and participation. This includes a profound relation to acts of witnessing, where the experiences and realities of others are key to inciting change. To hear and be heard feature as primary mechanisms for enactments of justice, supporting the essential foundation to conceptions of social equality and collective repair. This is not to suggest that recognition is only possible through the material fact of voice, or that hearing is only fulfilled by way of sounded events. Rather, notions of being heard are clearly metaphoric as well, in which the capacity to be recognized by others, as well as social and political systems, is worked through. Hearing and being heard thus stand for the urgency and need for acknowledgment, and which are equally grounded in understandings of voice in all its expansive and divergent manners, as what animates and fulfills human individuality and community.

For my purposes, recognition offers a framework for engaging voice and listening as they come to facilitate, manifest, and punctuate relations. This extends across times and scales, from the micro-dimensions or instances shaping daily life to broader macro-structures and histories that give definition to a politics of rights and recognition. In particular, bringing into focus a concern for recognition affords a view onto listening as deeply influential to dialogical acts and processes, keeping one attuned to the emergent meanings underpinning concern for others.

Parallel to the ways in which listening inwardly aligns with truth-seeking, self-determination, and a care of the self, listening-toward others is equally transformative. While listening is often perceived as a form of passive reception, a sitting back and taking in, listening also *impacts* that which it engages. Are we not intensely influenced by the listening given to us by others? From daily experiences of small exchange to deeper, more caring instances in which listeners

---

[1] The issue of recognition as a social mechanism is elaborated by Axel Honneth in his work, *The Struggle for Recognition*, which greatly informs my thinking on the topic. See Axel Honneth, *The Struggle for Recognition: The Moral Grammar of Social Conflicts* (Cambridge: Polity Press, 1996).

act as witnesses, listening is an essential form of generosity and compassion. Furthermore, knowing that someone is listening, we may adjust our behavior and way of speaking; we may even lower our voices so as not to be heard within a particular situation. Listening intervenes; it supports, encourages, incites, and it may also hurt, harm, control, and capture—it is far from passive or purely receptive. In listening to others we also open ourselves in ways that impact onto our individual, physical presence—what we hear can also change something of us, not only in terms of opinion or viewpoint but something of the body and the affective interlacing of self and others. As such, what becomes of ethical relations by way of listening? Are there particular insights to be found by considering listening's place within histories of struggle, and how it is understood to influence processes of truth and reconciliation? And further, what may a poetics of listening suggest in terms of contending with diverse human realities and their stories?

I'll follow these concerns by unpacking a set of theoretical perspectives in order to deepen understanding as to listening's role in nurturing social relations. This includes focusing on questions or modes of recognition, from the intersubjective and the shaping of oneself through another, to the challenges around legal or constitutional recognition of First Nations Peoples in the context of Australia (as a case in point). In thinking through the affirmative processes of recognition, I also strive to acknowledge critical debates that challenge recognition as a defining model for political action. As I'm concerned to pose, *listening-toward* wields input onto intersubjectivity, and the project of recognition, by engaging diverse positionalities and cultural understandings. Listening-toward is underscored as what can help in keeping close to struggles for recognition by *holding* difference.

The Way of Love, Poetics and Politics of the Not-Yet

The embodied, ethical dynamic articulated in listening-toward others finds an elaborated point of reference in the writings of Luce Irigaray, particularly in her book *The Way of Love*.

Central to Irigaray's project is a concern to challenge prevailing structures or ways of speaking, calling for a "new culture" of speech and, by extension, voice. For Irigaray, we do not yet know how to speak: "Our rational tradition has been much concerned with 'speaking about' but has reduced 'speaking with' to a speaking" that fails to truly encounter the difference of one another.[2] *Speaking with* thus calls us into a more nuanced form of relational engagement untethered from a prevailing logic of the absolute, one that can aid in challenging the languages, ways of speaking and the cultural logics grounded in a fear or distrust of difference—of that which falls outside the domain of a universal Truth. To speak with is to upset the tendency toward objectification, as aligned with mastery, which often imposes one set of truths over another. In contrast, *The Way of Love* maps ways of speaking shaped by listening, where the "ability to listen to the other" gives way to hearing a world of meaning different from one's own. Irigaray recognizes in the act of speaking with, or *speaking-with*, the possibility of holding a relation to difference, one shaped by a continuous relational or dialogical labor. As she asserts, "it is not possible to learn once and for all how to speak—at each moment the creative work of inventing a speaking is imposed."[3] In this shift from speech as an established form to something processual, horizontal, and discovered in the moment, speaking-with emerges as a co-creation, one that demands greater sensitivity for the meanings and experiences of others. The "sharing of speech," as Irigaray further names this process, emphasizes a relational intensity that makes of dialogue an ongoing invention. As she further suggests, "these words do not yet exist, and they could never exist in a definitive way. It is in a *new listening* to oneself and to the other that they will be discovered, pronounced" (my emphasis).[4]

Following the concept of the sharing of speech, I'm concerned to give greater attention to the *new listening* Irigaray emphasizes, and how listening is key to deepening processes of recognition. Recognition, within *The Way of Love*, is positioned as a deeply embodied, nuanced mutuality, an idealization of speaking-with that acts as a guiding principle or ethics. This is an emergent form of recognition, an ethics of concern and participation that works at fostering a new culture of speech, where "the word" is not a thing, but an invitation to share—a form of touch.[5]

⌒

If the sharing of speech names an emergent, ethical co-creation, what becomes of language within such a process? In what ways does speaking-with (as opposed

---

[2] Luce Irigaray, *The Way of Love* (London: Continuum, 2004), 8.
[3] Ibid., 64.
[4] Ibid., 50.
[5] Ibid., 18.

to speaking-about) shift something of oneself and the identity one carries—in short, how does one speak-with as well as listen-anew? Importantly, Irigaray proposes that the sharing of speech finds traction by way of *poetics*, where poetics acts as the creative basis of language and speech, and which supports the storying taking place between two. Poetics is highlighted as what makes of language a sensuality, "a language that creates, that safeguards its sensible qualities so as to address the body and soul, a language that lives."[6] Language by way of poetics becomes an erotic, soulful medium in which words are invitations to share, to move from a constitution of the One, toward the emergence of a "third world" between two. To speak-with, as Irigaray offers, is to *speak as if for the first time*. The relational scene of speaking-with makes of language and voice an embodied, collaborative journey, operating as an opportunity for discovering the richness of what we are or may become together.

Poetics is thus posed as being fully of language while exceeding its limits, making of speech not only an act of communication, an operational exercise, but an embodied, transformative movement, a *way of love*. To give weight and energy to the movement of shared speech, poetics integrates within its rhythms, its sensitivity for language as material, a profound relation to listening, for listening conducts a fundamental evocation of relation in ways that open onto the not-yet. While Irigaray calls us into speaking as if for the first time, such speech is nourished by a poetics of listening.

The Way of Love maps an ethical configuration for working at mutual recognition and respect, and calls for a new dialogical culture, demanding a reflection on what it means to speak and what speech can become. In drawing upon poetics as a means for fostering speaking-with, Irigaray offers an important challenge not only to our "rational traditions" of objectivity but, furthermore, to how those traditions have established themselves within contemporary systems of computation and finance. This finds a point of elaboration in Franco "Bifo" Berardi's examination of language's subsumption within financial capitalism's informational, globalized networks.[7] As he argues, dominant systems of financial markets upset the tangible, meaningful link between labor and value, between an embodied, tactile act and the understandings of (personal, social) value that follow. As a consequence, language and voice become floating signs untethered

---

[6] Ibid., 12.
[7] Franco "Bifo" Berardi, *The Uprising: On Poetry and Finance* (Los Angeles: semiotext(e), 2012).

from relational meaning, or placed within algorithmic datasets as part of a prevailing matrix of abstraction, thereby undermining "the affective potencies of language"[8] and the social connections they engender. Such affective potencies are those that keep close to the sensual vitality of embodied life, the social connections and "vibrations" of collective experience—the touch of words that supports the sharing of speech. "Neoliberal ideology pretends to be a liberating force that emancipates capital from state regulation, but it in fact submits production and social life to the most ferocious regulation, the mathematization of language."[9]

What forms of intervention can be made against the loss of affective potencies and the stripping away of the sensual meaningfulness of words? How to work against the obfuscation or break down of embodied, collective life by way of neoliberal systems with their emphasis on individual gain? Berardi finds an answer by way of *poetic language*, which is a language that celebrates the affective potency of words, wielding a counterforce to the mathematization and financialization of language. Poetry is positioned as a sensual weapon aimed against "semiocapitalism," and which may "start the process of reactivating the emotional body, and therefore of reactivating social solidarity, starting from the reactivation of the desiring force of enunciation."[10]

Berardi's arguments, along with Irigaray's concern for engendering a new culture of speech, highlights a general crisis of voice.[11] From the mathematization of language, and the algorithmic optimization of voice as data, as input, to the intensified polarization found in current social and political environments, voice is under strain. It is increasingly reduced, attenuated, figured in a set of simplified visualizations or soundbites, for instance, across social media platforms, and placed within an attention economy whose operations, as Berardi highlights, puts the voice to work within a frame of self-management, service,

---

[8] Ibid., 18.
[9] Ibid., 31.
[10] Ibid., 20.
[11] The question of a crisis of voice finds an important parallel consideration in the work of David Bohm. In his book *On Dialogue*, Bohm sets out to elaborate an understanding of dialogue as essential to society and the capacity for respecting others. Bohm is motivated by what he perceives as a "breakdown" in the ability to communicate across difference. Echoing Irigaray, he writes: "It is clear that if we are to live in harmony with ourselves and with nature, we need to be able to communicate freely in a creative movement in which no one permanently holds to or otherwise defends his own ideas. Why is it so difficult actually to bring about such communication?" See David Bohm, *On Dialogue* (London: Routledge, 1996).

Listening-toward

and profit. Under such systems, voice hurries itself toward an operational end, whereas poetry celebrates the fact of words as immersed in the affective fullness of embodied life. Poetic language is a living language manifesting the vitality of social worlds; it celebrates itself as an art of feeling, engendering paths of connection. As Fred Moten notes, "poetry is how things get together."[12]

↜

I'm concerned to follow these initial perspectives as a way to open a poetic path by which to approach what it can mean to speak and listen together. These are grounded concerns, shaped and urged on by the ongoingness of violence that seems to haunt not only political worlds and processes but even the arenas of art and culture, where the "freedom of expression" is increasingly strained.[13] If the word is an invitation to share, in what ways can words be found to contend with the deeply fraught realities that make it difficult to speak-with? How can a new culture of speech be truly supported, or planted within the daily scenes of a globalized and networked reality? These are questions and concerns that underpin *Poetics of Listening*, and which I find partial answers or support in poetics—for poetics manifests, as Moten further poses, a "refusal to enclosure."[14] This is a refusal that works at keeping to the outside, in the thick scenes of social life; it is what honors language as a biological force, as a commoning of words suffused with the vitality of shared meaning.

↜

In *The Metaphoric Process: Connections between Language and Life*, Gemma Corradi Fiumara poses the poetic figure of metaphor as a biological force, emphasizing the ways in which one *lives through language*. Echoing Irigaray's model of speaking-with, Fiumara writes: "Possible human worlds are collaboratively constructed and transformed through the unbreakable interaction of speaking

---

[12] Fred Moten, from a lecture, "Hesitant Sociology: Blackness and Poetry," held at the University of Chicago, spring 2016. Found online: https://www.youtube.com/watch?v=J5Zwuq898AY (accessed July 2024).

[13] As I'm writing this in the last months of 2023, there are many discussions, protests, and killings taking place, in particular in relation to the Israel-Gaza war. In the context of Germany, where I'm living, this is intensifying a longer debate around the freedom of expression, and what can and cannot be said in relation to the state of Israel. This is playing out within the context of contemporary art, leading to different institutional and individual challenges. As an important reference, see the case of *documenta fifteen* held in Kassel, Germany, in 2022. For insight into the discussion, see Martin Köttering Sabine Boshamer, eds., *The Controversy over documenta fifteen: Background, Interpretation, and Analysis* (Hamburg: Materialverlag HFBK, 2023).

[14] Moten, from a lecture, "Hesitant Sociology: Blackness and Poetry."

and listening"[15] and, importantly, rely upon "metaphorization." "It is our metaphoricity rather than our semantic use of discourse," she continues, "which enables us to create novel perspectives of whatever reality we inhabit and to experience it largely as a unity, as a whole, even though all its parts are not always exactly in place."[16] Fiumara's critical positioning of metaphor works at understanding language as integral to the biological ongoingness of human life and evolution. It figures language more as a process than a fixed code, one that proceeds by way of a "semantic motion," and how metaphoricity "enhances the practice of connecting diversities by juxtaposing terms which are distinct and incongruent."[17] These are perspectives that keep language close to bodily vitality and the affective potencies Berardi sees as critical to a meaningful life of social connection. As such, metaphor can be appreciated as what grants flexibility to the sedimentation of meaning, or the optimization of words. The metaphoric process pushes against systems of enclosure, breathing life into semiotic use and a purely "representationalist" approach to language. In short, Fiumara calls for deeper recognition of the "relational function" of language to which "the unbreakable interaction of listening and speaking" gives expression, placing language within the "precariousness, vulnerability and historicity of our own living conditions."[18]

I'm following Fiumara's relational approach to language as a complement to Berardi's call for a *poetic uprising*, drawing them together so as to think-with Irigaray's ethical model, where poetics is understood to give traction to the sharing of speech. Metaphor, or the metaphoric process, lends to how it is one may speak as if for the first time. As the imaginative figuring of ways of naming, of engaging new perspectives and of putting things together, metaphor lends to ways of relating as well—to "inhabit fields which previously appeared as opaque and unapproachable," especially when confronted by systems of enclosure.[19] These include the relational encounters and thick scenes of social life, where voice must find the words in approaching and holding difference.

Moreover, as the fundamental ground of poetics, metaphor is aligned with a paradigm of life in which language is no longer positioned as abstract, separate,

---

[15] Gemma Corradi Fiumara, *The Metaphoric Process: Connections between Language and Life* (London: Routledge, 1995), 9.
[16] Ibid., 10.
[17] Ibid., 14.
[18] Ibid., 9.
[19] Ibid., 21.

alienating; rather, it works at affirming life's relational journey in which language is fundamental, *biological*, steeped in the teeming festivities and frustrations, frictions and humor of a shared world. Metaphor turns words into invitations to share, where naming does not so much foreclose or delimit the nature of things, but incites curiosity, concern, a wish, or interest in meaningfulness. The ethical, relational scene of speaking-with is, to my ear, a metaphoric process, a poetic uprising that puts into motion the desiring force of enunciation.

↬

The relational scenario that Irigaray envisages positions one as an ethical partner, where the sharing of speech becomes the performative means for acknowledging and giving room to the differences of one another. Importantly, this entails contending with entrenched forms of prejudice and bias, as well as dominant structures that cut against the potentiality of social connection: that segregate, enclose, extract, or instrumentalize the affective potencies inherent to voice. These may be societal structures that contour where and how voices are heard, or economic systems that position voice and its value in ways that benefit a few; yet, they may also be internal, psychological structures, informing what one comes to anticipate, expect, or presume as to the performativity of voice and its meanings. These are all aspects that impact onto the idealized potentiality of speaking-with. In this regard, speaking-with is emphasized as a poetic force aimed at questioning the normative lines directing ways of approaching and valuing others; it works at questions not only of speech, but also that of identity and understandings of community.

Through an examination of contemporary social movements, and how the occupation of city spaces reconfigures the dynamics shaping communities, Stavros Stavrides offers a suggestive perspective to thinking an ethics of speech. In particular, Stavrides utilizes the figure of liminality as a way to envision new understandings of community, where community is less about "enclaves of identity"; rather, through the *commoning* of the city emerging by way of urban occupations (e.g., the movement of the squares in Greece in 2011), communities perform as interdependent entities, participating in a "network of communicating areas."[20] In the grassroots movements of urban occupations, people come together in new ways that bypass established institutional structures, putting into place an array of collectively organized, ad-hoc structures with the aim of supporting

---

[20] Stavros Stavrides, *Towards the City of Thresholds* (Brooklyn, NY: Common Notions, 2019), 43.

the movement and its people. From communal cooking and distributing food to providing care and treatment, from organizing demonstrations and assemblies to building systems of communication, along with all the small, emergent gestures and conversations that together act as a shared foundation, these are aspects that, for Stavrides, recreate the city as a commons. Within such a commons, community shifts from being an "enclave" to that of a "bridge," where localized actions link up in ways that unsettle existing identities, habits, ways of relating and doing politics. Permeable and liminal, the new configuration of community that Stavrides highlights is based on interdependence, which radically shifts an approach to difference and disagreement. "The act of recognizing a division only to overcome it, yet without aiming to eliminate it, might be emblematic of an attitude that gives to different identities the ground to negotiate and realize their interdependence."[21]

The concept of *liminal community* is helpful in broadening Irigaray's model of speaking-with; it opens onto practices that mobilize new social imaginaries in which identity is not restricted to its own enclave of meanings or territorial regions. Rather, for Stavrides identity is positioned as a means for holding difference—it is the basis for communicating with others, for realizing *their interdependence*. This finds further elaboration through a reflection on social ritual, in terms of the rites of passage through which identities are reworked within a given context. As he proposes, social rituals offer important structures by which "to be able to experience changes in identity, to be able to rehearse, test, check, and visit otherness," all of which "potentially means acquiring the power to negotiate with otherness."[22] Following these perspectives, can the scene of speaking-with be conceptualized as a social ritual, a process of co-creation through which one may rehearse, test, check, and visit otherness?

An ethics of speech may figure less as a fixed code of conduct and more as a liminal scene by which identities may be *put on hold* or *tried on*; where one is called into a situation that is "never definitive" and always "under construction,"[23] and through which, as Stavrides suggests, one may gain critical insight into how dominant powers come to define identity and the social roles one may play. For Irigaray, this entails wielding a challenge to notions of "mastery" and a logic of completion, the One, the Truth, deployed by dominant patriarchal systems.[24] To

---

[21] Ibid., 44.
[22] Ibid., 45.
[23] Irigaray, *The Way of Love*, 10.
[24] Ibid.

be always under construction can be appreciated as a confrontation with those systems and structures that direct (and hear) voice in restrictive ways, and that enclose language (as well as common spaces) within a particular economy of meaning.

$$\backsim$$

In *Auditory Poverty and Its Discontents*, Nina Dragičević deepens a critical view onto questions of voice by capturing the ways in which women's voices go unheard within patriarchal society. Importantly, Dragičević works at a greater intersectional perspective, in terms of underscoring how gender is embedded in realities of class and race; and further, how questions of class can be applied to the auditory, where hearing and being heard are shaped by a general state of impoverishment. As Dragičević suggests, under the force of a pervasive silencing, women must be considered as a specific "sonic and auditory class."[25] By examining the case of Nizama Hećimović in particular, who was brutally murdered by her partner in 2020 after reporting him to the police for domestic abuse, Dragičević questions how audible speech is politically charged, contributing to movements of resistance as well as violent acts of silencing.

> The *spoken* reports of rapes are producing the power institution to speak at some *later* time, and only after the number of violent attacks against women becomes interesting for the institutions to recognize it as *relevant enough* even to bother. And Nizama Hećimović was murdered because she had *reported* her soon-to-be murderer to the police. In terms of the male murderer's motive, Nizama Hećimović was killed precisely because of using audible speech in a setting where it can be recognized as relevant. But it wasn't recognized as relevant.[26]

Rather, the case of Nizama Hećimović exemplifies an auditory-class conflict shaping gender struggles and violence in which recognition is key to saving lives.

Dragičević's theory of auditory poverty can assist in mapping an ethics of speech as what contends with the *vocal economies* always already at work and which influence the conditions for recognition. From structures dominated by vocal norms that position some voices as more valuable or authoritative than others, to the struggles that demand new ways of speaking and communicating, vocal economies impact onto what a voice is and can be within a given situation. It is along these lines that struggles for recognition are always positioned in

---

[25] Nina Dragičević, *Auditory Poverty and Its Discontents* (Berlin: Errant Bodies Press, 2024).
[26] Ibid., 29.

relation to established structures and systems which come to socially, politically, legally define who is heard and in what ways.

The sharing of speech needs to be highlighted as never freely found, nor as a smooth affair; it is positioned precisely as a critical framework—a social ritual, a metaphoric process—so as to impact onto those sites and scenes where speech and voice are foreclosed or defined by systems of exclusion and prejudice, or simple neglect, by some speaking over others, and that lend to cultures of objectification, domination and discrimination. Irigaray's way of love is an ethical, embodied and intersectional argument aimed at challenging the habits and dominant structures shaping the ways in which hearing and being heard take place and are made meaningful. Moreover, it seeks to support and give courage to a speech full of listening, one that strives not to speak over others; rather, that language is something one always already carries, underpinned by the vocal norms and economies of given contexts, emerges as a ground by which to performatively, ritualistically, poetically "invent a speaking of one's own."[27] Such inventiveness must be positioned to include critical forms of listening as well.

I'm interested to think *listening-toward* as a particular mode of listening that contributes to the ongoing work of recognition. While listening clearly supports communication, participating in social exchanges, institutional operations, and the movements of daily life, it additionally facilitates experiences of recognition, as what impacts onto the ways in which participation and belonging are made available. As Dragičević argues, one may be heard within any number of situations, yet this does not necessarily mean someone is listening. Listening, in this way, entails action, responsiveness, change; it is a gesture where attention to others enacts care. Within the context of an ethical, political framework, listening is on the side of social justice.

These are the movements, the attentional powers, that make of listening neither passive nor active; that is suggestive for another vocabulary. And which carries my thinking, my research, toward the area of poetics. These are the social rituals, the network of communicating areas, the liminal work, where words become invitations to share, which are words not without critical weight—there is a great deal at stake within the move toward liminal community formations. The way of love is fraught with challenges, demands, with vulnerability—poetics as the refusal

---

[27] Irigaray, *The Way of Love*, 35.

to settle, to claim language as what keeps us alive, connected, in the thick scene of the common city, to speak as if for the first time as part of localized acts, puts one right in the middle of the fight.

⤳

The ethical work underpinning speaking-with is performatively expressed in Irigaray's use of the word *turning*—what she describes as a turning toward and then back. This turning becomes operative within Irigaray's philosophy, underscoring the physical, gestural, relational move that is the sharing of speech. In turning (or being turned) toward another, attention is articulated, given expression in the shifting of the body—a movement, a step, a pivot that announces interest and concern, however subtly or pointedly. This gesture carries an expression of regard, to signal a slight yet deeply pronounced alteration: turning pulls and pushes at a given order, a given arrangement, to open onto the not-yet, a becoming-with that captures the erotic potentiality of shared life. Turning, for Irigaray, is a primary step, one that invites interaction. Turning incites turning in return. Within such a complementary move, we already begin to invent something particular, what Irigaray highlights as the *creation of unique meaning*.[28] The move of turning—which is a turning that keeps turning—inaugurates a dialogical hospitality, a process of approaching, in certain ways, one another. This includes acts of speaking and listening, voicing and attending, giving and receiving—two ways of turning that are never so separate or dichotomous; rather, they oscillate upon a subtle threshold, giving way to a relational dance, an emergent scene, a social ritual: to feel along the way the positioning of each, a flexing and relaxing, a picking up and a letting go, a trying on and inventing. Turning thus names this relational dance as an embodied journey, "made of our flesh, of our heart,"[29] realized in this movement of *speaking-with / listening-toward*. I turn toward, I listen, and then I turn away, in wait; I lean in, I lean back; I give, in words that participate in the ongoing co-creation of speech, and then I receive, take, in the listening that gives way, that is also a time for pause, for being with myself at the same time—I take a breath, giving space for others to speak; I digest the words, and I also self-reflect, preparing my own words in return, in the turning that goes on and on, that is the creation of unique meaning. Such turning and re-turning emerges as an

[28] Ibid., xii.
[29] Ibid., 154.

affirmative positioning, a tussle, as what works at becoming-with, at fostering the working through and holding of difference.

&

Importantly, turning is a critical-creative move; it is to face the friend, the stranger as well as the enemy. It is a turning that is also unavoidable in moments, when one is called upon to face up to certain demands—I cannot turn away from responsibilities, or from particular systems that may force one to turn, or that restrict the capacity to turn freely. Turning, and the broader work of sharing speech, is always situated; it is a positioning, a mechanism of emplacement, operative within a greater assembly of language and power, identity and meaning, bodily ability and vocal economy. In turning toward, or in turning against, I may also recognize the struggles of others—to *bear witness* to those who are denied access and whose own capacity to turn, or turn away, is restricted. Within this socio-ethical schema of turning, listening contributes, for listening is often what incites one to turn: the *new listening* that Irigaray highlights as central to speaking-with may be found precisely in the ways in which listening turns us, keeping one exposed to the ongoingness of surroundings and the lives of others. This integrates, by way of listening's holding of difference, the capacity to attend to the fullness of others, to the deeply nuanced stories people carry. It is along these lines that listening contributes to wielding a more supple politics when it comes to holding and acknowledging the complexity of individual lives.

&

The artist and scholar Rajni Shah offers insightful views onto listening that seek to map an equally nuanced appreciation for its positive impact onto understanding and experiencing relationality. Stemming from their work in theater and performance, Shah is concerned to bring attention to the dynamics between performer and audience, explicitly turning toward the broader aspects that surround a given action or content. This includes, for example, inquiring into the "framing" that occurs in the staging of performance, how performances act to "gather" audiences, functioning to "host" others as well as how audiences become hosts themselves, for instance, in the listening that "holds" the stories being told.[30] These areas of focus are reflective of a broader concern for the relationship between listening and theater Shah addresses. Underpinning and guiding their *Experiments in Listening* is an understanding of listening as what

---

[30] Rajni Shah, *Experiments in Listening* (Lanham, MD: Rowman & Littlefield, 2021), 45.

can help broaden attention, to figure a subject position shaped by compassion and care, and that suspends the "imperative to act" so defining of theater as well as the greater arenas of social and political life. Listening, instead, allows for holding still, for attending to who or what is there; it is enabling of focusing across foreground and background, shifting the lines demarcating what we may know as content and context. As Shah suggestively offers, a commitment to listening as a practice is on some level a commitment to "not-knowing," for listening is the very thing that allows for dwelling within a space of uncertainty. It is the means by which to suspend the imperative to act, as well as the imperative to know (driven by our rational traditions).

By way of an examination of listening and theater, Shah's work opens onto questions of dialogical experience, highlighting what it means to be an *audience for others*. Being an audience for others is to conduct acts of holding, it is to gather the stories being told; furthermore, it provides a relational model for shared acts of speaking and listening that open onto "different ways of being together with strangers."[31] These are ways that, echoing Irigaray's notion of the sharing of speech, move toward "a common and collective consciousness" where individual opinions are put to the side. Instead, the holding of attention Shah positions as key to thinking a relation between listening and theater, a relation equally pertinent to everyday life, is one defined by a *third thing*. Extending from the writings of Jacques Rancière, a third thing comes to underscore performance as what is "owned by no one," but which "subsists between them, excluding any uniform transmission, any identity of cause and effect."[32] Positioning listening as what allows for bringing focus to what is often deemed peripheral to theater, categorized under the terms "hosting" or "framing," as well as care, Shah shifts the very terms of performance. Rather than the staging of an act, Shah figures a model of performance directed by listening, the relational meanings that emerge by holding a space of collective consciousness, and that "allow us to meet through the 'third thing' of the performance."[33]

↩

Rajni Shah's deeply nuanced perspectives on listening can contribute to thinking further as to listening's role in challenging entrenched structures defining ways of speaking and relating. Returning to Irigaray, *The Way of Love* is an invitation to

---

[31] Ibid., 51.
[32] Jacques Rancière, quoted in Shah, *Experiments in Listening*, 51.
[33] Shah, *Experiments in Listening*, 58.

join—to step in, to enter—in the processual shared worlds that constitute social existence and whose relational urgencies call for greater care and reciprocity. These include the deep struggles and conflicts that demand attention, as well as considered practices. To turn may also be to turn away completely—it might be to cut the bonds that link to situations of violence, control, domination. Even in the ongoing co-creation of speaking-with one is never free from any number of ideological positionings and languages, histories of violence, the ongoing challenges around racialization, ableism, and sexism, for instance. These are part of the work of speaking-with, and which come to inform the tensions shaping encounters across difference. To turn and re-turn, to *speak-with / listen-toward*, is to work at calling into question the defining limits of recognition itself. This is essential to Irigaray's arguments—the way of love is a demand, a challenge to ourselves, and to the social and political systems that surround; it contends with the structures and semantics of language, the speech that one carries, already formed by the histories of self and community, family and society, and the ideologies that define how it is one understands what it means to be attentive. The way of love is a dance of war as well, a civic fight, a societal argument, a discursive or semantic intervention; it is the showing of (poetic) force as much as the expression of generosity and compassion—it is, if anything, the articulation of a deeply nuanced form of relational labor and commitment, an ethics that works its way across social structures, vocabularies, histories. Its destination is never so certain or clear. Yet love names this process, this struggle, as a type of risk that must be taken—that one takes as one's own. For love gives profoundly to ensuring and enriching human survival, and more, to finding the courage to go on, to make this life and the life of others all the more livable; it is what lifts up, even as it may push down—even as it may hurt, love is what endures as the belief in others and oneself.

The Third Voice, Third Listening

I want to further an examination of listening in the context of recognition by shifting from Luce Irigaray's model of speaking-with toward a consideration of the work of Jessica Benjamin, and in particular her concept of the Third. In doing so, I hope to elaborate an understanding of listening's role in supporting an ethics of difference, especially in terms of how we may deepen a sensitivity for dialogical labor as a co-creative undertaking.

In her psychoanalytic work and theories, Jessica Benjamin argues for an intersubjective model, one that necessitates a more relationally aware approach to therapeutic process, not to mention broader social repair. As she outlines in her book *Beyond Doer and Done To*, "the matter of how we come to appreciate the other's separate existence, how we evolve through a relationship where each is the other's other seems to be the rightful concern of a psychoanalytic theorizing of intersubjectivity."[34] Central to her focus is a concern to establish methods attuned to recognition as an affirmative experience, where recognition helps in establishing greater reciprocity by "destabilizing" the often entrenched structure of analysis that positions the analysand as "an object of need."[35] In contrast, a model of intersubjectivity is grounded in recognizing "the presence of two knowing and not-knowing subjects in the room—each one potentially engaged in recognition of the other's alterity."[36] This includes understanding how analysis itself can often reinforce existing patterns of domination by positioning the analysand as being under the authority and power of the analyst. If the analyst takes on the role of the *doer*, and the analysand that of the *done to*, as someone *going through* analysis, the overall process of therapy may inadvertently perpetuate a structure of domination, reducing the transformative potentiality of repair. It is in light of such an understanding that Benjamin poses the concept of the Third.

The Third is articulated as a process by which "we implicitly recognize the other as a 'like subject,' a being we can appreciate as an 'other mind,'"[37] and which can assist in upsetting a relational dynamic that may locate one against or over another; rather than conceive of the other as positioned between difference and sameness, the Third is figured as *holding the tension of recognition* situated between two. It keeps in place a necessary mode of coordinated collaboration, or what Benjamin highlights by the phrase "doing *with*" (as opposed to "doing *to*") and which thirdness comes to designate.[38]

Furthermore, Benjamin sees in the Third a potential means for challenging systems of domination more generally; whether within the constructed scene of analysis or across any number of situations, developing practices of

---

[34] Jessica Benjamin, *Beyond Doer and Done To: Recognition Theory, Intersubjectivity and the Third* (New York: Routledge, 2018), 2.

[35] Ibid., 3.

[36] Ibid.

[37] Ibid., 4.

[38] Ibid., 5.

intersubjectivity, for Benjamin, is to work at challenging a model of power based on "doer and done to." The Third thereby comes to name a relational, intersubjective process by which persons engage in mutual concern; this includes the ability to work through the complex range of private struggles, especially in terms of navigating the layered or sedimented traumas some may carry and that call for greater attention and care. Thirdness names a work of co-creation that values one another's contribution to a shared world.

↢

Benjamin elaborates the Third as a process by distinguishing particular modes of thirdness, each of which helps give further detail to its dynamics. For example, the *differentiating Third* emphasizes the necessity to hold onto individuality; while the Third calls for intersubjective engagement, demanding that one gives oneself over to others, and the emergent identities and meanings that arise, for Benjamin this does not entail a losing of oneself. Rather, thirdness requires that one hangs onto individuality while surrendering to the cultivation of the Third— what Benjamin describes as a "differentiating-while-joining movement."[39] The differentiating Third assists in reminding of this crucial movement.

Furthermore, Benjamin distinguishes what she calls the *moral Third*, which helps one appreciate how intersubjectivity, and the cooperative sharing of a certain time and place, brings with it an ethical value. The encountering of each, the turning and re-turning as Irigaray highlights, establishes itself around forms of (unspoken) agreement, a type of "law of connection" as Benjamin suggests; the languages, vocabularies and gestures that contribute to thirdness all emerge as uniquely tuned expressions cultivated over time and shaped by what each brings to the relationship. The living nature or quality of the Third can therefore be judged as to its ebb and flow, its success and security as well as its failure or rupture. The moral Third thus speaks to the qualities and values defining the ongoingness of shared connection, making of a relationship a "lawful world,"[40] one whose organization is particular, helping to acknowledge when something goes wrong. This entails the ability to then take responsibility for its repair. To build and rebuild a lawful world is founded on recognizing the emotional, structural, and moral life of that world.

Finally, Benjamin poses the notion of the *rhythmic Third*, as part of the greater dynamic of thirdness. The rhythmic Third captures the ways in which

[39] Ibid., 51.
[40] Ibid., 6.

thirdness entails a deeply embodied presence inherent to being involved with others, and which is brought forward in crafting the Third as a process of collaborative coordination. This may echo the sense of movement Irigaray maps, where turning shapes the sharing of speech as a process of affective attunement. These are rhythmic dynamics which require a sensitivity for the body's place within the nurturing of dialogue, and especially for working at repair as the capacity to respond to the hurt of others as well as oneself. Additionally, the rhythmic Third underscores the importance of play and improvisation, to being responsive to the living temporalities and spatialities contouring the Third. To shut the space at times, or to leave open; to work at closure, or to let go, these are gestures that shape the Third as a shared world, and which necessitate sensitivity for the present moment as well as the capacity to improvise.[41] Importantly, for Benjamin, the rhythmic Third has a deeply affirming quality, where play and improvisation help sustain humor, the joy of doing things cooperatively, of being in this world together. Returning to the space of analysis crucial to Benjamin's arguments, rhythm helps give movement back to the body so as to allow for new understanding, to help overcome feeling stuck.[42]

Underpinning the different modes of thirdness Benjamin details is the fundamental necessity to surrender oneself to the emergent dynamic of the Third. Surrendering for Benjamin, though, must be contrasted with submission; rather, one surrenders as a fully constituted individual, finding in thirdness the potentiality for connection, individual growth, and for sharing in a greater process aligned with human flourishing.

Importantly, for Benjamin, the Third is posited as a transformative container for enabling acknowledgment of the suffering of others. Approaching each other as partners in a process of co-creation, of maintaining a lawful world, impacts greatly on overcoming injury. For Benjamin, such ethical, relational work is based on the ability to extend oneself beyond one's identity, especially when confronting histories and experiences of abuse. To identify, as Benjamin argues, with those

---

[41] Ibid., 144. Benjamin emphasizes the importance of improvisation by posing the statement "Yes, And" as opposed to "No, But"—which suggests a general ability to incorporate play into the psychoanalytic process.

[42] Benjamin's concern for bringing play and improvisation into processes of therapy, in order to restore movement, finds further expression in Susan Raffo's therapeutic work which I explore in more detail in Chapter 3. See Susan Raffo, *Liberated to the Bone: Histories, Bodies, Futures* (Chico, CA: AK Press, 2022).

that may hurt us, as well as those we may come to harm, acts as a generative basis for working at repair. This includes the necessity to move beyond a restrictive position of self-protection and dissociation; instead, it is important to *hold a connection to suffering*, acknowledging thirdness as an ongoing tension, a labor, rather than as a state of stillness or resolve. Holding a connection to suffering is to be attuned to the sensitivities underpinning recognition, as what requires constant attention, invention, and reinforcement as well as mutual support. While this may appear as rather weighted, it may also be expressed by the joy experienced in *participating in others becoming something they are not-yet.*

Within such processes, speaking contends with the vocal economies that influence what can be said and where. These are situational, historical coordinates that mark out a vocal territory, a structuring that inflects one's sense of having a say and of being heard. To work at thirdness is to inhabit as well as modulate given vocal economies, finding support at times while also working against the defining force they often impose. To speak as if for the first time, to surrender to the process of the third, may be to foster a critical engagement with the situational powers and normative structures often defining speaking, lending instead to the cultivation of *vocal ecologies.* Alongside or within the vocal economies surrounding and influencing voice and the sharing of speech, vocal ecologies are to be found, nurtured, inhabited, where voice figures as a channel for other bodies, other agencies and words, and whose "profit" benefits a greater good. Voice need not always be that which works at individual agency. Rather, it can be conceived as a distributed form, as a contribution to the co-creation of meaning.

Conceptualizing vocal ecologies finds a point of reference in Marlene Schäfers's research into practices of vocalizing found in Kurdish communities across Turkey.[43] In particular, Schäfers reflects upon the tradition of *kilam*— which are songs usually of love and loss sung at weddings, funerals, and other instances of mourning or celebration—and how Kurdish women have found an emancipatory potency in the tradition more recently. Schäfers argues that, while voice is positioned as the basis for individual agency within a liberal Western perspective, valorizing acts of speaking up or raising one's voice, in the context of *kilam*, voice is never simply one's own. "In the Kurdish context where I conducted research, voice often became detached from the subjects who uttered them,

---

[43] Marlene Schäfers, *Voices That Matter: Kurdish Women at the Limits of Representation in Contemporary Turkey* (Chicago: University of Chicago Press, 2023).

expressing not the emotions of the self but that of others."[44] As Schäfers presents, Kurdish singers, or *dengbêjs*, are often employed or called upon to speak on behalf of others, to express the hardships as well as joys of Kurdish life, and importantly, to bring forward a collective affective intensity. "These were voices capable of moving listeners to tears, making them shiver, or, as local idioms put it, 'burning their hearts' thanks to the trembling of a vowel or the weight of a poetic image."[45] Fundamental to Schäfers's research and arguments is a concern to hear in the vocalizing of Kurdish women *dengbêjs* an expression of voice that is less centered on individual empowerment, and instead, on wielding a form of "social labor."[46] This includes shifting the emphasis from voice as a question of representation, as what works at social and political recognition, and toward an engagement with its audibility and tonality, and the emotional, affective impact voices can have.

As social labor, voices circulate as a collective medium, giving expression to the feelings and experiences of others; it works at binding community together, capturing and manifesting emotional life, the loves and losses, the dreams and hardships defining of individual lives and which are collectively experienced. It is along these lines that understandings of speaking-with may take on additional meaning. And where the poetics underpinning its performance may gain further traction. From the co-creative process of the sharing of speech to the affective potency of poetic language, voice moves from being wholly constituted by individual acts, as being representative of the self, toward operating as social, dialogical labor; it also works at holding a connection to suffering, attending to the traumas, the struggles, and the living nature of community, helping to speak the unspeakable and to carry collective memories. Following these perspectives, thirdness can be cast as the nurturing of vocal ecologies, where voice is not simply representational of oneself, but affords ways of speaking with and through each other, of hearing voice as an ecology of relations and affect.

In following Benjamin's concept of the Third, Irigaray's model of speaking-with, and the social labors of voice that *bring listeners to tears*, intersubjectivity may be conceived as transformative—as what participates in the configuration of a liminal community, giving support to communicating across and because

---

[44] Ibid., 5.
[45] Ibid., 6–7.
[46] Ibid., 7.

of difference. As Irigaray notes, something unique emerges in the midst of the sharing of speech: a dwelling or dimension. This becomes suggestive for conceiving of a *third-sphere*. Neither public nor private, this shared dimension is understood to carry the reverberant potential found in being heard; it gestures toward the possibility of realizing interdependence by way of localized acts of negotiation—a dimension that both conducts as well as gives shape to the liminal work of thirdness. The third-sphere is a *commons*, realized and held within instances of communication—"For the common is that which is always at stake in any conversation: there where a conversation takes place, there the common expresses itself."[47] As a commons, it is made and remade along the way, continually invented and held, let go and made again. The commons evoked by way of conversation, within the scene of speaking-with, is one that appears within existing spaces and situations, taking root in particular instances while diffusing at times—the third-sphere carries all the promise and potentiality, labor and affect of thirdness, giving it a container, a common spatiality, a living ground.[48]

Within this context, the modality I'm elaborating as listening-toward can be further conceputalized as *third listening*. Third listening is a listening by way of intersubjectivity, a listening specific to the ethical work of speaking-with—which is equally suggestive for a notion of *third voice*. What becomes of the voice when partnering in the sharing of speech? Does something change of the voice when approaching conversation as the very thing which carries the commons, makes it possible? As Schäfers suggests, voice need not be tied to representing a self, or to semantic use, but it may circulate as an affective potency, a social labor by which personal experiences are stitched into a collective fabric—to emphasize "broader socio-affective patterns."[49] Following such views, and those of Irigaray and Benjamin, voice shifts its orientation more overtly toward the *third thing*—as that which is between

---

[47] Cesare Casarino and Antonio Negri, *In Praise of the Common: A Conversation on Philosophy and Politics* (Minneapolis: University of Minnesota Press, 2008), 1.

[48] In posing the idea of the "third-sphere" I'm aware of Homi Bhabha's concept of Third Space, as well as the larger area of Third Space Theory, from Lev Vygotsky to Edward Soja. While I acknowledge these theories, and how they also may inform Benjamin's thinking on thirdness, I'm more drawn to Benjamin's work and her way of positioning thirdness, which is less about cultural representation, identity politics and sociolinguistic factors. For more on Homi Bhabha's concept of Third Space in particular, see Homi K. Bhabha, *The Location of Culture* (London: Routledge, 1994).

[49] Schäfers, *Voices That Matter*, 56.

us. And which can be thought as part of the commoning dynamic of the third-sphere.

Extending or enlivening what one knows of oneself and others, third listening gives support to speaking *as if for the first time*. This may be a listening that moves itself from the perspective of oneself to that of another, but also to that of a *We*, a listening that reaches toward and that settles itself within the third-sphere. Third listening is not only a directed form of listening; rather, it is prone to being displaced, *refracted*, bent by the rhythms of intersubjectivity—a *new listening* pulled along by others; and one defined not only by the entrenched realities in front, but equally by the not-yet that provides a horizon to the third-sphere. Is not thirdness, in fact, what exposes us to the unrecognizable, keeping one open to emergent meanings and identities? To the possibility of trying on otherness? And which supports the commons as that which needs to be continually renewed, nurtured, defended, and made meaningful? While thirdness is posited by Benjamin as a relational model in support of mutual recognition, it is fundamentally a rhythm, a liminal work, an ethics that positions one *at the beginning*—even while we may develop relationships over time, building memories together as well as patterns of behavior, to be familiar, thirdness asks that one be in the present, to keep involved in the ongoing holding of connection, in the maintenance of socio-affective patterns and common worlds. This places one at the beginning, *under construction*, and where mutual recognition is figured as an ongoing work, a commoning practice, a response-ability. Third listening is what keeps us returning to each other, keeps us close to tears—that follows the social rituals as means for reaffirming common bonds, feeling them again and again as if for the first time. Third listening, therefore, invites a metaphoric process, anchoring itself in the affective potencies and emergent meanings of poetics—for it is poetics that refuses enclosure, keeping us involved in the conversation as what carries the potentiality of the common.

It is a social labor that—while working at all the ups and downs of this life and living world—is always close to the pleasure, the joy, the lightness of being together, the erotic sensuality of doing things with others, the families and friends that may challenge and hurt at times, but which bind me to the art of living, together, and that I want to carry with me into this writing, today, to put it here, like a sun around which constellations of voices, memories and songs hover.

74 *Poetics of Listening*

Heart Listening and the Uluru Statement

Questions of voice and recognition move across personal, interpersonal, community, and societal contexts, accenting the importance of *having a say* as part of broader social, political representation. Within the context of a poetics of listening, this is understood to gain traction by way of listening's influence. To argue for a relation to voice that keeps close to listening is key to working at intersubjectivity, and the recognition that one is deeply dependent on others, that identities and communities are made and unmade together. Within such a construct, something of the voice must be understood to shift. To speak *as if for the first time* radically intervenes onto how a voice performs, behaves, sounds, and resounds, placing all that it says within an emergent scene where presuppositions are put on hold. As Jill Stauffer argues in *Ethical Loneliness*, to truly bear witness to another's past experiences and life stories one must set the conditions in which such stories can be told on their own terms.[50] This entails a form of listening that keeps one exposed to being moved, interrupted, strained—a *listening as if for the first time*. And which I'm aiming to elaborate through the poetic figure of third listening. This is clearly akin to the *new listening* Luce Irigaray positions as key to the sharing of speech, and which further elaborates voice as social labor, as shared affect.

I want to further explore these issues by considering the case of the Uluru Statement from the Heart. Bringing focus to this particular case can allow for extending critical thinking on listening and recognition by shifting from the dialogical scene performed between two, and the process of the third as found in the context of psychoanalysis. Can we further conceive of thirdness on the level of societal challenges, national debates, historical struggles? Jessica Benjamin suggests as much, posing the maintenance of the third as important for addressing unfinished histories of collective trauma. The Uluru Statement from the Heart speaks toward such concerns, figuring voice and the importance of having a say as fundamentally operative within the context of Indigenous struggles in Australia.

The Uluru Statement from the Heart is a statement written by 250 delegates as part of the First Nations National Constitutional Convention held in May of 2017

---

[50] Jill Stauffer, *Ethical Loneliness: The Injustice of Not Being Heard* (New York: Columbia University Press, 2018).

in Uluru, Australia.[51] The statement was developed following the establishment of a Referendum Council in 2015 in collaboration with the government of Prime Minister Tony Abbott and opposition leadership. Following a series of crisis meetings led by Indigenous leaders and government officials, with the aim of instituting constitutional recognition, the council emerged as a result of the decision to hold a referendum on the issue of constitutional change (which led to the Constitutional Convention as a means for bringing Indigenous communities together to debate on the nature of the referendum and constitutional reform).

As a result of the Constitutional Convention, and a series of dialogues taking place prior, the Uluru Statement from the Heart functions as a formal petition to the Australian government calling for constitutional recognition of First Nations Peoples. This is elaborated through three propositions, including (1) the establishment of an Indigenous Voice to Parliament, (2) a Makarrata Commission aimed at supporting agreement-making through treaties, and (3) overseeing a process of truth-telling for the nation. Each of the propositions are based on long-standing neglect on the part of Australian governments to make amends for the country's colonial past and present by acknowledging structural problems within the country when it comes to the impoverishment of Indigenous communities. The fact that First Nations Peoples are "the most incarcerated people on the planet" (as noted in the Uluru Statement) is but one indication of a greater structural issue. Importantly, the Statement works at rectifying current structural problems by enshrining within the constitution the Voice of First Nations Peoples. This would manifest through establishing a legal body ("the Aboriginal and Torres Strait Islander Voice," or what has become better known as "The Voice") that would have the authority to make representations to Parliament and the executive government on matters relating to Aboriginal and Torres Strait Islander Peoples. Additionally, the Parliament would have the capacity to make laws with respect to the Voice. Through the establishment of such a body, Indigenous people would be ensured greater representation within the government and involvement in related acts of legislation especially pertaining to their communities. This would structurally guarantee that regardless of changing governments, as well as changes within Indigenous leadership, Aboriginal and Torres Strait Islander Peoples would continue to have a say in policies that concern them most.

---

[51] For more on the Uluru Statement from the Heart, and to access the Statement itself, see https://ulurustatement.org/ (accessed July 2024).

Following the announcement of the Uluru Statement, which was subsequently produced as a painting containing references to Aboriginal creation stories, Thomas Mayo, a Kaurareg Aboriginal and Kalkalgal, Erubamle Torres Strait Islander, and delegate to the convention, set out to present the sacred statement to Indigenous communities across the country in order to gain support for the referendum. In Mayo's account of the Statement, published as a book under the title *Finding the Heart of the Nation* (2019, second edition 2022),[52] emphasis is continually placed on the diversity of opinions and views held across Indigenous communities and territories on the topic of recognition and reform; the fact that the referendum itself was opposed and challenged by some Indigenous leaders, and further, that some delegates to the Convention walked out of the discussions, is highlighted as an essential component of the story of the Statement and its achievements. Such diversity and differences are given fuller expression in Mayo's publication, which primarily consists of portraits of people the author met and interviewed along the journey made in organizing support for the referendum. These are heartfelt and challenging encounters, exchanges and stories that underpin the work of the Statement itself, which is to be found not only in the final act of holding the referendum (which took place in October 2023 and resulted in its rejection) but in all the labor and love, fear and hope, laughter and sense of deep accomplishment. And which Mayo works at honoring in the many narratives he offers. This finds poignant reflection through the ways in which he expresses responsibility, humility, and dedication to the project. Mayo acts as activist *and* caretaker, organizer *and* witness, whose own struggles and self-doubts are equally full of hope and a belief in people.

Carrying the rolled-up Statement in his truck as he drove across Australia over a period of eighteen months, Mayo's journey is one of transformation; he comes to carry not only the colorful canvas, and all the collective work gone into its production, but equally a process of learning how to listen. "When I started writing the stories of these pages, I was worried my writing wouldn't do them justice. It was difficult at first. Listening is a language in itself, I discovered. But with each interview I connected with the person and the writing became easier, because I learnt to listen."[53] Mayo's book is an *invitation to listen* to Indigenous

---

[52] Thomas Mayor (Mayo), *Finding the Heart of the Nation: The Journey of the Uluru Statement from the Heart continues* (Richmond, VIC: Hardie Grant Explore, 2022).

[53] Ibid., 63.

Listening-toward

voices and their spirited stories, but also to Mayo's own listening as he journeys, learning of peoples' convictions and concerns; it is moreover an invitation to Australians to listen in ways that might "change the Australian Constitution so that First Nations Voices are *always* heard."[54]

The story of the Uluru Statement offers important perspectives in terms of reflecting upon the intertwining forces of power, history, recognition, voice, and listening, the expectations and disappointments surrounding the ongoing struggles of First Nations Peoples. It further helps elaborate what might constitute an ethics of *speaking-with/listening-toward*, showing dialogue as profoundly transformative when coupled with a language of listening—a *third listening*—that, as Stauffer suggests, sets the tone by which to extend one's own listening habits. This is a form of *heart listening* as Mayo names it, one that finds guidance by way of the relational, transformative reach listening conducts. This is carried across Mayo's account, which tells of late night campfires full of intimate conversations, communal songs, and affirmations of the Statement, as well as presentations in front of corporate executives and legal firms which, as Mayo reveals, turned some toward a Yes vote.[55] Heart listening is also a listening that follows stories of the heart, those of Indigenous activists who, over the years, have worked tirelessly at social change. As David of the Noongar people offers, "My family have been fighters for a long, long time. And I speak in regards to my grandmother, riding around on a horse with a petition as a nine-year-old that her father wrote up, trying to get his children to be allowed to go to school."[56] Such heart listening is an echo to Irigaray's way of love, where love names a commitment to others, one that "invites humanity to shine through the dark well of ignorance."[57]

These are stories and experiences that Mayo thoughtfully shares. Yet, they also rub against the political realities in which state power is difficult to shift. As the rejection of the referendum suggests, the deeply nuanced call for heart listening, which is a listening guided by a belief in compassionate action and the shaping of change through affectionate acknowledgment of wrongdoing and hardship, confronts a potential limit when it comes to shifting public opinion.

∻

---

[54] Ibid.
[55] Ibid., 136.
[56] Ibid., 124.
[57] Ibid., 136.

The Uluru Statement from the Heart comes to confront larger debates regarding the politics of recognition. As Glen Sean Coulthard critically argues in *Red Skin, White Masks*, recognition can function as a mechanism in which dominant systems of settler-colonialism are reinforced by their ability to define the very terms through which recognition, and the possibility of fuller social and political participation, is deployed. In other words, in being granted or "accorded" to Indigenous people, recognition can function to perpetuate the power of a given colonial state along with its political, economic systems.[58] Furthermore, it potentially deepens the ways in which Indigenous communities come to *identify* with the prevailing authority of the state and that expresses itself through a complex array of "psycho-social effects" in which colonized populations internalize "the derogatory images [of themselves] imposed on them," thereby transforming "the colonized population into *subjects* of imperial rule."[59] These are critical perspectives and realities that complicate the ways in which recognition is understood to automatically benefit marginalized and disenfranchised communities.

It is by way of these two sides—from the objective, in terms of entrenched structures of state power, to the subjective, where colonized persons are internally held captive—that Coulthard works at challenging recognition as a mechanism. Following such arguments, Coulthard instead maps what he terms practices of "Indigenous resurgence" founded on acts of *self*-recognition, which are acts that "turn away" from dependency on the colonial state.[60] This includes recognition of Indigenous enactments that seek to challenge the "legitimacy of the settler state's claim to sovereignty over Indigenous people and their territories on the one hand, and the normative status of the state-form as an appropriate mode of governance on the other."[61] Furthermore, acts of *self*-recognition enhance greater recognition of the cultural practices and knowledges on the part of Indigenous communities which, as Coulthard notes, "have much to offer" relationships between peoples and the natural world "built upon principles of reciprocity and respectful coexistence."[62]

---

[58] Glen Sean Coulthard, *Red Skin, White Masks: Rejecting the Colonial Politics of Recognition* (Minneapolis: University of Minnesota Press, 2014), 30.
[59] Ibid., 31.
[60] Ibid., 153–4.
[61] Ibid., 36.
[62] Ibid., 48.

The aspects that Coulthard identifies as problematic to recognition as a political mechanism can be seen as operative within the Voice referendum. As a project, the Voice aimed at constitutional reform to ensure greater political recognition for Indigenous people on the part of the government and nation. Importantly, this was not about changing language or wording, as was accomplished in 1967 with a referendum on constitutional reform aimed at ridding the constitution of specific prejudices as to "race."[63] Rather, the Voice proposed changing aspects of the legal structure of the country. This would have entailed greater political will, as well as acceptance of a stronger Indigenous presence within government. It therefore sought to appeal to the state, understanding that having a rightful place in the government would ensure an Indigenous perspective when it comes to lawmaking. Neil Pearson supports such an understanding, arguing it is time the nation allows Indigenous people to have the "responsibility" for their own development.[64]

Importantly, as the Indigenous lawyer and key proponent of the referendum Megan Davis argues, the Uluru Statement and Voice referendum are significant because they express an approach to reform fully designed by Indigenous people, arising out of a lengthy process of dialogue and debate among Indigenous communities and delegates. As such, it wholly speaks toward critical enactments of self-determination directed toward greater representation and participation in national bodies of governance. "A First Nations voice in the Constitution would empower Aboriginal and Torres Strait Islander peoples with a mechanism to be heard on our own terms, so that we are treated more justly and humanely than in the past."[65] This is echoed by David Noongar, when he comments: "So, when we considered the Voice proposal, I thought it was ideal because, personally, I could see how it worked. It's unfinished business. We had back then and still have all these bureaucrats in between that are pretty much helping to undermine the whole process for Aboriginal self-determination and self-management. We need to take control."[66]

---

[63] For an insightful presentation and analysis of the 1967 referendum, see Megan Davis and George Williams, *Everything You Need to Know about the Voice* (Sydney: UNSW Press, 2023), 35–58.

[64] Noel Pearson, "A Rightful Place," in *A Rightful Place: A Road Map to Recognition*, ed. Shireen Morris (Carlton, VIC: Black, 2017), 80.

[65] Megan Davis, "Self-Determination and the Right to Be Heard," in *A Rightful Place: A Road Map to Recognition*, ed. Shireen Morris (Carlton, VIC: Black, 2017), 141.

[66] Ibid., 130.

The example of the Voice provides a compelling expression of the ways in which recognition remains a key social, political mechanism, one which is never fixed or static but is continuously debated and invested in. As Davis elaborates, the dialogues organized throughout 2015 and 2016 leading up to the Convention brought forward a range of critical discussions on what constitutes "recognition," which "combined to instigate a shift from the focus on 'recognition' being on 'race' and racial non-discrimination to true First Nations empowerment and self-determination."[67] It was about "power and authority" as opposed to symbolic change. "The voice is about *active* participation in the democratic life of the state"[68] and about "truth-telling" in which First peoples' histories and experiences could be told and given "acknowledgment by the nation."[69]

I highlight these aspects to consider in what ways the idealization of speaking-with, as a model of ethical, relational co-creation that works at holding a relation to difference, confronts long-standing structures defining a given (settler-colonial) society. And how listening and recognition are deeply entwined, appearing across personal lives and interpersonal communication, as well as community struggles and social movements. As democratic governments are founded on the "voice of the people," how opportunities are provided for voices to be heard on their own terms is crucial. This is precisely what the referendum sought to provide, and which the Voice also worked at deepening. Yet, given the rejection of the referendum it remains to be seen in what ways recognition of an Indigenous voice would be implemented within the country, and what effects this might have on a structural level. The call for a rightful place on the part of Indigenous people remains pressing. This is a call, as Pearson notes, for a "bicultural future."[70]

↬

As I queried earlier, what becomes of the voice within the construct of speaking-with? Does something change of the voice? And what is the "new listening" Irigaray highlights as central to an emergent, ethical model of dialogue? I find partial answers in Thomas Mayo's example, where the author's own voice is constituted by the voices of many others. His is a form of *listening activism* aimed at recognizing the voices of people as populated by the voices of land,

---

[67] Ibid., 137–8.
[68] Ibid., 130–1.
[69] Ibid., 141.
[70] Pearson, "A Rightful Place," 77.

community, by history and, importantly, struggles for recognition. Mayo's book is an elaboration of this listening act, aiding in the heartfelt politics of the Uluru Statement. It is along these lines that *Finding the Heart of the Nation* performs the voice as a social labor aimed at securing greater recognition on the part of a broader citizenry. This is a moral, affectionate, political work that seeks to remind people of history, struggle, the values of land and ancestry, while appealing to a horizon of change, a becoming-nation shaped by the not-yet recognizable: a *bicultural future.*

I take Mayo's heart listening then as a practice, an activism that, while seeking recognition on the part of the government and nation, aims to do so on its own terms: these are the terms the painting of the sacred Statement itself carries, for such an object, marked by the cultures, the languages, the heritage and cosmologies of Indigenous people, delivers to the nation a call to shift, to turn, to recognize, so as "to be more sensitive to the claims and challenges emanating from these dissenting Indigenous voices."[71] For these are voices that not only challenge but offer opportunities for reconciliation.

In her work on intersubjectivity, Jessica Benjamin highlights the process of the Third as what positions us as witnesses for each other. Within the co-creative, emergent dynamics of thirdness, one takes on the role of witness for another, attending to what others come to say or shy away from. The showing of ourselves, in the rhythms that punctuate and inflect the Third, becomes the ground for a pronounced form of recognition, one that gives room for the weaknesses and the truths, the silences and the noises, for what can be said and what remains unspoken. Importantly, Benjamin is concerned to elaborate the Third as a framework to be applied in acknowledging and working through greater histories of conflict and abuse across a given society. As part of such a project, witnessing is cast as essential. "In witnessing and confirming what has taken place," Benjamin writes, "we affirm that the victim is worthy of being heard, deserving of dignity, of recognition for suffering and caring protection."[72] Witnessing is deeply influential in terms of enabling truth-telling and a greater process of reconciliation.

To elaborate this perspective, Benjamin offers a reflection on the Truth and Reconciliation Commission (TRC) taking place in South Africa starting in 1996.

---

[71] Coulthard, *Red Skin, White Masks*, 36.
[72] Benjamin, *Beyond Doer and Done To*, 90.

The commission functioned as a private and public court, where victims as well as perpetrators of violence under apartheid could offer testimony. This included research and investigation into alleged crimes, as well as how political parties and other institutions and businesses in the country contributed to maintaining discriminatory and abusive practices. Importantly, the commission created a powerful context for addressing histories and experiences of violence, with the overall aim of moving forward with establishing democracy in the country. Developed within the context of the Mandela government, reconciling the deep divides across the country, especially between the powerful white minority and mostly poor Black majority, was understood as essential. The commission therefore served multiple purposes, and over the course of its work running until its closure in 2000 (and the establishment of the Institute for Justice and Reconciliation), it compiled an important dossier documenting human rights abuses starting from 1960.

A controversial step made by the commission was to allow applications for amnesty to be presented. By granting this right the commission sought to both deepen knowledge as to the structure and activities of the apartheid government, while also nurturing a greater process of reconciliation, where perpetrators of violence and their victims could confront each other outside a system of judgment and punishment. Such a move met with fierce criticism, yet it proved consequential to the process. Chaired by Desmond Tutu, the commission carried a larger moral mission, one which was to generally impact positively onto the nation.[73] By creating a platform aimed at reconciliation, the commission gave room for the airing of grievances, the acknowledgment of suffering, and importantly, pleas for forgiveness, where the nation could bear witness to its own internal challenges as well as movements toward securing a future to come.

For Benjamin, the commission offers an important expression of the Third on a national level, where the process of witnessing contributes to healing the wounds of an unfinished history as well as supporting greater civic discourse aimed at resisting terror. She writes: "Recognition gives validation to victims that their injury matters, but also restores the connection to truth and the social bond with the larger Third that is inevitably denied during the exercise of violence."[74]

---

[73] For a concise overview of the Truth and Reconciliation Commission process in South Africa, see Mary Ingouville Burton, *The Truth and Reconciliation Commission* (Auckland Park: Jacana Media, 2021).

[74] Benjamin, *Beyond Doer and Done To*, 218.

Citing Pumla Gobodo-Madikizela, a clinical psychologist who served on the commission, Benjamin emphasizes the necessity to reach out toward others in a "spirit of compassion instead of revenge."[75] This is no easy task, and Benjamin is sensitive to the challenges as well as the impossibility for some to offer gestures of compassion.

The breaking down of a system defined by the unequal relation of oppressor and oppressed, of doer and done to as Benjamin names it, and the unmasking or demystification of dominant power, are vital steps in recovering from histories of sustained political violence. For in such a move resides the seeds of new relations, and a new moral, political order. This includes the transformative work found in truth-telling. As the TRC created a space for truth-telling, both victims and perpetrators could confront each other on more equal terms, where stories of suffering and damage could be heard and acknowledged, and where telling and hearing the truth contribute to restoring a sense of humanity. Importantly, this extends both ways, where perpetrators may tell of their experiences and express remorse for their actions, enabling victims to witness their oppressors as emotionally and morally vulnerable, and where victims can tell of their hardships while facing their oppressors and through which their humanity may be recognized.

In reflecting upon her own experience of the TRC, Gobodo-Madikizela offers a compelling view onto the transformative power of reconciliation and, in this case, how the commission provided a crucial opportunity for witnessing the vulnerability of those who previously held power. "When violators of human rights allow themselves to be emotionally vulnerable, they are giving others a chance to encounter them as human beings."[76] While processes of truth-telling, of reconciliation and witnessing, are extremely challenging and fraught with pain and anger, Gobodo-Madikizela evokes a hopefulness in the TRC as a project— and in other situations where truth and reconciliation commissions have set out to address histories of oppression. These are complex processes that move across emotional, psychological lives and political, social structures and histories; as moral, national projects, truth and reconciliation commissions speak toward the importance of acknowledging the suffering of others on a national scale, of giving time and space for the difficult work of shared recovery. This integrates

---

[75] Pumla Gobodo-Madikizela, *A Human Being Died That Night: A South African Woman Confronts the Legacy of Apartheid* (Boston: Mariner Books, 2004), 45.

[76] Ibid., 16.

within its process and performative staging crucial acts of hearing and being heard, of voicing and of witnessing, of appearing before one's own victims or oppressors, confronting the brutal realities that bound each together in a system of violence and hate. Witnessing, as Benjamin argues, works at restoring the dignity of lives so vital to the project of freedom and justice.

↬

Damien Freeman and Nicola Hunter emphasize the importance of reconciliation in the context of Australia, while acknowledging how it remains elusive and difficult. Part of this reality is the degree to which truth-telling has been avoided, stripping communities and the nation of a much-needed process of repair. As they note, truth and reconciliation processes provide important opportunities for publicly discussing memories and documenting historical truths, "thus enabling the parties to move forward together with a greater sense of mutual resolution and understanding in relation to past experiences."[77] Furthermore, such processes provide space for shared healing and recovery, so that "past conflicts can be resolved and relationships positively transformed."[78] This is not to overshadow how reconciliation is a fraught process, full of anger, resentment, hurt, and the wounds of unresolved history. Dylan Robinson, a xwélmexw scholar and artist, reminds of these challenges, highlighting how truth and reconciliation forums may too often supply participants and audiences with good feelings while failing to engage the deep work still needing to be done, especially when it comes to political, economic, or legal change. He importantly calls for being aware of how the "affective component" of reconciliation may engender hope in ways that are detrimental to effective transformation.[79]

The urgency around truth-telling and reconciliation is embedded in the Uluru Statement from the Heart, and the larger project of the Voice, which calls for truth-telling as part of its mission. Returning to Benjamin, as part of these processes are the ways in which they bring forward a pronounced form of witnessing. Truth-telling may be about airing grievances, discussing the past and acknowledging suffering, yet importantly, it is also about creating an environment in which those involved may act as witnesses for one another. Witnessing makes recovery possible.

---

[77] Damien Freeman and Nicola Hunter, "When Two Rivers Become One," in *A Rightful Place: A Road Map to Recognition*, ed. Shireen Morris (Carlton, VIC: Black, 2017), 188–9.

[78] Ibid., 189.

[79] Dylan Robinson, *Hungry Listening: Resonant Theory for Indigenous Sound Studies* (Minneapolis: University of Minnesota press, 2020), 231.

Central to witnessing is the act of giving narrative to trauma as well as experiencing being listened to; while trauma can be tied to an event from the past, the act of speaking aloud, of giving narrative to one's experience in front of others, confirms the experience itself—such acts make the experience known. As Dori Laub notes, the knower of trauma is both the victim as well as the listener, the one in the position of receiving the narration which, in the case of truth-telling and more formal structures of national reconciliation, includes all parties involved. Importantly, by participating in the knowing of the experience, the listener emerges as a "co-owner" of the traumatic event. As Laub notes, "through his very listening, he comes to partially experience trauma in himself."[80] This is a deeply challenging position, especially if the listener has direct experience of the trauma being addressed and narrated.

Witnessing is fundamentally an act of listening. And within the context of truth and reconciliation, it puts into play a form of collective listening that greatly assists in working at shared recovery and healing—as Benjamin continuously reminds, thirdness is a process, not a thing; it is not necessarily something arrived at, completed, fulfilled; rather, it is expressed in the enactments and gestures that work at holding a connection to suffering. As such, it necessitates a collective holding, a coordinated collaboration, which gives support especially when truth-telling may feel painful. When it comes to addressing past experiences and histories of violence and abuse, to finding ways of achieving mutual recognition and resolution, to challenging and combatting structures that keep in place systems of settler-colonialism, listening is needed. This includes recognition of how listening can also be exhausting, riddled with pain, annoyance, with having to possibly hear something that feels violating, *unlistenable*.

Love of the World

I've been working through questions of listening and recognition, giving attention to the ways in which listening-toward others participates in struggles for recognition. From the immediate experiences of being with others, working at the dialogical and social labors by which to hold a relation to difference,

---

[80] Dori Laub, "Bearing Witness, or the Vicissitudes of Listening," in *Testimony: Crises of Witnessing in Literature, Psychoanalysis, and History*, ed. Shoshana Felman and Dori Laub (New York: Routledge, 1992), 58.

to the greater social movements that seek legal, national recognition so as to be more fully heard, listening is emphasized as central. As part of this, the notion of third listening is put forward to deepen a view onto listening's ability to foster a shared world, as well as shared responsibility for the making and unmaking of identities and communities. Third listening is a poetic listening, a listening from the heart that keeps close to the sensuality of words and their affective potencies. As Gemma Corradi Fiumara posits, the poetic figure of metaphor is a biological force, one that helps in inhabiting new perspectives, engendering new ways of communicating and relating. Metaphor, or the *metaphoric process*, gives greatly to the dialogical, social labors in which voice works at an affective ecology of relations—a third-sphere. These are aspects that contribute to processes of truth-telling and reconciliation, to how it is one may find the courage and the words when facing one's oppressor or victim. As Jessica Benjamin emphasizes, restoring dignity to broken lives is crucial for repair. Within such a context, hearing and being heard operate as literal as well as metaphoric capacities and experiences that underpin justice. To be a witness to others is to be a listener which, as Dori Laub emphasizes, is to take on the role of *guardian*, giving acknowledgment and care for the trauma of others. These situations and processes are never without challenges, interruption, breakdown. The dialogical, social labor inherent to speaking-with is riddled with tension, disappointment, anxiety—the Third is a process; it is an ongoing endeavor, of turning and holding, defending and protecting, petitioning and witnessing.

⤳

In considering these different perspectives, I hope to contribute to building a discourse, a practice, one that can enhance listening's affirmative role in struggles for recognition. Listening-toward extends an invitation to share, to turn and in turning, to hold difference, inaugurating a space, a shared dwelling, or third-sphere. This has led me to further appreciate Luce Irigaray's use of the phrase, *the way of love*, as an overarching framing to her conceptualization of speaking-with. The holding of difference listening-toward labors at is, as the author suggests, expressive of a position of love. The way of love is a gesture of radical care, it is caring for the attention given and received, that is called for in nurturing greater relational value and the affective potencies of speaking-with. It is along these lines that I want to conclude by thinking listening *as* love.

In his theoretical work on recognition, Axel Honneth underscores experiences of love as the precondition (a "first stage") by which recognition is established and made meaningful as a social mechanism.[81] This is founded on understanding love as being bound to "primary relationships," from friendships to parent–child relations through to the intimate sphere of romantic relation, all of which hold within them a profound *affectional reciprocity*. Primary relationships, importantly, become a first instance in which the social mechanism of recognition articulates itself, for primary relationships are where individuals find their "being through others." Importantly, as Honneth is concerned to emphasize, this is never a stable, fixed condition—recognition is a struggle, and in the case of love, includes a tension between attachment and independence, between togetherness and self-actualization. Love thus comes to figure as a general structure for all ethical life, "For it is only this symbiotically nourished bond, which emerges through mutually desired demarcation, that produces the degree of basic individual self-confidence indispensable for autonomous participation in public life."[82]

While recognition may be confirmed through legal proceedings, on the level of rights, and it may operate to garner a sense of social participation through expressions of community, love names a primary, enduring basis for recognizing the needs of others as well as experiencing one's own worth and meaningfulness by way of others. Furthermore, love carries an aspect of faith, for to love is to believe in others. As Simone Weil states, "belief in the existence of other human beings as such is love."[83] To love, for Weil, is to keep close to the facticity of others, to recognize each for who they are, rather than wanting them to become something other, or projecting onto others an ideal image. Such a view leads Richard Gilman-Opalsky to suggest that love assists in overcoming forms of discrimination, for love *humanizes* persons—to see others as individuals rather than as things or objects of desire (Gilman-Opalsky underscores how desire is too often confused with love). Love further entails a profound emotional sharing, thereby "deprivatizing" states of happiness, grief, pleasure, and pain.[84] To love is to feel with others, giving way to an understanding of love as a connective tissue. It expresses itself in how one *participates in others becoming something they are not-yet*.[85] Finally,

---

[81]   Honneth, *The Struggle for Recognition*, 95.

[82]   Ibid., 107.

[83]   Simone Weil, quoted in Richard Gilman-Opalsky, *The Communism of Love: An Inquiry into the Poverty of Exchange Value* (Chico, CA: AK Press, 2020), 19.

[84]   Gilman-Opalsky, *The Communism of Love*, 21.

[85]   Ibid., 31.

as Gilman-Opalsky argues, love emerges as a form of public power. Extending from Honneth's suggestion that participation in public life is supported through experiences of the mutual bond found in intimate relations, love is carried as a general internal structure for engaging with and being part of a shared world. The "communism of love" as Gilman-Opalsky terms it, positions love as what makes community possible in ways that extend beyond the familiar and immediate.

⌐⌐

How is love and listening connected? In what sense is *speaking-with/listening-toward* an expression of love? Are there dangers to be considered in posing love as an ethical, political ground for enhancing the collective good? How can love figure, like listening, as input into the work needed to change societies, nations, governments when it comes to moving recognition toward greater levels of social, structural transformation? As love, listening can be appreciated to support a model of power based on care, compassion, on building trust and community, and that encourages human flourishing. This finds echo in the work of bell hooks when she writes, following Martin Luther King Jr.'s belief in the power of love as what may lead toward a more just future: "I share that belief and the conviction that it is in choosing love, and beginning with love as the ethical foundation for politics, that we are best positioned to transform society in ways that enhance the collective good."[86]

Such a view is reflective of how I'm conceiving a poetics of listening—to follow the ways in which listening holds difference, and in holding gives room to a diversity of voices, languages, meanings, and worlds. If the "communism of love" reminds of love's ability to strengthen our commitment to each other, it moreover enhances collective forms of power, especially in terms of listening beyond ourselves. "Choosing love we also chose to live in community," hooks writes.[87] In following hooks, I'm led to consider that such a choice may also include *choosing to listen*—choosing to undertake the work of listening, as what contributes to an ethic of love. Listening expresses a love of the world; it is what turns us, commits us to each other, and to a common good. The ethic of love that hooks calls for is far from a "sentimental" expression; rather, it is a call to deepen the joy of a collective work, one that fosters "communion with a world

---

[86] bell hooks, "Love as the Practice of Freedom," in *Outlaw Culture: Resisting Representations* (New York: Routledge, 1994), 247.

[87] Ibid., 248.

beyond the self, the tribe, the race, the nation"—to work together at healing "our wounded body politic."[88] Choosing love for hooks is to choose to move against domination. Such movements, as Thomas Mayo suggests, entails learning to listen by way of the heart, by way of love, for love is a belief in what others are and can become. And for what we can do together.

[88] Ibid., 250.

3

Listening-with: Sympathy, Bodily Life, and Healing Justice

The workings of inner voice, and the deeply influential processes of social and political recognition, contribute to understanding listening as transformative to individual subjectivity and community building. By way of listening's attentional power, forms of personal orientation and self-awareness are fostered, supporting a principled life and expressions of ethical know-how. This extends across social worlds in which listening becomes vital to self-determination and self-esteem: to be heard as an individual is to be acknowledged by others; it is to experience a sense of acceptance and participation within given communities and societies. To listen is to also give acknowledgment; it is an act or gesture that attends to others, that bears witness, and that often works to give room for others to speak, to participate, and to gain agency.

Furthermore, listening is essential to care and caritative practices. In fact, listening's influence and impact are deeply tied to bodily life and experience, keeping one close to an embodied awareness, where attention to others moves by way of affective connection. Listening is the means by which to nurture empathy, to feel with others; it follows and supports bodily life while opening paths toward broader metaphysical, spiritual dimensions. Although listening can appear as rather quiet, as something cerebral or passive, it is fundamentally felt, impassioned, and it impacts onto embodied experience. In what ways do the reflections and realizations prompted by inner voicing shape bodily vitality, health, and social behavior? In being recognized by others, what becomes of the body—are there noticeable signs or shifts in bodily composure and well-being made manifest by feeling acknowledged, heard, attended to? And what are the consequences or effects of listening—do we not listen in order to be moved and affected as well? To experience pleasure and joy, to discover and relate to others? In listening out for answers, for the reverberations of insight and epiphany, are we not opening our bodies to a certain influence? A direction to be taken, a gesture to be performed, a feeling to be shared?

The capacity to listen to oneself, and to participate in the struggles and well-being of others, can be said to change something of the body. It is my perspective that listening greatly participates in the embodied work of living and caring, providing a means for staying connected to bodily health and healing. To listen is often to *listen-with* the body, keeping in touch with oneself as a feeling, sensual body while equally coming close to others as fully embodied persons. In essence, listening is the expression of an embodied intelligence and lends greatly to processes of repair.

∽

It is my concern to deepen an understanding of listening's place within caring practices and in what ways it contributes to influencing bodily life. Listening can be appreciated as a means for nurturing awareness of one's body and its state of health, and in doing so, to foster a sensitivity for the lives of others. As I'll develop in this chapter, listening affords recognition of the *languages of the body*. From psychological, emotional states to physical conditions, bodily awareness is profoundly transformative, helping to regulate personal well-being. This includes being aware as to how one feels within given environments, how contexts and their conditions impact onto the body and one's sense of comfort. This extends to an appreciation for how personal well-being is always influenced by living conditions and the broader historical forces that shape individual lives. As I work at showing, *interconnectedness* is an expansive weave that integrates not only the immediate conditions of places and people, but questions of history and politics, intergenerational bonds, and the societal structures that emplace, embed, and orient people in certain ways. To speak of bodily awareness is to open onto recognizing a more holistic view, one that also requires a more holistic approach to health and healing.

How does listening participate in nurturing bodily awareness? In what ways do healing practices and care work entail a skill of listening? These are questions that I'll follow, posing *listening-with* as a particular modality. This leads to emphasizing listening as a language of connection, of sensitivity and healing, a language that is also aligned with poetics. Importantly, listening-with must be understood to extend beyond a sound-centered perspective; rather, highlighting listening as a bodily practice, as what contributes to processes of healing and the maintenance of vitality, opens onto a broader view, where listening is positioned as a *way of feeling*. While listening-into is to attend to the inner dimensions, to cultivate self-knowledge and to work through the influencing force of an external world, listening-with is positioned as a modality that *follows* the body, that carries and cares in ways that impact the vitality of bodily life. As such, I'm interested in how it lends to bodily intelligence, a way of being with the body and the bodies of others, one grounded in the experiential. Integrated within these considerations is a focus on the affective tonalities or "currents" underpinning consciousness and being with others. Drawing from affective neuroscience, and theories of the new unconscious, listening-with emerges as a critical means by which to attune to the body and all that it carries. This includes sensitivity for past and ongoing experiences of violence and harm, the unfinished histories that keep open certain wounds, especially for marginalized communities. To engage in care work is to nurture a greater care culture in which listening acts as a vital contribution.

Bodily Power, Therapeutic Work

In *Beyond the Periphery of the Skin*, Silvia Federici argues that within today's capitalistic environment it is essential to reappropriate the body. She writes: "Our struggle then must begin with the reappropriation of our body, the revaluation and rediscovery of its capacity for resistance, and expansion and celebration of its powers, individual and collective."[1] To bring attention to the body's intrinsic powers is to learn from its languages, its rhythms: "Our bodies have reasons that we need to learn, rediscover, reinvent. We need to listen to their language as the path to our health and healing, as we need to listen to the language and rhythms of the natural world as the path to the health and healing of the earth."[2] Federici's proposition is suggestive for understanding listening as a question of embodiment and bodily vitality or power. As with the cultivation of inner voice, listening to the body is underscored as key to a care of the self. Yet, in what sense can the body be listened to? How might such listening be understood as the basis for countering capitalism's appropriation and exploitation of the body as a power and force? And which can enable solidarity across planetary ecologies and more-than-human others? Federici embraces the potentiality of listening as

---

[1] Silvia Federici, *Beyond the Periphery of the Skin: Rethinking, Remaking, and Reclaiming the Body in Contemporary Capitalism* (Oakland: PM Press, 2020), 123.
[2] Ibid., 124.

a transformative capacity, whereby listening to (or *with*) the body affects change, particularly in terms of reworking its situatedness within dominant systems of capitalistic exploitation. Yet, the capacity to retrieve something of bodily power, as the creative force of vitality, is never so simple; whether under the rhythms and structures of contemporary capitalism with its extractivist practices, the defining labors that situate and strain one's body (some more so than others)— that call one into a range of particular performances—or through the social, technical mechanisms that require the ongoingness of an emotional, cognitive work, the body is positioned to lose much of itself. What are the defining features of bodily power? And in what ways does the body become available to listening's recuperative influence?

⌣

Echoing aspects of Michel Foucault's theories of the care of the self, which integrate a process of inner listening in the cultivation of *logos*, Federici opens another perspective, one closer to the work of somatic practices. A care of the self, following Federici, positions listening as what affords ways of attending the body as a biological intelligence or natural vitality. Such a view finds echo in the many sites and situations of health care and somatic therapy, where care workers attend not only to particular ailments or symptoms but also to the various signals of the body and what those signals often tell. Having the capacity to sense the fullness of the body and its changes is often crucial for proper diagnosis and treatment, not to mention the more tender and considered gestures in support of another's comfort. Listening helps in recognizing the highly nuanced and holistic world of bodily vitality. The body has its own logic, its own language, and learning this language allows for greater awareness as to its health and what constitutes care. A care of the self is thus founded on processes that move from the inner voice and the shaping of a reasoning individual, to an awareness of bodily health and the somatic signals or stories that require greater sensitivity, where the state of the body is recognizable through deeply supple forms of attention. Developing a listening awareness can be seen to contribute profoundly to well-being, both for oneself and for others.

In her book, *Liberated to the Bone*, Susan Raffo offers a range of insightful perspectives onto questions of health and healing, as well as listening's contribution to care work. As a craniosacral therapist, Raffo is dedicated to finding ways of attending to the body and all that it comes to carry and endure. Fundamentally, this entails recognizing not only the immediate injuries some may suffer; Raffo brings attention instead to the ways in which bodies are burdened by histories of violence that may span generations. As she highlights, "there is impact with violence, there is impact with pleasure, and then there is what happens after that impact, the echoes that carry forward."[3] For Raffo, and for the broader cultures of care work, what we know of the body is never strictly confined to the experiences of individuals and immediate symptoms or pains. Bodily life, instead, is recognized as part of a greater whole that includes a range of social, economic, psychological, emotional, and spiritual experiences. Furthermore, bodies are histories in themselves, biological, genetic, cultural, political histories that define much of their abilities and tendencies. Our bodies are the manifestation and expression of all these histories, the intergenerational bonds and cultural genealogies, the languages and meanings that inscribe a plethora of defining values and viewpoints, that emplace and orient in certain ways, and that often lead bodies into particular forms of strain. As Raffo argues, to work at healing is never strictly about individual health; rather, healing is a political act, one that directs itself toward the larger project of *healing justice*. Healing, for Raffo, fundamentally starts with ending violence.

Importantly, Raffo brings focus to the deep or slow violences inherent to settler-colonialism and the systems of racialization that have negatively affected generations of Black, Indigenous, and People of Color (in the context of North America, which is the main focus of the author). These unfinished histories wield their influence onto the physical well-being of individuals and communities, but they also carry over onto the land itself. Raffo's *Liberated to the Bone* begins with the question: "What does it mean to do healing work, to do any kind of change work when the land below your feet still carries stories that are not finished?"[4] These are "original wounds" perpetrated by settler-colonialism and the imposition of systems based on the owning of land and people.[5] And which continues as part of a greater cycle of conquest, from the colonizing Europeans who fled their own form of persecution only to work at enslaving others, through to the ongoingness of violences shaping the lives and health of the poor. As Linda Villarosa argues in *Under the Skin*, racism actively underpins health in the United States.[6]

---

[3] Susan Raffo, *Liberated to the Bone: Histories, Bodies, Futures* (Chico, CA: AK Press, 2022), 59.
[4] Ibid., 12.
[5] Ibid., 16–17.
[6] Linda Villarosa, *Under the Skin: The Hidden Toll of Racism on Health in America* (New York: Anchor Books, 2022).

In calling attention to the "original wounds" of land and people, Raffo seeks to *ground* her practice, and the work of healing in general, recognizing that in enacting care it is essential to know of the unfinished histories that "shape the space of our practice and the people who come to see us."[7] Importantly, pursuing the work of healing justice necessitates that such knowing is undertaken not only "with your mind" but with "your whole self": "When I use the phrase 'healing justice,' I am reflecting on how the systems we seek to change outside of our bodies are also carried within our bodies."[8] Knowing of unfinished histories, of genealogies of violence, carried as original wounds into personal lives and the life of society, is to know by way of the whole self, knowing of one's own place within particular systems. Such knowing, as Raffo argues, is possible only by way of "the felt sense," which comes to communicate by way of poetry: "The cells of the body communicate with us through poetry, through story, image, and metaphor. This is how we end up with a felt sense of something rather than only an intellectual understanding." Echoing Federici's call for reclaiming the body as a path toward health and healing, Raffo further suggests that "this felt sense, this way of knowing from the body up, is how transformation takes place."[9]

↪

I want to follow Raffo's perspectives and concerns, along with Federici's, to think further about health and healing as work that addresses original wounds, and that gains traction by way of a poetics of listening—this is a work, a poetics, that explicitly draws forward the felt sense as a means for change, for recuperating and reclaiming bodily power. Importantly, as part of healing justice, health and well-being are not only conceived as individual concerns or issues but extend toward social, collective, or communal and national embodiments. Healing justice radically moves across individuals and communities, and as Raffo highlights, across histories and nations which includes the question of land. It is moreover positioned to challenge economic and medical structures, emphasizing care as a political issue.

In her article "On Care and Citizenship," Elke Krasny reflects upon the artistic work of Simone Leigh, in particular her project *The Waiting Room* presented at the New Museum in New York in 2016.[10] As a project, Leigh's *The Waiting Room*

---

[7] Raffo, *Liberated to the Bone*, 22.

[8] Ibid., 25.

[9] Ibid.

[10] Elke Krasny, "On Care and Citizenship: Performing Healing (in) the Museum," *Passepartout—New Infrastructures* #40 (2020): 3–28.

references the tragic incident of Esmin Green, a Jamaican cleaner who died while waiting for treatment at the Brooklyn Hospital after being involuntarily admitted for psychiatric care. Leigh's project asks for a deeper engagement with the politics of care, questioning in what ways the health care system in the United States unevenly cares for people, where the poor and People of Color are especially disadvantaged. Yet, *The Waiting Room* not only brings forward critical perspectives onto a care injustice, it moreover fills the museum with care practices, creating a number of spaces and situations where care can be newly enacted. As Krasny suggests, "commemorating and honoring Green's life and death, *The Waiting Room* provided the kind of care that might have prevented her from falling into despair and from being involuntarily admitted to the hospital."[11] From massage therapy and community acupuncture to herbal and plant remedies, from meditation and yoga to safe spaces for discussion among women of color, Leigh performs self-organized care in challenge to the racist workings of healthcare in the United States. In short, the project sought to take back care from an exclusionary system. This included referring visitors to a greater history of health practices and knowledge, specifically drawing upon those found on the slave plantation and in Black diasporic communities across the country. As Krasny highlights, "emphasizing this parallel and alternative history of Black healing, which includes collective practices such as song or dance, is in and of itself a contribution to healing as it strengthens the memory of Black opposition to health discrimination, thus foregrounding endurance and resistance rather than focusing on the violence and trauma of victimization."[12]

Considering Krasny's examination of Simone Leigh's work, questions of original wounds are emphasized in ways that also support forms of resistance and the recuperation of collective care practices. These are practices that keep hold of the ground under the feet of communities, that carry the knowledge of folk remedies as well as the stories carried down across generations supplying shared understanding of pain and injury along with approaches to treatment.

Throughout her work on healing justice, Raffo offers insight into somatic understanding and practice, acknowledging how violence and trauma are carried by the body and how it may surface in various ways, moving across generations and by way of structures of racial, misogynistic prejudice as well as through ableist understandings of wellness. Importantly, persons not only experience

[11] Ibid., 14.
[12] Ibid., 15.

violence and trauma, but they may come to reinforce such experiences through actions that move their bodies in particular ways, that place one within structures shaped by violence, and that may lead to perpetuating their influence. In what ways can one work at shifting structural violence, to upset how abuse becomes normalized? Through what means might we attend to deeply held negative patterns and pains that inhabit bodies? Leigh's *The Waiting Room* gives expression to navigating these questions, finding creative routes for recovering repressed medicinal knowledges, for deepening understanding of bodily life on a holistic level, and for sharing in shaping a more caring future centered on community and the common good. This includes giving room for listening's guidance, its capacity for attuning to the felt sense and all that it garners.

↜

To listen somatically, as Federici calls for, is to reclaim something of the body; it is to find ways of reconnecting to its *natural power*. Listening to the body is to "befriend" the layers of its nature, its stories and systems, as well as its yearnings and aches. It is to bring compassion to all that it carries or is burdened by. As Deb Dana highlights through her work in polyvagal theory and practice, listening enacts forms of self-care so as to help "regulate" the body's responses to perceived or experienced danger, which results in flight or fright, in protecting or shutting down, and which severs a connection to well-being.[13] Self-compassion, being a friend to oneself, listening to what the body tells, all assist in bringing one back into a state of connection.

Alongside such views, a number of questions may be raised: if listening is shaped by the very systems it seeks to upset, how might it perform a countermeasure? Does not my listening itself carry all the structures and histories of violence along with it? That is, in what ways can listening truly support an end to violence and the work of healing justice? To negotiate the dangers that continuously influence what I may know of the body? It is along these lines that it must be emphasized that bringing listening and compassion to the body names a practice—it is deep work, change work, and it is a radical position to take, because it must tread through histories of injury and prejudice, it must labor against systems of destruction so as to reconnect with a living world, and it must go against what Rupa Marya and Raj Patel term "colonial medicine."[14] This is

---

[13] Deb Dana, *Anchored: How to Befriend Your Nervous System Using Polyvagal Theory* (Boulder, CO: Sounds True, 2021), 31.

[14] Rupa Marya and Raj Patel, *Inflamed: Deep Medicine and the Anatomy of Injustice* (London: Penguin Books, 2022), 20.

grounded in recognizing the impact of histories of settler-colonialism that have instilled ways of thinking and practicing medicine that fail to address structural violence, and which adversely affects Black, Indigenous, and People of Color in particular. "Most doctors—most humans, really—have unwittingly inherited a colonial world-view that emphasizes individual health, disconnecting illness from its social and historical contexts and obscuring our place in the web of life that makes us who we are."[15] The authors work at expanding a critical view onto illness that acknowledges how individuals are deeply impacted by systems shaped by legacies of settler-colonialism and made to bear their ongoing effects. "Our concern is that the modern medical industry patches up bodies broken by the same system through which medicine itself was produced."[16] This is a system defined by "practices of domination" and which continues apace, enacting forms of oppression and occupation that damage ecosystems, nations, communities, and individual lives.

These are perspectives that stand behind Federici's call to reclaim the body from out of the capitalistic stranglehold on the web of life. And which may lend gravity to practices of listening to and with the body—a listening that works its way against systems that extract embodied power, and that purport to care for its pains while furthering a structure of violence across the globe. As Marya and Patel emphasize, it's crucial to decolonize medicine today so as to "rehumanize" not only people's pain, but how dominant systems understand their work. Decolonizing medicine starts with "repairing those relationships that have been damaged through systems of domination,"[17] allowing for a reconnection to the web of life: to protect the planetary, social ecosystems upon which life is based. Listening-with the body is a work of reconnection.

〜

Healing justice may suggest political, social, and cultural actions, all of which are essential in reworking systems of ongoing abuse. Yet, healing is fundamentally spiritual, it is grounded in attending to the broken rhythms of those who suffer, who hold trauma, to bring them back into alignment with themselves, and which comes to impact a greater community and ecology of living things—that is profoundly collective and centered on understandings of the common good. It also gives challenge to approaching the body as only ever socially constructed,

---

[15] Ibid., 12.
[16] Ibid., 19.
[17] Ibid., 22.

as bound to discursive powers. As Federici reminds, the body has been nurtured through millions of years of "coevolution with our natural environment" as well as through "intergenerational practices" that have given to the body a structure of needs and desires.[18] These are needs and desires entwined with the natural environment, where the warmth of sunlight, the green of trees, the replenishing power of water, the need and desire for touch, for sleeping and making love, all come to define the body as a natural power. And which are there, as a structure of needs and desires that are equally spiritual—as what binds to a greater state of vitality and connection. Living well is never simply about biological function—it is quite clearly something more. To care for others is also often guided by a desire to do good, to improve the life experience of others; it is informed by compassionate recognition of a greater whole, a common good, whether of an individual as a living ecosystem, or further, toward that of a communal or planetary world. To recover bodily is to recover something of that wholeness.

In order to elaborate an understanding of listening's influence on bodily vitality and power, I want to turn to practices of meditation, in particular following the writings of Willa Blythe Baker, a practitioner of Buddhist meditation and Founder of Natural Dharma Fellowship in Boston. In her publication *The Wakeful Body*, Baker invites readers into greater understanding of the body as a natural base of unity, that is, of mindfulness. "The body holds the key to mindfulness,"[19] Baker posits, for it is by way of the body that one may retain or recover a connection to spiritual wakefulness. Such views are based on recognizing how subjectivity, as the manifestation of a process of socialization, is often challenged by an inevitable schism within the body itself. Baker recollects that as a child she experienced her body as a "landscape of feeling" and sensation, where the body is shaped and informed, supported as well as scarred by its environments, by those who give care and by all the experiences of love and fear, joy and danger; these come to define the landscape of feeling (or, the *experiential body*) and which is carried in how one comes to experience the fullness of bodily life. Moving into adulthood, for Baker, was to shift from the experiences of the landscape of feeling and sensation into a body "formed by concepts, opinions, and ideas."[20] No longer aligned with feeling, the body is understood by way of concepts and judgments,

---

[18] Federici, *Beyond the Periphery of the Skin*, 119.
[19] Willa Blythe Baker, *The Wakeful Body: Somatic Mindfulness as a Path to Freedom* (Boulder, CO: Shambhala Publications, 2021).
[20] Ibid., 2.

susceptible to dominant social codes and meanings that become incorporated into one's "body image" (or, the *concept body*). For Baker, such a process speaks toward a certain *bodily grief*, whereby one mourns the loss of sensations and the intensities of bodily feeling. In contrast, a body of concepts comes to dominate, which often sets the body against itself.

The Wakeful Body is a guide for reclaiming that original wakefulness, for aligning with the natural vividness the body experiences and offers. "The body dwells in the here and now"[21]—it is *naturally awake*, giving continual guidance for how to relate to the world in which one lives. Importantly, for Baker, the body is approached as a unity with multiple layers, each with particular functions or ways of opening oneself to experiencing the present. These layers of embodiment, following yogic philosophy, are termed "the Earth Body," "the Subtle Body," and "the Awareness Body." Through particular meditations and practices, each layer of embodiment may be approached, lending to how one may specifically experience the physicality of the body, the energetic and affective qualities of embodiment, and finally, the layer of consciousness, and how a sense of awareness can pervade the body. From the physical ground of the body to the energetic, nervous dimensions of feeling, and through to a somatic consciousness, in which awareness fills the body, each layer of embodiment contributes to nurturing a relation to the body as the basis for mindfulness.

⟿

Throughout *The Wakeful Body*, the author is concerned to emphasize mindfulness—from the Sanskrit term, *Smriti*, which means "that which is remembered"—as a "faculty of attention" cultivated by way of practices. Mindfulness, therefore, is a faculty of attention that works at remembering our original wakefulness, it is to *keep in mind*, holding attention to that which is immediately present; it is to stay in the present, to stay wakeful. Importantly, as Baker highlights, within the original Sanskrit term, mindfulness does not necessarily equate solely with the mind, in terms of cognitive awareness; in fact, being mindful is equally a question of bodily awareness. Thus mindfulness names a greater perspective onto the practice of attention itself, as what mends or assuages feelings of fragmentation, of being burdened by everything that severs a connection to oneself.

---

[21] Ibid., 6.

Such views may help in understanding Federici's call for reclaiming the power of the body. This reclamation is guided by the intuitive understanding of the body as a carrier of a natural power, an original wakefulness, and through which one attunes or returns to the primary landscape of feeling, which is also to feel involved in the vitality of a greater experiential world. To reclaim the body is to reclaim the capacity for awareness, along with how such awareness may assist in negotiating situations that obfuscate, interrupt, exploit, and generally injure the body. Mindfulness, and the practices that support ways of keeping close to the felt sense, become acts that also challenge systems that situate the body for their own gains as Federici highlights, and which may also be broadened, to consider a range of contexts in which bodies are made to endure particular modes of labor, life, education, or treatment—situations that strain the body, that make one ill, that exploit or extract all types of energy and value from its vitality. While there are critical views to be made onto contemporary cultures and discourses of mindfulness today, and its uptake within forms of marketing and lifestyle, such cultures equally speak toward the complex ways in which bodies are put under strain, made to suffer, pushed to new forms of exhaustion as well as debilitated by a range of discourses, systems, and institutions. These are aspects that, for Susan Raffo, become central in terms of deepening the discussion around slow violence and the urgencies underpinning healing justice. Reclaiming the power of the body is to reclaim *your body story*, to reawaken to the body's "divine memory" or intrinsic knowledge—which is fundamentally a knowledge of how to live.

↩

To return to the body is to also return to listening. As Federici articulates, *we must learn to listen to the languages of the body.* This is fundamental to the cultivation of attention called for in practices that seek to open paths toward finding *the body in the body.* As Baker highlights, "meditation is a form of deep listening" in which "we are listening to the inside world, to the subtle symphony of our own embodied experience."[22] In this way, meditation is about learning to listen, of enhancing one's listening as a power of reconnection. Listening, as Baker describes, is an "art of pause"[23] through which to keep attentive to the layers of embodiment, from the earth of the deep body to the sky of bright awareness, from the cells that speak in poetry to the unfinished histories that

---

[22] Ibid., 53.
[23] Ibid.

Listening-with   103

hold the body down. "Listening to your body as an ongoing practice can help you notice the dissonances between body and mind sooner. If you learn to listen to your body's situational awareness and become attuned to its messages, you will discover some deep truths."[24]

Feeling-Thinking, the Caring Communion

A care of the self is a care of the body; it is a listening-with that gives room to all that the body is, knowing of oneself as a vitality expressive of a state of health as well as history and stories of self and community. While I'm focusing on listening as part of somatic practices of health and healing, it needs to be appreciated how listening is only part of a larger story of the body; there are many other important tools, practices, ways of treating and caring, that must be acknowledged. In this regard, listening is positioned as a contribution to knowing the story of the body and its place within a range of discourses, cultures, and knowledges. Listening comes to act as a guide, an *art of pause* by which to gain greater awareness of feelings and energies, and how the body *speaks*: how it tells about itself, gives indication, how it receives and channels, signals and requests, through different voices, frequencies, and layers. As Baker reminds, often one must pause, to remain still so as to hear all that the body communicates, offers, needs. The inner voice of a reasoning self is ultimately centered by way of the body and the living dynamic of the felt sense. Such bodily intelligence may come to show a less binary construct in terms of how understandings of emotion and thought, body and mind, are often dichotomously positioned.

In his influential research, the neuroscientist Antonio Damasio highlights the connection between feeling and the brain, arguing that the emergence of feeling as a capacity has given humans the ability to attend in ever-complex ways to the challenges of survival. It is by way of feeling that bodily intelligence expands. Importantly, feelings for Damasio are always *hybrid*, in terms of arising from within the body while telling us something of that body; they are of the body while signaling to the brain the state of itself. As Damasio summarizes, "we feel because the mind is conscious, and we are conscious because there are

---

[24] Ibid., 60.

feelings."[25] Feelings help us care for ourselves, to know what the body needs, to also sense the world around and, as such, are fundamental to consciousness. From feelings of hunger to those of pain, the body speaks in ways that make of the nervous system a sounding board: I am continually in touch with myself, listening for signals of what the body feels while signaling back, through any number of actions, adjustments, shifts in rhythm and practice. "Feelings let the mind know, automatically, without any questions being asked, that mind and body are together, each belonging to the other."[26] This moves beyond primary feelings defined by the basic needs of the body; feelings, moreover, help establish a greater "emotional knowledge," where joy and fear, love and hate, move human consciousness into more complex experiences and ways of living. To know of oneself is to feel oneself in ever-attentive, conscious, and caring ways. This extends toward feeling the body as part of a greater environment; feelings may feel internal, but they are equally arising by way of experiences of place and what it means to live within particular societies. Furthermore, the hybrid nature of feelings, as Damasio asserts, may assist in moving beyond the often entrenched views that define the body as the domain of feeling and the mind that of reason. Feelings, rather, upset "the classic void that has separated physical bodies from mental phenomena."[27] In other words, feelings are important carriers of consciousness, establishing the neurological, affective ground by which human life unfolds.

⌐

In following Damasio, I'm led to consider the ways in which listening helps in attending to the body, specifically enabling a holistic view and understanding of oneself and others. Listening may be appreciated as what helps keep one close to a form of consciousness that is *full of feeling*, that is shaped by the bridging of body and mind often occluded (if not policed) by the belief in their separation. Listening puts us back together, honoring the ways in which feelings are fundamentally ways of knowing. This may be a vital capacity listening supports, figuring an intervention onto the binary constructs that would keep bodies here and minds there, and by extension, emotional knowledge and intellectual work at odds—that valorizes the concept body over the experiential body. The

---

[25] Antonio Damasio, *Feeling and Knowing: Making Minds Conscious* (New York: Pantheon Books, 2023), 110.
[26] Ibid., 122.
[27] Ibid.

Listening-with 105

power of the body Federici works at reclaiming, as that which can carry us into a politics of transformation and renewal, takes its guidance by way of listening's ability to know of the body and its languages, which are languages of feeling and connection; they are languages of *the body in the body*, of the felt sense, languages of the cells, languages to hold onto when one is scared, in need of help. These are *hybrid* languages that speak by way of a *feeling mind*, a *thinking body*. They are languages that help "me feel my way through spaces of not knowing, the necessary spaces where difference emerges."[28] For Raffo, these are restorative languages to "savor in my mouth, listening to how they sound and to what echoes inside of me in response."[29]

≈

I've been highlighting the ways in which listening enables forms of self-care as well as a care of others. And how such views can contribute to healing justice, to finding ways of contending with the ongoingness of violence. Furthermore, listening as care, as critical forms of compassion and bodily awareness, deepens an understanding as to the particular features defining a poetics of listening. It is my view that to *listen-with* is to figure a poetic link to the vitality defining embodied life; it is not only to sense but to move that sensing into forms of understanding, ways of feeling-knowing the body and addressing all that it carries as well as offers. To listen-with the layers of the body, from the earth of physical instinct to the sky of awareness, is to discover the living poetry of bodily vitality. This finds support in how Raffo understands anatomy—as she suggestively states, "anatomy is poetry."[30] It is poetry in that anatomy is the organic experience of life; it is the living composition we know as *the body*, one whose vitality is a never-ending story of encounter and experience, health and passion, tissue and bone, coevolution and intergenerational practices. "Learning anatomy is not about assigning facts to parts but about sensing in and becoming that anatomy. It's about experiencing our own lives in a place of nuance and detail, completely and always connected."[31] Knowing anatomy is to know of the body as poetry rather than a "set of facts"—it is to enter into an intuitive relation to the life of embodiment, its organic vibrancy and dynamic layers, its natural powers and unfinished histories. In this way, poetics names a form of sensing

[28] Raffo, *Liberated to the Bone*, 25.
[29] Ibid., 25–6.
[30] Ibid., 39.
[31] Ibid., 38.

and knowing that is *sympathetic*, that is adept at knowing by way of the inside, knowing of the body as it lives and breathes, aches and celebrates, desires and grows as well as lessens. This is further accented in Baker's own reference to poetry within the context of meditation; as she offers, "poetry is the language of the body."[32] Poetry turns us toward the meaningfulness of embodied life, that which is "below the skin"[33] and which, as Baker and Raffo both outline, allows us to feel and express the interconnectedness so defining of bodily vitality.

Within such a poetic construct or view, listening is positioned as an essential capacity. Listening aids in knowing what the body feels, and feeling what the body knows. It follows the surface vibrations of day-to-day experience, the trembling of hunger, ache, desire, and need, as well as the deeper echoes that carry lineages of both slow violence and slow love, all the relations that sit within the folds and fevers of the flesh. Listening-with is a craft of touch and care that works at holding and handling the tender dimensions of embodied life, the hurt as well as the joy. As a caring, protective act, listening assists in forms of touch, whether in the physical massage of another's body, the nursing or the comforting one may give, or in the gestures, the speaking, the quiet offered within the arenas of talk and relation. Listening wields a force of sympathy and empathy, of acknowledgment and care, that honors and elaborates the poetry of anatomy. Such a force is fundamentally expressive of bodily power in all its personal and interpersonal breadth, its social and political potentiality, contributing to the maintenance of oneself and others, as well as to restoring and repairing the injured or broken.

From the hands that have nurtured me, the support structures that allow me to live, or that weigh down on what living can be, to the air and food I take in, am given, enjoy, and that populate and nourish bodily vitality, or that undermine the fullness of a healthy life, these are forces and matters that I collaborate or contend with, that nurture and intervene, that love and enrich, or injure, and to which listening is turned to enact its attentive, knowing touch.

⤳

In her reflections on care work, Susan Raffo suggests that acts of healing must proceed with two open hands, where one hand may work at holding the pain, the suffering, experiences of violence, and the other may hold love, connection, a belief in recovery and change.[34] Such two-sided holding, I believe, is precisely

---

[32] Baker, *The Wakeful Body*, 14.
[33] Ibid.
[34] Raffo, *Liberated to the Bone*, 56.

the holding listening may also enact. A holding that simultaneously may grasp the specificity of individual life and suffering, the hurt and the longing others carry as shaped by personal experience, along with grasping a way forward, a holding that opens onto paths of repair—that is adept at evoking a future to come. As the composer Pauline Oliveros suggests, *deep listening* is the ability to simultaneously listen across scales, from minute detail to an environmental context, from the here and now to the then and there.[35] Such movements, as I'm hearing them, include the capacity to move across temporalities, from the past and present to a future to come—to gain a sense for how to move again, against the confines and blockages of past injury. In the context of healing practices, deep listening figures a holding environment, an art of pause, in order to give room to all one carries, placing loss and memory in one hand, while evoking an opening, a path of repair, one made possible by placing love in the other hand. It is by way of such holding that "we listen and support the body itself to find its own way."[36] These are deeply restorative movements, accenting the poetic power of listening as that which assists in feeling the deep tissues of time and memory, as what is able to notice and give room to all that continues to echo within and across bodies and generations, and that helps in imagining a future.

This finds critical elaboration by Camilla Koskinen and Unni Ä. Lindström in their work on listening in the context of caritative practices. As the authors argue, listening is essential for nurturing the "caring communion" between caregivers and those in need.[37] Their understanding of the caring communion opens onto the larger field of nursing, highlighting the ways in which nursing integrates an active and effective form of listening. This extends from the ability to listen to patients, not only about particular ailments or pains, but also how nurses lend an ear to the telling of life stories. Given that nurses often encounter people at their most vulnerable, accompanying them as they endure pain and suffering, not to mention possibly confronting the end of life, having the capacity and skill for giving comfort as well as "sharing the lived experience of the patient" is incredibly transformative.[38] Nursing must be appreciated as care work deeply aligned with listening. As Paula Kagan reports, "people desire to be listened to

---

[35] Pauline Oliveros, *Quantum Listening* (London: Ignota Books, 2021).

[36] Raffo, *Liberated to the Bone*, 70.

[37] Camilla Koskinen and Unni Ä. Lindström, "An Envisioning about the Caring in Listening," *Scandinavian Journal of Caring Sciences*, vol. 29, no. 3 (September 2015): 548.

[38] Sheila D. Shipley, "Listening: A Concept Analysis," *Nursing Forum*, vol. 45, no. 2 (April–June 2010): 125.

more than anything else during their experiences with health professionals."[39] It becomes important then that health professionals foster listening skills, and further, that environments in which care is delivered function as listening spaces.

Johanne Thingnes Leira, a nurse working in Norway, highlights that she often observes how doctors fail to listen to patients as they rush from one to another; for her, nursing is about providing the empathy patients long for, which includes building trust and acceptance.[40] "Listening in a nonjudgmental and accepting manner may offer a sense of emotional release for patients as well as provide the nurse with valuable information regarding the patient's condition."[41] This moves beyond what patients actually say. Leira reveals that for her listening is about "getting to know the patient" holistically; it is "listening for a long time" so as to be attentive to shifts in facial skin coloration and rhythms of breathing, "how their eyes appear"; whether they are afraid, anxious or calm; whether a patient is taking care of themselves while in hospital, what they are eating; and whether they are alone or with family members.[42] These are ways of listening that can reveal a lot about the health of a patient and aid in "understanding the whole person."[43] Such an approach is also about recognizing the "resources of the patients" themselves, and how these contribute to treatment. Leira's views can be seen to support the notion of the "caring communion" Koskinen and Lindström underscore, where listening works at protecting the life of others. Listening *as* protection gives much to "transforming loneliness into communion," restoring the will to live which patients may lose.[44] These are radically tender and engaged enactments, shaping what it means to live and die well.

In considering somatic practices and cultures of care work, listening emerges as an active contributor—a generative, attentive means for learning and following the language of the body. This equally leads to ways of knowing, to gathering insight as to the state of things, the feelings and conditions of others. Listening can be said to wield a force that is more attentive than directive, more conductive than performative. As such, it elaborates agency by way of radical receptivity and

---

[39] Paula N. Kagan, "Feeling Listened To: A Lived Experience of Humanbecoming," *Nursing Science Quarterly*, vol. 21, no. 1 (January 2008): 59.
[40] Johanne Thingnes Leira, in conversation with the author, 2023.
[41] Shipley, "Listening: A Concept Analysis," 129.
[42] Leira, in conversation with the author, 2023.
[43] Shipley, "Listening: A Concept Analysis," 130.
[44] Koskinen and Lindström, "An Envisioning about the Caring in Listening," 553.

compassion, a caring positionality. In doing so, listening opens onto what I want to highlight as *poetic knowledge*. Following the philosophical work of James S. Taylor, poetic knowledge is underscored as a *first knowledge*, as it is grounded in the senses and cultivated through an *inclination toward noticing* indicative of a poetic sensibility.[45] (This finds echo in Gaston Bachelard's proposition that in the "poetic image" lies the origins of consciousness, a first flowering.)[46] As a first knowledge, poetic knowledge is *connatural*, in that it emerges by way of attuning to life-worlds and tends toward a participatory mode—it is fundamentally in touch with and touched by environments, by the movements of things and the presence that surrounds. This is akin to Willa Blythe Baker's notion of the experiential body, as an original body constituted as a "landscape of feeling" that extends across one's body and the environment. As a *connatural* knowledge, poetic knowledge is a *sympathetic* form of knowing: it is a knowing by way of the inside. Poetic knowledge is a feeling, sympathetic form, which can be appreciated to align with the felt sense as well as a listening capacity— what Bachelard highlights by way of his understanding of reverie as poetic consciousness: "Poetic reverie listens to the polyphony of the senses,"[47] giving way to an expanded consciousness. These are poetic dimensions and capacities that resonate with care practices that specifically aim at a holistic approach, that draw upon the body as an intrinsic natural power, a language. What kind of language is this? A language of wholeness and connection, of spiritual wakefulness and sensation, a language of poetry. And that gives way to sympathetic knowledge, as a knowledge of the whole person. It is my view that to know the whole person is to know poetically.

Poetic knowledge, as founded on a *connatural* resonance with the life of things, and that figures a knowing by way of the inside, speaks toward Raffo's and Baker's understandings of poetry as the *language of the body,* one that keeps close to vitality and its fluctuations. It moreover aligns with somatic practices

---

[45] James S. Taylor's work on poetic knowledge as a first knowledge echoes with the notion of an "art of noticing" developed by Anna Lowenhaupt Tsing in *The Mushroom at the End of the World*, which suggests that deepening the capacity to notice assists in fostering greater understanding as to social, relational, planetary interconnectedness. See James S. Taylor, *Poetic Knowledge: The Recovery of Education* (Albany: State University of New York Press, 1998), and Anna Lowenhaupt Tsing, *The Mushroom at the End of the World: On the Possibility of Life in Capitalist Ruins* (Princeton: Princeton University Press, 2015).

[46] Gaston Bachelard, *The Poetics of Reverie: Childhood, Language, and the Cosmos* (Boston: Beacon Press, 1971), 1.

[47] Ibid., 6.

and the work nurses perform, where attending to the wholeness of persons gives way to holistic forms of care—and the cultivation of the caring communion. Consequently, poetics emerges as radically supportive of a *paradigm of life*, aiding in recognition and valorization of the life of things; it underpins those practices that attend to others in times of need, that bring sensitivity to the pains people carry or endure, affording ways of holding with both hands.

It is along these lines that a poetics of listening may be cast as what helps support the move toward reclaiming bodily power. From attending to the wholeness of persons, bringing care and compassion to people's lives, to working at healing justice, as grounded in recognition of history and land, and the capacity to feel by way of the felt sense, sympathetically gaining knowledge of all that people carry—these are perspectives suggestive for deepening understanding not only for the necessity to reclaim the body but also for the ways in which a poetics of listening contributes.

Holding-listening, listening-with, a listening with two hands, these are gestures attuned to the feeling mind and thinking body, and they speak toward ways of knowing defined by a poetic sensibility. As Taylor suggests, poetic knowledge is an intuitive, sympathetic knowledge, it is knowing from the inside and that keeps one close to the stories of the body. These are stories of birth, of love and pleasure, stories of community and of loss, hopes and hardship—all the original wounds of history and remembrance. Learning the language of the body, the language of poetry, emerges as fundamental to healing justice—to challenge systems that work by way of domination and the exploitation of all things vital. As Bachelard suggestively notes, "poetry helps one breathe well."[48]

Currents of Sympathy, Poetics of Healing

In considering listening in relation to questions of care, and how it is a reclamation of the body becomes essential to living well, a sense for a greater holistic approach and understanding is brought forward. As Federici's argument suggests, reappropriating the body and its value is about putting the body back together; it is about taking the body back from systems that break it down,

---

[48] Ibid., 182.

atomizing and reducing its fullness. It is also about recovering something of the spirit of the body, knowing its power as connected to the broader web of life. This is further suggested in the project of healing justice and how Susan Raffo calls for understanding bodies as communities, as histories, as poetry. Never a singular, self-contained body, but rather one always already interconnected, embedded in relations, and therefore suggestive for holistic, sympathetic forms of knowledge.

I'm interested to consider further how it is that listening may bring us back to the body, keeping one close to its languages, its vitality, its divine memory. And which entails reclaiming a holistic relation, where interconnectedness is recognized, felt, lived. In her book *Influx and Efflux*, Jane Bennett addresses the question of interconnectedness from a number of compelling perspectives. In particular, she poses the issue or figure of sympathy, or what she terms "circuits" or "currents of sympathy," as an energizing guide in understanding interconnectedness.[49] Drawing upon a greater history of philosophical, scientific, and esoteric accounts, sympathy is utilized to address the atmospheric, magnetic, and vitalist connections that come to pass between bodies, that hold bodies together, or that animate organic and inorganic matters alike. From celestial movements to human connection, sympathy is posed both as a moral register of common feeling, often identified with acknowledging the pain of others, and also as a naturalistic force. Currents of sympathy speak to the "affective tonalities" that pass across and through bodies and things, subjects and objects, humans and more-than-humans. Such currents are material ambiences or resonant flows—the "influx and efflux" of influence and attraction, a being-with that is always already a weave of affective movements. For Bennett, sympathy figures a connective threading that accounts for a flow of "communicative transfers" between living things.[50]

Importantly, Bennett's ideas may assist in understanding interconnectedness less as an emotional building of relations, and more as an affective current that moves across the personal and impersonal, the near and far. Here, the body participates within a greater material ecology of things, where porosity and openness are situated as a power enabling a more "visceral" communicativeness. Such affective, impersonal force Bennett warns is not without its challenges.

---

[49] Jane Bennett, *Influx and Efflux: Writing Up with Walt Whitman* (Durham, NC: Duke University Press, 2020), 29.

[50] Ibid.

Currents of sympathy may also be captured within projects and systems of exclusion; they may be directed in the service of forms of manipulation and control. Sympathy comes to signal a world of pressures and impressionability, of leanings and learnings that constantly position, enliven, agitate and impact the body. These are the ongoing movements that underpin a first knowledge, where bodily power is *connatural*, woven into a greater ecology of relations.

The concept of currents of sympathy names a materialist, interconnected force that manifests in the nuanced, affective tonalities passing across and through personal and interpersonal worlds, while also opening onto the gestures one may make on behalf of others: the sympathetic, compassionate actions in support of those in struggle or need, and that extend across the personal *and* impersonal, the familiar *and* the less-than-familiar. While humanitarian projects are given traction through articulated forms of policy or politics, these are equally informed by a *sympathetic knowing* attuned to the violences and injuries some are made to carry and which tremble the greater weave of interconnectedness. Currents of sympathy, in this context, are not strictly about the individual capacity to sympathize with others—of having or expressing compassion; rather, Bennett considers a more materialist approach, shifting from the "emotional" and toward the "gravitational": sympathy as what gives charge to things, positive and negative, full and empty—what pulls at us, or pushes at the material arrangement of things. Subsequently, Bennett opens a rather counterintuitive perspective on what constitutes (political) action. As she argues, the direct enactments of (political) action may find additional routes by attending to the affective, impersonal forces that define a common world—moving from an emphasis on taking a position to that of the cultivation of *disposition*.[51] These are routes suggestive for understanding listening as a particular kind of force, one that conducts rather than performs, and in doing so, opens onto more holistic approaches to enacting change.

⤿

What forms of awareness are enabled within a framework of sympathetic knowing? If, as Raffo argues, the impact of violence onto people comes to echo forward in many complex and hurtful ways, in what sense can listening attend to such echoes, supporting a range of gestures, responses, caring? Are there particular ethical perspectives called forth when engaging the connective

---

[51] Ibid., 109–18.

Listening-with   113

threading of sympathy? Sympathy can be understood to figure an *ecology of feeling*, which gives way to a broader construct of community and connection. In other words, sympathy affords ways of elaborating what community is or may be by acknowledging, as Bennett suggests, personal as well as less personal forms of interconnectedness. As such, it extends beyond an immediate circle of relations, affording responsiveness to a greater world of others.

It is along these lines that the therapeutic practices of healing Raffo works at may be positioned. Healing justice acknowledges how individuals are affected by an array of direct and indirect others, by those who have cared for, that continue to care, and by those that may have harmed, or that continue to harm; by the unfinished histories of certain societies and nations, and that run through communities, generations, like currents of energy, to influence the life one may lead, as well as all that a body may carry. Health and vitality are shaped by innumerable forces and structures, human and more-than-human, personal and impersonal, from legacies of love and violence to systems of support and abuse. To work at healing is to work at addressing these interconnected realities.

〜

Moving from somatic practices of healing to the sympathetic currents that define interconnectedness, I'm concerned to deepen an understanding as to what's at stake in reclaiming bodily power. That is, how the reclamation of the body can enact forms of intervention onto scenes and systems of abuse. As Simone Leigh's critical-creative work demonstrates, reclaiming the body is about reclaiming agency over its well-being, especially in terms of histories of Black pain.

Jane Bennett fosters additional views onto these concerns by mapping an "energetics of ethics."[52] Emerging from within a broader argument on enchanted materialism, Bennett works at appreciating ethical behavior as a question of affect—how ethics is lived and given weight in a world in which agency is felt as distributive, as constituting a shared reality. The energetics of ethics is positioned so as to capture the affective (or sympathetic) dimension and its impact onto responsiveness and responsibility for others. In short, ethics as energetic figures an interconnected world in which human behavior follows from feelings of participation and involvement, their limitations and potentialities within given contexts. Such views nurture a greater sense for the sympathetic currents that

---

[52] Jane Bennett, *The Enchantment of Modern Life: Attachments, Crossings, and Ethics* (Princeton: Princeton University Press, 2001), 155.

pass across bodies and places, and contribute to acts that work on behalf of others.

Bennett's energetic theories are given further footing by way of Francisco Varela's lectures on ethical know-how.[53] Varela provides a view onto ethical behavior built upon a focus on the immediate ways in which people respond to others. Importantly, Varela upsets the idea that ethical behavior is equated with forms of moral deliberation and judgment. Ethical behavior is, instead, responsive to an immediate situation, manifesting ways of coping with the present. Through such perspectives, Varela asks for deeper consideration of immediate forms of coping—to shift focus from ethical behavior as based upon moral deliberation and judgment, and to consider the gestures and acts that come to reflect an understanding of what is good and needed. Ethical *know-how* rather than *know-what* is foundational to Varela's arguments and can be seen to follow emerging understandings of human cognition, which increasingly recognize how a great deal of decision-making occurs on an unconscious level. The "new unconscious," as it is termed, reveals that human behavior is far less directed by parts of the brain in which conscious thought is taking place. Instead, emotions are fundamental and have been discovered to influence much of what we understand as conscious thought. Driven by advances in medical technology, the new unconscious has spawned a new field of study, "affective neuroscience." Echoing Damasio, Leonard Mlodinow suggests that "where we once believed that emotion was detrimental to effective thought and decisions, we now know that we can't make decisions, or even think, without being influenced by our emotions."[54]

Such views are suggestive for what Varela highlights as a "radical paradigm shift" within the cognitive sciences, which emphasizes "situatedness" and the "concrete, embodied" nature of knowledge.[55] Cognition, for Varela, is expressed through the immediate handling of things, in the touching, feeling, moving acts that bring one into contact and which draws forth a knowledge of environments and oneself. "Thus cognition consists not of representations but of *embodied action*" (emphasis in original).[56] Situatedness provides the basis for what

---

[53] Francisco Varela, *Ethical Know-How: Action, Wisdom, and Cognition* (Stanford: Stanford University Press, 1999).
[54] Leonard Mlodinow, *Emotional: The New Thinking about Feelings* (London: Penguin Books, 2023), xiv.
[55] Varela, *Ethical Know-How*, 7.
[56] Ibid., 17.

Varela highlights as "readiness-for-action," which is built upon a history of lived experience and that figures itself throughout everyday situations. Ethical know-how thus proceeds by way of a history of embodied experiences and lived situations; it is grounded in the affective tonalities that shape much of one's behavior, and that pull one in and out of the intensities of relational contact and currents. Bringing focus to know-how, the situated and embodied qualities by which knowledge of others and responsiveness become learned, is important so as to accent bodily intelligence as what may guide behavior within particular situations.[57] Such intelligence is elaborated by Bennett, in particular when she calls for greater sensitivity for the affective tonalities of self and other. If agency is to be understood as shaped by the affective tonalities passing across bodies and places, as well as the languages and systems that impact onto individual lives, then it is essential "to listen to the subintentional aspects of the self" so as to better attune to the particularities of given situations.[58] These subintentional aspects, and the understanding of know-how Varela poses, echo with the field of affective neuroscience, which increasingly recognizes the impact and influence of feelings. Within the configurations of know-how and the energetics of ethics shaped by the connective threading and felt awareness of bodily life, listening comes to assist in defining "tactics of the self" on an embodied, affective, and responsive level.[59] To listen is always already a *listening-with*, as it nurtures bodily awareness, keeping one close to the "subintentional" so defining of the self and its place among others. Moreover, listening fosters an "enchanted sensibility"—a feeling for interconnectedness, a sympathetic knowing—that may sensitize one to the vulnerabilities and uneven realities shaping much of the world.

～

From care and repair, and the ethical know-how supported by listening's affective reach, to currents of sympathy that move across bodies and places, I'm tracing a view onto listening as one that supports bodily intelligence. To *feel* is to resonate in so many ways with all that surrounds, all that moves in and of the body, this body I am, and from which I also come to act with and for others. To care is to listen for the signals and stories, to follow the affective tonalities and unfinished histories that bodies hold and also produce, bringing forward a sensitivity for others, into the hands and onto the world. Listening

---

[57] Ibid., 31.
[58] Bennett, *The Enchantment of Modern Life*, 155.
[59] Ibid.

methodologies are deeply intuitive—as Raffo suggests, listening is there as an embodied form of knowing, as a tactic, a way of knowing the whole person, and its place within caring practices is essential. It does much in attending as well as working at shifting legacies of violence, to give support to healing justice by way of its critical, sympathetic, feeling-thinking capacity. This extends across diverse scenes and situations in which bodies struggle, positioned within systems of abuse or discrimination, and where listening emerges as medicine itself.

The Native American poet Joy Harjo offers insightful perspectives in this regard, in which poetic writing allows one to keep close to the collective world of the *spirit body*—the songs and stories that carry us in times of crisis, and that offer their guidance. "Language is a living being"[60] for Harjo, and it is by way of language, with its lyrical magic and sonorous evocations, that one may find ways of combatting systems of oppression. Harjo can be heard to engage poetics as a means for reclaiming the power of the body Federici identifies, as what lends to speaking a "prayer language."[61] This is a language that keeps close to living worlds, that supports ways of communing with the "beauty weaving mountain and the sky" on certain mornings; it is a language that breathes and where words become a form of ceremony, an act of creation. "The poet listens with pen, pencil in hand, or hands poised above the typewriter or keyboard, adrift in the orality of making words and finding out where they are going."[62] Poetry feels its way, finding out by way of a sympathetic approach.

The poetic journey Harjo describes is one also marked by loss—it is a ceremony that addresses histories of violence underpinning Indigenous struggles in North America, and that attends to "memories of fracture, as if all the broken pieces have voices, and they call me back to witness."[63] By way of poetry, Harjo finds a means, a weapon, a medicine, to work against histories and their ongoing violence, that affords a path for accessing the "voice of inner truth," which is a voice aligned with the "wisdom of eternal knowledge."[64] This is a wisdom found *under the skin*, one whose voice "speaks softly" and that carries and provides the "deepest knowing"—and toward which listening is turned, as that which follows and finds direction. "Listen with your ears, your eyes, your throat, your abdomen, your toes." This is a listening that leads to the poetic path,

---

[60] Joy Harjo, *Catching the Light* (New Haven: Yale University Press, 2022), 8.
[61] Ibid.
[62] Ibid., 17.
[63] Joy Harjo, *Poet Warrior: A Memoir* (New York: W. W. Norton, 2021), 50.
[64] Ibid., 44.

Listening-with

to the ceremony of words, to acts of creation and survival and healing, a poetry that can "bring rain, turn the heart of a lover, speak truth in a dying country, undo the rein of a dictator."[65] These are poetic spells and conjurings founded on the lessons listening grants, to spirit a prayer language full of lost voices as well as the voices that endure, that are born in the wake of words and the wisdom they honor and carry—a "listening by way of the belly."[66]

~

The poetic wisdom Harjo shares, as a writing-ceremony of reclamation, returns us to the sympathetic perspectives Bennett maps; currents of sympathy that may carry—along their vibrant, resonant, and connective threading—a range of voices and knowledges. From Raffo's somatic acts of healing justice to Baker's wakeful meditation practices, from Bennett's affective tonalities to Harjo's poetics of eternal knowledge, we are immersed in a cosmos of feeling-thinking, of sympathetic knowledge, where listening-with the body—or *by way of the belly*—becomes anchoring, energizing, transformative. A listening that helps us harmonize with the "humming sound" within. This is a humming, a vibration, as Harjo suggests, of the heart and whose resonance is the foundation of a care work, an energetic ethics.[67] An ethics that follows the interconnectedness of living things, and which finds articulation in the protest song "Water Is Life" written in support of the water defenders of the Dakota Pipeline Protests in 2017 and to which Harjo contributed the introductory lyrics: "Those who saw into the future predicted the destruction / If we didn't listen. The earth began crying out for us to stand up. Defend the water. Stand up!"[68]

I pause, listening to the song, following all these threads passing across ideas of the body and my own body as I sit here, writing, listening, and further, passing through histories of domination and empire, which are still in the present, still making new histories and trauma, in the ongoingness of war and political violence, in how it is that conquest proceeds, I pause so as to stand up, to listen out, to honor all those who fight and fall, who write the poetry and who call for deep medicine, and who give greatly to my own ability to write this story, for what I hope will be a better future to come.

---

[65] Ibid., 42.
[66] Ibid.
[67] Ibid., 116.
[68] "Water Is Life," written by NM Water Is Life, released on November 19, 2016. https://nmwaterislife.bandcamp.com/track/water-is-life (accessed July 2024).

Trans-figuring Bodily Power, to Be a Body for Others

Embodied listening, a *listening-with* that holds the body, that follows its pleasures and pains—attuning to the poetic language of the cells, the anatomy, as a landscape of feeling, and that functions as the energetic ground by which to attend to others. The power of the body Federici highlights is found intrinsically, immanent to its physical vitality, its structure of needs and desires, and which is deepened through its connection to a greater living world. The breathing force of embodied power is one that finds its momentum, its expressivity by being part of the life of an outside: the interconnectedness that makes of the body something more than itself. As such, the body emerges more as a milieu than a container, more a fold than a plane, more a fever than an identity. To know of the body is to sense its limits, the borders of itself as touched and impinged, as cooperative and interrupted, as gifted and responsive, where the potentiality of its becoming is integral to its nature. If listening is part of the body's story of connection, it is by way of its capacity to open the body to itself, giving traction to inhabiting a state of interconnectedness where one knows of oneself as energetic, and where know-how and the readiness-for-action are a fundamental strength. As Federici insists, listening may return us to ourselves as bodies full of feeling. Listening is supportive of bodily vitality, contributing to processes of healing, nursing, and taking care. It does so by *enlivening* the capacity for connection and invention— for an energetic readiness that is foundational to acts of creation, protection, a reaching out.

Extending from these perspectives, I'm interested to move the focus toward reflecting on other types of somatic practices. And to consider in what ways listening contributes not only to care and the well-being of others but also to making changes to what the body is. What forms of embodiment does listening incite, support, nurture? As I've been arguing, to listen-with is to find ways of keeping close to the body as a power, one that carries the sympathetic, connective potency of a first knowledge. This is a body full of voices and stories, whose truth is carried in the loves and pains, the histories and how one may come to notice the beauty weaving mountain and sky. From such a perspective, the body is a movement always in search of greater connection and flourishing. This is a body that, as Joy Harjo offers, works its way toward *catching the light*.[69] It is along these

---

[69] Harjo, *Catching the Light.*

lines that the power of the body is also found in its ability to adapt, to survive, and to operate as a medium of transformation.

~

Catherine Clément's philosophical work on the topic of delirium offers insight into the transformative potential of embodied forms of listening. For Clément, delirium gives expression to bodily vitality, articulated through a range of practices, rituals, gestures, and enactments; from music to dance, festivity to feasting, delirium is operative within society and expresses moments of heightened sensuality and ecstasy. Here, delirium, or what Clément further articulates through the musical notion of "syncope," puts one in touch with an affirmative "eclipse of individuality."[70] Delirium is positioned as an essential mechanism that fulfills something of the body by way of its undoing, a certain *going beyond itself* that specifically interrupts or delays individuality. This eclipse, this opening, importantly contains a return, a reclamation. "Remember the definition of syncope in music: a note lags behind and anticipates the rest of the movement."[71] Syncope thus names a performativity located within the "composition" of a social ordering which introduces delays, breaks, dissonance; syncope is a waiting, a pulling back, and then, suddenly, a return that synchronizes once again. Syncope is a fainting *and* a recovery: to fall, to miss the beat, and then to recover, to find the tempo again, which figures itself as a projection toward the future, from dissonance toward "resolution."[72] Delirium, and the movements of syncope, name a certain ritualistic, recuperative process that moves the body elsewhere, and then back.

~

If syncope is fundamentally a rhythmic process, where missed or dropped beats give room for an extended breath, a sensual intensity, a transition, it brings forward a pronounced relation to time. What does it mean to be *in time* or to *keep time*? These are ways of following a given pattern, aligning with a system or structure that shapes one's movements and defines trajectories. Being-in-time is to be emplaced within a greater chronology—such is the dynamic of tempo, one that situates the body, its biological, social rhythms, within a given order or frame, and which gives way to interruptions, missed beats, detour and improvisation.

---

[70] Catherine Clément, *Syncope: The Philosophy of Rapture* (Minneapolis: University of Minnesota Press, 1994), 1.

[71] Ibid., 119.

[72] Ibid., 120.

These might be considered as breaths, rests, moments of overexcitement or rupture found in letting go or racing ahead. Even while patterns emerge across all types of times and spaces, environments and communities, to be in time carries with it an ongoing tension that turns tempo into a socio-affective construct.

This includes challenges around *keeping up*, where certain bodies may not have the ability to keep in time. Chronology is also *chronopolitical*, suggesting that syncope, as that instant of affirmative delirium, is also sometimes an issue of ability—one may veer off because one cannot go on. Syncope—and related syncopations—come to carve out a time of refuge, to give room for other temporal imaginaries and needs, for taking a break. Such an eclipse of individuality can be a reminder of how certain bodies may be tensed by given orders, from spatial to temporal, social to economic. This is certainly part of Clément's philosophy of delirium, which calls for an appreciation of the living, organic nature of embodied experience and that integrates how it is one may keep up. "Syncope *creates* delay and accentuates it by prolonging time,"[73] figuring gaps for other ways of being in the body. In lagging behind, or dropping the beat, syncope may not only figure a delirious instant, it moreover interrupts an overall system, inviting or demanding an alteration of a greater compositional order—it may, in fact, allow for breath precisely when it is most needed.

Clément's syncope is transformational, *transfigural*—one comes back to oneself by way of a detour and where listening participates in exposing oneself to the raptures of a musical event, the performative tensions of being-in-time, and the potentiality of a chronopolitical delay or digression.

The syncopated return Clément highlights as part of a philosophy of delirium speaks toward the recovery of a natural power. The rhythmic reworking of temporal ordering is part of reclaiming the body as a power, of delaying the ongoing progression of capitalism's tempo that Federici seeks to counter. This finds support through Judith Becker's invaluable work on deep listening in the context of trance ritual and other ceremonial events. "Trancing," as Becker describes, is intimately tied to music, and can be found in a range of ceremonial events appearing across cultures and societies in one form or another. For Becker, trancing crucially relates to deep listening as the capacity for emotional responsiveness and heightened sensitivity to sound and music.

---

[73] Ibid., 81.

Listening-with   121

Following from the work of Pauline Oliveros, deep listening emerges as key to fostering trance and near-trance states, which, within the context of Becker's studies into religious ceremony, gives expression to a highly unique form of embodied, musical cognition. This includes recognizing the ways in which music works to bring "into existence other times, other places, other beings."[74] For the trancer, one journeys into a zone of contact with sacred worlds where "alternate selves and alternate places and alternate times" become dramatically real. As Becker elaborates, "trancers experience a kind of syncope, an absence, a lapse, a 'cerebral eclipse' "[75] conditioned by a listening process that is both "physical *and* psychological, somatic *and* cognitive," and which supports particular forms of knowledge inaccessible outside of trance states. These are deeply physical experiences, where trancers enter into prolonged states of ecstasy through heightened exertion and arousal, primarily through extended periods of drumming and dancing, that also give embodiment to unique forms of communicativeness. Importantly, it is by way of trancing that individuals and communities maintain contact with the sacred and divine, and which is often connected to acts of healing. As Becker chronicles in the context of Sri Lanka, the Sanni Yakuma ritual is performed so as to help the sick.[76] Consisting of eighteen different forms of masked dance, the ritual enactments call upon the demons thought to have infected the ill, and through a series of dialogues and dances, are finally banished back to the demon world. The ritual is led by a shaman healer along with a small troupe of healers who play *yak bera*, or "demon drums." At certain heightened moments during the nighttime ritual, healers will convulse and collapse with flaming torches held between their teeth, marking the appearance of the demon.

Throughout trance rituals, the shaman or healer dies in order to be reborn; they fight off demons causing infliction and suffering, exorcising and channeling illness through their bodies so as to restore the patient as well as the community. As Clément suggests in her theories of delirium, the shaman must journey to the other side, they must die as well as find the means to recuperate themselves by way of all types of magic. This is the dynamic of syncope the author works at outlining, where the eclipse of individuality is embedded within a larger act

---

[74] Judith Becker, *Deep Listeners: Music, Emotion, and Trancing* (Bloomington: Indiana University Press, 2004), 27.

[75] Ibid., 25.

[76] Ibid., 31.

122 *Poetics of Listening*

or mechanism of sickness and healing, collapse and recuperation.[77] And which shows the body as a natural power in connection with sacred worlds.

↠

Throughout her work, Becker is concerned to interrupt the long-held view that trancing is strictly physiological, that it is grounded in relations between music, primarily rhythm, and bodily arousal and reaction. In contrast, following research within neuroscience, Becker argues for a more holistic view, to appreciate music cognition and the psychological, neurological dimensions active within trance, and more broadly, deep listening. Within such a view, embodiment itself is highlighted as the physical domain of *felt-consciousness*. Importantly, the knowledges that emerge through such intense bodily states and experiences arise out of and speak toward a cultural community aligned with particular worldviews or cosmologies of belief. Trancers are carriers of culture and they provide channels to the sacred and divine, reinforcing key narratives held by the community through an ongoing illumination and states of revelation. Yet, the mystical knowledges afforded access by way of trance and deep listening are not the only present knowledges; as Becker notes, trancers have the capacity to "control" the rather "uncontrollable" arena of emotions, bringing forward alterations, new dimensions, ways of being. In essence, trance and deep listening become mystical, cultural practices. They are highly conscious, active, aware states of body and mind, and they work at processes of transfiguration or emergent forms of embodiment. And which activates what Clément envisages as the "acoustics of the soul," in which dissonance acts as an important moment of rupture and transition, allowing for a reinvention of harmony and a return to wellness.[78] To move close to the divine by way of trance is to stay connected to the body as sacred, where the force of *felt-consciousness* opens onto revelation and reinvention—a continual re-creation and reaffirmation of bodily power.

↠

Trancing, transfiguration, syncope, and the mystical enactments heightened by way of listening-with return us to understandings of bodily power. These are movements or perspectives that emphasize practices of embodiment as vehicles for countering histories and systems of abuse, of overcoming injury and illness—and that one may work at in order to heal as well as contribute to the

---

[77] Clément, *Syncope*, 102.
[78] Ibid., 120.

project of healing justice. Somatic listening practices open onto a knowledge of interconnectedness, an ethical know-how shaped by affective tonalities with their sympathetic currents that pass across bodies and places, and furthermore, across terrestrial and mystical worlds. By way of such transformational configurations, the body may come to emerge as *transfigural*, where listening contributes to embodiments of sensitivity, transition, invention, and connection—to the channeling of spirits, or the speaking of a prayer language. This is part of bodily power, lending to the ability to contend with forces that constrain, delimit, abuse, or make ill. From the healing work of craniosacral therapies and the meditations that aim at recovering the fullness of the self, to reawaken the body, and further, from the energetic ethics and know-how that attune self and other by way of a felt sense, the sympathetic currents, and that lends to engaging eternal, mystical knowledges, embodiment becomes an ongoing expression of a shared vitality—it is the work of creation, a protective action, a reaching out.

These are understandings and knowledges carried additionally in certain dance practices, which equally speak toward bodily power and the sympathetic modalities by which to cultivate the felt sense. One such methodology that can contribute to awakening the body as a power is that of Body Weather developed by Butoh dancer Min Tanaka. Body Weather investigates the nature of the body and its place within a broader environment, understanding this as constitutive of the body itself—the body is never an isolated object, but is rather situated within a connective threading, or for Tanaka, an ongoing *weather system*: bodies constantly change, as the weather does, through an interconnectedness with its surroundings.

Tess de Quincey, a choreographer based in Australia and active in Body Weather practice, describes it as such: "In Body Weather we try to train the subconscious listening of the body / training the instinctive responses / opening up the intuitive / training the intelligence of the body / to be articulate."[79] Body Weather is founded on recognizing the body as reflective of a greater organic process of change, fluctuation and maturation, of transition, and which figures as the basis of its intelligence, of knowing its place within a given environment, how its movements relate to other movements, affecting and being affected as

---

[79] Tess de Quincey, "Thinking through Dance—Dancing through Thought," Sydney Seminar for the Arts and Philosophy: Ideas in Movement—about Dance, May 22, 2005. Found on artist's website: https://dequinceyco.net/archive/articles/ (accessed July 2024).

124 *Poetics of Listening*

it goes. These are sensitivities that define the practice which, as de Quincey highlights, lend influence to how one may relate to broader social encounters or political atmospheres:

> How do we meet each other? How do we embrace difference and conflict? And what of alienation and disempowerment? How do we greet those from elsewhere? A Swedish politician said that she sees culture as being the ability to meet someone in the eye. But the Japanese for example might not agree with that. The eye is too direct. The atmosphere of the body and its subconscious readings provides the borderlines of negotiation.[80]

Shifting from the eye to the atmosphere of the body, de Quincey follows Body Weather as what may support acknowledging the body "on its own terms." And which provides a path—a choreographic ethos—for how to meet each other, which is to "touch an underlying common nerve."[81] These are methods and approaches, ways of feeling-thinking that seek to move with a body-community, by way of the common nerve (echoing Bennett's "currents of sympathy"). "In essence Body Weather searches for an emergence of the intelligence of the body—the body on its own terms, the body speaking. Min [Tanaka] coined the expression a thinking body, encouraging a listening onto the state of constant change both inside and outside the body."[82]

Body Weather, and the subconscious listening it works at training, is suggestive for deepening a view onto listening-with and the affordances it offers; these are ways of tuning and attuning, of following the language of the body, a language of currents and the common nerve, and where dance may support, by figuring a movement-ethic, a way of stepping with deep regard.[83] Body Weather,

---

[80]   Ibid.

[81]   Ibid.

[82]   Tess de Quincey, "Body Weather—Dance in Practice," article found on artist's website: https://dequinceyco.net/archive/articles/ (accessed July 2024).

[83]   Tess de Quincey offers an example of a Body Weather exercise:

> We have an exercise in Body Weather called "wind." / the image is that you are a plant in muddy ground with deep roots / you are pliant, like a reed—with viscosity, juicy but holding emptiness. / your base position is neutral standing / your partner gives stimulation into your body as wind / your body follows the point of entrance and the length of the stimulation as far as it lasts—the feet aim to maintain their roots into the ground, and then you return to neutral standing / you don't add, don't embellish, you just follow accurately the stimulation you receive / and the further out you go, the deeper you have to ground yourself / you can also give wind simultaneous to receiving wind. but you can't refuse / you have to accept. de Quincey, "Thinking through Dance—Dancing through Thought."

and the bodily intelligence it seeks to enhance, may teach how to move within turbulent times.

Joy of Dance, a Celebration

Throughout this chapter I have been expanding on the particular modality of listening-with. This has included engaging with questions of care and healing, practices of embodiment, and how bodies are carriers of intelligence and felt awareness. Fundamental to these reflections and arguments is the appreciation for how listening is often called upon as that which can *follow* the body, learning its languages, its powers. Across therapeutic and meditation practices, for example, listening is positioned as necessary in order to work through held trauma, to expand the capacity for mindfulness and living well. And further, listening appears as essential for attuning to a world of others, for fostering a *readiness for action*, in terms of protecting others and maintaining or restoring dignity to individual lives. How we come to know the *whole person*, from past experiences to their state of well-being today, is predicated on listening's crucial involvement.

Embodied life is no smooth affair; rather, it is a rough, shimmering world full of journeys and passions, labor and love. Things push against, as one pushes back, figuring all types of collaborative strategies, all forms of accommodations and resistances, movements and struggles. To *listen-with* is to know of the body's ongoingness, its wisdom that collects over time, which is personal as well as planetary, geological, genetic: all these vibrations and reverberations of voices, gestures, histories, and practices figure as part of what one may come to sense and do as one participates, as one lives, grows, breathes, hurts, loves, diminishing as one goes. Through such deeply material-spiritual work, the power of the body Federici speaks of may be less static as one may think, less singular or even containable; rather, such power is founded on the body's interconnected nature, its immersion in sympathetic, poetic, and mystical knowledges, supporting ways of moving and responding, being there for others—*a body that becomes a vehicle for other bodies.*

In emphasizing the urgencies around reclaiming the body, Silvia Federici points to listening as a way of contending with dominant powers, especially those aligned with capitalism and its extractive, exploitative systems. Listening gives way to knowing of the body as a creative force, a vitality that is fundamental

126 *Poetics of Listening*

to nurturing and caring for a greater common good. Knowing of the body as interdependent, as *connatural*, and as what can offer itself in acts of compassion and healing, listening keeps one close to the fact of a critical togetherness. Such affordances emerge through the ways in which listening is able to assist in attuning inner and outer worlds, earthly and divine others, as well as past and future; to notice and recognize that which surrounds, in terms of the structures and systems that impact onto bodily life, not to mention the demons that are always nearby, along with the deep and personal stories resounding within. As an art of pause, one that readies oneself for the light of poetry as Harjo suggests, listening is wed to the felt sense through which care for oneself and others is fostered. And which must be appreciated to impact onto the vitality of the common nerve.

↫

If listening is operative in nurturing bodily care, and helps guide in processes of repair, it does so by also being aligned with pleasure and the joys of bodily sensation. To write from and with the body, as Hélène Cixous argues, is to shudder the logic of a patriarchal language and discourse that often dominates by repressing the fullness of the body; it is to upset the ways in which some are positioned as Other, especially those cast as being outside a defining rationality— as having *too much body*.[84] From music to dance, ritual to celebration, the tender and forceful refrains and rhythms that send the foot tapping and the body moving, listening as a language of the body manifests in an array of joyous actions and experiences. In fact, the things we listen to have the power to fully move us beyond ourselves—it may be to fall into states of trance and ecstasy, where the ability to commune with spirits is made profoundly manifest, or it may be to find pleasure in doing good for others, feeling moved by their life stories, their vulnerability. It is along these lines that a poetics of listening features, supporting ways of being in the body that are transformative, transfigural, that are full of feeling and that work at defending the fullness of bodily life. While listening assists in attending to the body, in caring for difficult journeys and the pain of others, it also opens toward processes of recovery through feelings of happiness, exuberance, pleasure. Listening excites the body in so many enriching ways.

---

[84] The concept of writing the body, of *écriture féminine*, is developed by Hélène Cixous throughout her work, and is foundational to her thinking. See her seminal essay "The Laugh of the Medusa" (1976). Hélène Cixous, "The Laugh of the Medusa," *Signs*, vol. 1, no. 4 (Summer 1976): 875–93.

As part of her call to reclaim the power of the body, Federici finds an important point of reference in dance. As she poses, "dance shows the intelligence of the body"—it gives indication as to that natural power she identifies as coursing through our bodies. By way of dance we learn of the body as a deeply dynamic and creative vitality, and as profoundly connective as it reaches out, extends, synchronizes, breaks away, through movements that elaborate the primary tempo of breath and heartbeat, amplifying and celebrating the power of bodily life. A standing, a rotating, a turning, or holding still, and that may afford, as Clément reminds, a time and space for contending with existing regimes of rhythm and reason. As "the exploration and invention of what a body can do,"[85] dance expresses a logic of the body—it is, for Federici, a philosophy itself in terms of articulating a way of moving in the world—a reasoning found in sweat and extended arms, laughter and the joys of a syncopated movement. Dance is guided by listening-with, as one collaborates with the body, follows its language, its imagination, its power, bringing these forward in a mode of celebration, coordination, and improvisation, through movements that seek to define their own time and space, and how it is we may partner with others.

Dancing is also a working through of the ways in which the body is shaped by its situatedness, as it is located within systems of discourse, economy, labor, and socialized structures, all of which impress onto bodily life an array of meanings, orientations, figuring oneself along particular lines, by way of particular time signatures. The body is *patterned*, stitched into social fabrics and temporal orders through which movements are shaped and produced, given traction or definition. To lean in or out by way of listening is to become adept at participating in currents of sympathy that are equally currents of our times.

These are inquiries and enactments that are understood to help contend with ongoing injuries, as well as what may lend to crafting tactics of the self: bodily tactics, ways of listening, sympathetic and compassionate gestures, the dance steps that may follow and also bend the beat, to take pleasure in the diverse ways we may experience the vitality of the body, alone and together. Here, the project of listening-with is aimed at elaborating the sensual languages and poetic rhythms, the feeling-thinking awareness and wakeful understanding, as what may affirm as well as reclaim the energetic breadth of embodied life.

---

[85] Federici, *Beyond the Periphery of the Skin*, 123.

4

Listening-against: Power, Negative Method, and the Diplomatic Arts

There are numerous instances in which social or political conflicts and crises demand more robust and sustained forms of dialogue. These are instances often shaped by power relations, where statecraft and the work of diplomacy are required to deploy a range of gestures as part of processes of negotiation. Or, instances where nongovernmental agencies, social workers, and peace keepers work at localized conversations, to support communities burdened with disaster or violence. Within such instances, finding the means for truly hearing what communities need is urgent. While power and its deployment of force may lend to systems of domination, as that which "holds the reins" and dictates the terms, power is equally found in compassionate action, in gestures and policies that deepen support for others, and that wield a strength that is also vulnerable, gentle, loving. Between these polarities, how ideas of the common good, justice, and political process are understood impact greatly onto people's lives.

Across structures and scenes of political struggle, how can listening contribute? In what ways is power and listening related, and how does listening figure within conceptualizations of justice? As Andrew Dobson argues, democracy itself is founded on a belief in responsiveness, where citizens expect to be listened to by their leaders.[1] Such views extend more generally, positioning listening, and its presence as well as absence, as a measure of good government and how its political systems are felt to be participatory.

As I'm concerned to consider, understandings of listening within the context of democracy and citizen power give greatly to shaping governmental procedure and responsiveness, as well as processes necessary for justice-making. If listening is seen as vitally important in supporting participation and fair government, it

---

[1] Andrew Dobson, *Listening for Democracy: Recognition, Representation, Reconciliation* (Oxford: Oxford University Press, 2014).

is also on the level of giving room for the expression of what Arnold Mindell highlights as "the deepest feelings and dreams" of people.[2] While democracy may articulate itself upon a foundation of citizen power, it can only truly realize itself by shifting the rhetoric from "power" to "awareness." Awareness, for Mindell, names the *inner work* necessary for both individuals and organizations to thrive; like individuals, organizations are also "haunted" by repressed feelings, unheard voices, unrecognized dreams and fears, and they must work at emotional awareness, for organizations are *living systems* rather than simply mechanical entities.[3] Such views lead Mindell to argue for a model of "deep democracy," as democracy built upon an awareness of the "dreaming background" to any given community, organization, constituency and assembly.[4]

It is my interest to consider listening in relation to questions of power, and how it is positioned or instrumentalized in the service of different political agendas and struggles. And furthermore, how listening may contribute to the inner work underpinning deeper forms of democracy. This includes a reflection on listening as a technique of surveillance, where individuals and communities may be captured or controlled by way of auditory devices, by systems that *listen in*, or that instill a sense of fear by way of a greater apparatus of domination. To listen within such instances is to police the discourses and vocabularies, the speech and activities of others with the aim of curtailing opposition or potential threats. The capacity to surveil a population is central to what is understood as the maintenance of security, as well as at times that of oppressive systems. Moreover, listening also fights back by way of the act of whistleblowing—to *break the silence* on certain behind-the-scenes activity, allowing for greater transparency. What falls within hearing range is therefore defining of certain political, social orders, and the values embedded therein. To do the work of listening is central to how we understand politics itself.

Within the systems and structures that work at surveilling, we find an extremely pronounced interweave between listening and machines: techniques of surveillance are fundamentally driven by advances in technology, and as such come to articulate a relation between listening and machines—a history of

---

[2] Arnold Mindell, *The Deep Democracy of Open Forums: Political Steps to Conflict Prevention and Resolution for the Family, Workplace, and World* (Charlottesville, VA: Hampton Roads, 2002), 3.
[3] Ibid., 4.
[4] Ibid.

listening includes a history of technology, a history that invariably influences the movements and abilities of power. The capacity to extend listening beyond the perceptual limits of the physical body is a fundamental perspective when considering questions of the political. How do such capacities and experiences alter what we come to know as listening? As a great deal of listening today is directed or made possible by technologies, how has this affected a relation to power as well as understandings of democracy? And with the advancement of artificial intelligence, how are new forms of machine listening changing cultures of voice and public discourse?

Such questions and views turn us toward the rich and complex arena of human-technical assemblages; from early speaking machines to cyborgian bodies, from cochlear implantation to radiophonic voices, human-technical assemblages articulate forms of speaking and listening that are collaborative, tensed by ethical concerns and political agendas, and strangely *biomechanic*. They open up creative, artistic possibilities and cultures, while also lending to any range of systems of control. We have been listening through and with machinic others for a long time. How do human-technical assemblages relate to the arena of politics, the work of democracy and the movements of diplomacy as well as protest? If the power of listening is one that aids in conflict resolution and peace-building, as well as in engaging systems that overstep ethical and political limits when it comes to rights and freedoms, in what ways does this suggest a particular type of knowledge? And how does such knowledge impact on how one may approach political struggle and the urgencies around state violence, for example? Is it feasible to work at building *listening institutions* as what may set the conditions for listening cultures? And how might such affirmative views balance with the need, at times, to *not* listen? Listening is clearly at the heart of power, and is fundamentally a power in itself.

Techniques of Surveillance, Machine Listening

In his book, *Noise: The Political Economy of Music*, Jacques Attali gives an analysis of power by way of noise—noise, for Attali, is "the source of power."[5] Such a view is founded on positioning noise as a type of raw matter, a radical force out

---

[5] Jacques Attali, *Noise: The Political Economy of Music* (Minneapolis: University of Minnesota Press, 1985), 6.

of which meaning, identity, and society emerge. "With noise is born disorder and its opposite: the world."[6] The very question of order, toward which power directs itself, finds its endless source in noise which it essentially appropriates, captures, controls; noise is harnessed as the energetic charge of life, the force of innovation, of crisis and change. While power may work at fixing a given order, as a structuring of bodies and identities, communities and societies, it is equally informed if not driven by rupture, chaos, breakdown—within an order of power these too are incorporated, made operative. As Attali goes on to suggest, noise comes to underpin any number of social, ritualistic forms, one being that of music (as well as carnival). Music is presented as "originating in ritual murder, of which it is a simulacrum, a minor form of sacrifice heralding change"; furthermore, as part of traditional forms of religious and political power, music "signified order" while also prefiguring subversion.[7] Within the context of power, music is a site of contestation, conflict, a material-symbolic scene always pulled between order and rupture, control and resistance. It is brought under the banner of national identity, for instance, to reinforce tradition, to give narrative to stability and the continuity of a given power structure, *and* it is always intervening onto what Jacques Rancière terms "the distribution of the sensible"[8]—as a noise that comes from below, or from within, to force into view alternative meanings, to interrupt so as to allow other voices to be heard. It is through this general framework that Attali opens a greater discussion on noise and power, music and society, sound and economy and, further, to recognize listening as key to the flows and operations of the political. "The technology of listening in on, ordering, transmitting, and recording noise is at the heart of [power's] apparatus."[9] To capture, take over, or hack such technologies is fundamental to upsetting regimes of control.

Listening is therefore deeply political; it forms the basis of power, in terms of surveilling the movements of opposition, gauging the tone of popular opinion, identifying the presence of dissident views, while also supporting humanitarian initiatives, ways of mobilizing the power of people, attuning to the needs of others through compassionate action and a belief in the common good. Even within the noisy dimension of inner life, listening is what enables ways of negotiating

---

[6] Ibid.
[7] Ibid., 4.
[8] Jacques Rancière, *The Politics of Aesthetics: The Distribution of the Sensible* (New York: Bloomsbury, 2013).
[9] Attali, *Noise*, 7.

power's influence: to work through all the directives, voices, and influences of an external world imported into the body, incorporated into the languages and viewpoints one may use and hold; listening searches, is reflective and engaged, to assist in staying in touch with an inner truth. Listening *listens back* against power while cultivating its own form of empowerment.

Importantly, this includes the ways in which listening moves across individual and collective worlds, becoming a means by which to contribute to a greater community. This finds expression in how writer, musician, and Michi Saagiig Nishnaabeg scholar Leanne Betasamonsake Simpson speaks about listening from within an Indigenous perspective: "I think individuals are responsible for listening to their own truths and listening to the sound of their own heart, for self actualizing, and for figuring out how to contribute to the community in a good way, in a productive way, in a way that generates more life."[10] Simpson elaborates this essential view by emphasizing the need to move beyond the highly individualistic dynamics of colonial-capitalistic societies, to stay close to the breadth of relationality so defining of life. As she continues, "It's important to figure out your own voice and to use your own voice, to listen to yourself, I think, as a life practice, but that's always going to be in conversation with all of these other beings that you're sharing time and space with, because we're relational, and because what I do impacts other life beings."[11]

The flows and tensions moving across these listening positions, and listening effects, find a point of amplification by way of machines. With the emergence of artificial intelligence, who or what is listening is stretched beyond the physical body, complicating the issue and limits of political, ethical, and legal accountability.[12] Or rather, with the introduction of *listening agents*—that occupy a position between human and machine, between affective sensitivity and algorithmic computing—new forms of control as well as empowerment are given traction, along with new forms of politics and economy, and ways of being heard. What happens when voices are generated as clones of another? No longer simply a synthesized, automated voice, but a replicant of an existing voice, especially one that may occupy a position of power? Voice cloning raises

---

[10] Leanne Betasamonsake Simpson and Kite, "Discussion with Leanne Betasamonsake Simpson," *Ear, Wave, Event*, no. 7 (Spring 2023): 2.
[11] Ibid.
[12] Cathy O'Neil, *Weapons of Math Destruction: How Big Data Increases Inequality and Threatens Democracy* (London: Penguin Books, 2017).

challenging questions, furthering a greater discussion as to what constitutes voice within a digital age.[13]

While voice has long been untethered from its embodied home to inhabit an ambiguous position between the actual and virtual, between terrestrial and transmitted worlds, the voice clone opens a new uncertainty and potentiality. It is both tied to the actuality of a person, signaling back to a given identity one may know and recall, while being able to *speak for itself*. This is a voice that no longer needs its original body or mind but is generated by way of existing samples or datasets. While the disembodied voice of radiophony and telephony has long populated the globe, the voice clone resides within the now ubiquitous data stream and may participate in any number of conversations. It is not so far to imagine that one day we will be able to clone our own voices, or those of loved ones, so as to be able to converse in the future.

Voice cloning captures the original view posed by Attali in terms of power's relation to noise, and how listening moves across different modalities, from dominant systems of control to emergent forms of resistance, from listening as what eavesdrops onto citizens and listening as what empowers greater communal relationality. The voice clone may equally migrate across these polarities, affording new methods of control, of coding or over-coding the inherent noise of life's articulations, while figuring all types of vocal resistances, where being heard may find new paths, new politics, and partnerships.

⤺

Machine listening, and the algorithmic systems now shaping a great deal of society and individual lives, raises key questions as to what counts as recognition: from voice recognition to voice cloning, the ways in which machines come to identify people, to create profiles and databases on individuals, presents urgent challenges to democratic society.

Ramon Amaro, in his book *The Black Technical Object,* presents a deeply engaged reflection on the politics of facial recognition technology, particularly in relation to questions of race. Central to his analysis is a concern for the ways in which machine learning sits uncomfortably alongside race, revealing or reinforcing embedded discriminatory structures found in dominant white

---

[13] For more on voice cloning, see Michael Teich, "AI Voice Cloning—and Its Misuse—Has Opened a Pandora's Box of Legal Issues: Here's What to Know," *ipwatchdog,* August 9, 2023, https://ipwatch dog.com/2023/08/09/ai-voice-cloning-misuse-opened-pandoras-box-legal-issues-heres-know/ id=163859/# (accessed July 2024).

society. This is founded on the fact that such technology is created and defined by dominant tech companies in the United States whose programmers and executives are predominantly male and white. Such a reality contributes to forms of bias, positioning whiteness as the norm. As the author elaborates, machine learning technology "is preconditioned by a process of human relations that has already conceived of Black beings as objects among other objects" and are therefore "always already externally fragmented and thereby readied for algorithmic reassembly through the white imaginary."[14] To elaborate such concerns, Amaro cites the example of Joy Buolamwini, and her project Aspire Mirror. Developed in 2016, Aspire Mirror is described as a device that "enables you to look at yourself and see a reflection on your face based on what inspires you or what you hope to empathize with."[15] As Amaro highlights, during the testing phase of the project, which relies upon facial detection and tracking software, the artist encountered difficulties, as the software could not detect aspects of "her presence due to her dark skin tones and facial features."[16]

The question as to the racial biases of AI software is central to Buolamwini's own research and work, leading her to advocate for greater understanding as to "algorithmic harm" and the ways in which AI technologies need greater accountability. This equally pertains to voice recognition software along with emergent voice cloning technologies. Machine learning is an arena in which a politics of the senses is placed within struggles around recognition itself— whether one is recognized as such by machines has become equally a political issue, shifting the terms of what traditionally has been understood as social and political recognition: while individuals and communities may strive for recognition within social and political worlds, through any number of institutional and noninstitutional processes, machine recognition is becoming increasingly influential. As companies implement voice and facial recognition tools across workplaces, housing and home environments, social and political institutions, urban and civic spaces, it becomes imperative to advocate for better practices.

---

[14] Ramon Amaro, *The Black Technical Object: On Machine Learning and the Aspiration of Black Being* (London: Sternberg Press, 2022), 13.
[15] As found on the project website: https://www.aspiremirror.com/.
[16] Amaro, *The Black Technical Object*, 41.

Returning to Ramon Amaro and his concerns for the politics of recognition and technology, machine learning is important for how it operates by way of existing assumptions and stereotypes defined by dominant white society, where identity is always already housed within a greater form of categorization. "In this way, machine learning is not causal of racial categorization. Machine learning is the expression of a signal that alerts us to an individual and collective condition that finds its most prized value in the categorization of life in order to facilitate meaning through external affirmation."[17] To be recognized or not by machines is to already (unwillingly) participate in a system of bias and the "epistemic logics of racial exclusion" in which "Blackness, as such, is always already incompatible with the algorithmic milieu."[18] For Amaro, this impacts not only on existing social and political realities, and the lives of people of color; such discriminatory systems work against life itself, constraining the dynamism of people and communities to yet another system of categorization and where the "operation of individuation is furthermore relegated to a series of representations among a falsely unified species."[19] Such "freezing of individuation" finds further expression in voice recognition software; while machine learning may follow human behavior and expression, it equally requires that one learns *how* to be recognized by the machine. This includes a process of adapting to the behavior of the machine and related software protocols. For example, in the article "Dragon NaturallySpeaking: Being Listened to and the Subservience of Speech," Eeke van der Wal reflects upon her experience using the voice recognition software Dragon NaturallySpeaking.[20] Following physical injuries due to extended computer use, van der Wal started working with Dragon, which allows for a hands-free experience. Yet, the possibility of using one's voice to command the computer revealed a number of unexpected challenges as well as insights. Crucially, it became imperative that van der Wal fit her own speech to that of the software; this included modulating her non-native English, learning particular commands in order to properly compose sentences, and distinguishing command from sentence content through nuanced forms of inflection. In short, Dragon dictates the way in which a user speaks and composes sentences. To highlight this experience, van der Wal offers this example:

---

[17] Ibid., 35.
[18] Ibid.
[19] Ibid., 56.
[20] Eeke van der Wal, "Dragon NaturallySpeaking: Being Listened To and the Subservience of Speech," *Soapbox: Practices of Listening*, vol. 1, no. 1 (Fall 2018): 41–63.

I *comma* however *comma* did not know beforehand that in English *open quote open parenthesis close parenthesis close quote* are called *open single quote* parentheses *close single quote* and I had to learn that Dragon responds to commands such as *open quote* open parenthesis *close quote comma open quote* close parenthesis *close quote comma open quote* open quote *close quote comma open quote* comma *close quote comma open quote* full stop *close quote comma open quote* new line *close quote comma* etcetera *choose option one full stop.*[21]

As the above example highlights, commanding computer usage through voice recognition software is no simple affair. As van der Wal suggests, such forms of interface reveal a more complex relation, one that for the author is suggestive for a posthuman positionality. "Dragon is no longer simply a tool or technology to be used by its user, but instead becomes an active participant in this relation."[22]

Following from this realization, the question of recognition is founded less on a human-centered construct of agency; rather, as van der Wal argues, the notion of an independent subject whose voice may work at willful control is destabilized. Instead, voice is fundamentally subordinate to a greater relation with machinic others. As the author goes on to infer, listening emerges as deeply operational. In fact, through coming to terms with processes of mediated voice recognition, it becomes less clear what constitutes agency, or where it comes to be located: does it reside in the act of speech, in the voice of the one who speaks, or in listening, and in the listening act?

While machine learning and the algorithmic realities of AI confront us with new challenges, and new forms of potential capture and control, manipulation and fake realities, they also come to participate in new articulations and methods of agential arrangements. As Amaro queries in his discussion around machine learning and race, "what if this Black technical object was to interact with the logics of machine learning beyond the desire for recognition and reinforcement of its existing rudimentary operations? What if we, the Black technical object, were to travel through the algorithmic as that which enacts its own form of reason, to arrive at a self-actualization?"[23]

The Black technical object emerges by way of the rudimentary operations of machine learning with their structural bias's, while posing a certain excess, a move

---

[21] Ibid., 46.
[22] Ibid., 49.
[23] Amaro, *The Black Technical Object*, 14.

from within being-object that works at another form of travel and arrival. These are human-technical moves, science fictional moves, moves that stare back at the omniscient eye of the machine, or that work at *scratching* the code. One arena in which such moves may be found is certainly that of hip-hop, which articulates the self-actualized reasoning of the Black technical object by way of the turntable. Warren C. Longmire suggests as much in his article "Odd Futures: How Hip Hop Defined Post-Modernism," positioning hip-hop as the foundation to postmodern culture (particularly in the context of the United States).[24] Fundamental to Longmire's analysis, and understanding of the postmodern, is the technique of "remixing"—remixing articulates a cultural shift from singularity to multiplicity, from reified form to assemblage of matter, from the expression of unique meaning to the sampling of existing work, from the aura of genius to the grooves of the DJ. With the emergence of hip-hop in the Bronx in the 1970s, DJing moved out of the disco and into the hood where, as Longmire argues, remixing came to define an "art of bricolage" that would speak to poor Black neighborhoods (and beyond) in ways that postmodern visual art never would.[25]

Such an art of bricolage does not begin, though, in the Bronx, but finds its origins in Kingston, Jamaica, and the sound systems of the 1950s and 1960s that would define Dub reggae, Ska, and subsequent cultures of turntablism. It is this larger African, diasporic history that Longmire invites us to attend to, and in doing so, to recognize how hip-hop is grounded in technical innovation, or rather, in an intelligence of technique.[26] Instead of casting hip-hop as a cultural product, Longmire emphasizes it as *science*, one that works on existing technologies—from turntables to sound systems—to invent new techniques of production and performance. These are technical innovations that, while based on creative forms of appropriation, hacking, sampling, and assembling, came to impact onto the production of music technologies.[27]

It is by way of the science of hip-hop that Longmire's views may contribute to thinking along with Amaro's Black technical object. While hip-hop may not

---

[24] Warren C. Longmire, "Odd Futures: How Hip Hop Defined Post-Modernism," in *Black Quantum Futurism: Theory and Practice*, vol. 1, ed. Rasheedah Phillips (Philadelphia: Afrofuturist Affair/House of Future Sciences, 2015), 61.

[25] Ibid., 63.

[26] Ibid., 70.

[27] For an insightful documentary on Afrofuturism and its impact onto music technology, see the film *Mothership Connection* (1995) by Black Audio Film Collective.

necessarily figure within questions of machine learning, and debates around AI, it readily articulates ways of traveling through the algorithmic milieu, the circuits and technological mechanisms of production and reproduction, to turn against the codes of (Western) music in acts and journeys of self-actualization. Such practices and enactments figure a subjectivity that *listens-against* the directives of dominant systems; that posits a listening agency by which to inhabit the logic of machines, shifting the codified and categorized in support of new emancipatory expressions. These are gestures that echo Jacques Attali in his appraisal of power's relation to noise, for hip-hop traditionally disorders dominant white power structures by way of a sustained agitation— from the scratch to the remix, the break to the slide, hip-hop stages a range of interruptive performativities onto the musical orders of white society. This is an art of bricolage that supports "another kind of mythology," one constituted by "a sequence of temporal fragments not joined together but disseminated through repetitions and different modes of enjoyment, in memories and successive knowledges."[28]

As I've been considering, listening and power are profoundly interlocked and come to define a political arena in which who or what is heard, who or what is listening, shapes a particular social or institutional order. This includes a concern for power's relation to technology; from voice's position within new algorithmic systems to questions of race and machine learning, dominant power is founded on its ability to extend its (sensorial) reach through a range of technical platforms. Such perspectives, and systems, entail a relation to counter-techniques, and the gestures and enactments by which the marginalized or dispossessed pry open unlikely routes, finding ways of recoding or overcoding the protocols and machines of power. These are methods or gestures of traveling through the mechanisms, the algorithms, the material-technical platforms and instruments, to manifest all sorts of performative-technical moves and itineraries. It is along these routes that listening becomes radically influential to the ways in which power and empowerment both function.

---

[28] Michel de Certeau, quoted in Frank Farmer, *After the Public Turn: Composition, Counterpublics, and the Citizen Bricoleur* (Boulder: Utah State University Press, 2013), 35.

Listening as Diplomatic Force

In holding a time and space, listening does much to open that space, prolong that time, allowing for things to be said and life stories to be heard. As such, it greatly supports the previously unsaid in finding articulation, thereby shifting the lines demarcating the listenable. From listening to the body as a path toward health and healing, as a means to reorient the bonds that may situate persons in particular ways, to recognizing the voices of communities that call for attention, listening moves us, may act as the basis for movement and the reordering of a given time and space. In this way, it poses an approach to action and agency that aligns with responsiveness, with radical openness, thereby lending to the valorization of dialogue and the fostering of cooperation. While the outspoken articulations of voice are fundamental to political actions and institutions, there is a way in which verbalizations can take over in their rush toward conclusions or opinion-making (not to mention being bent by pressures to conform to dominant views). In response, listening, and the attentional work it conducts, is often what is so needed, enabling if not demanding that one truly hear the speech of others as well as all that resides just out of earshot—to dwell in a space of complexity. As Gideon Calder argues, if the voices and views of others are to matter, especially those marginalized by dominant systems, it is essential that "they are listened to, and listened out for."[29] This is a crucial distinction which can contribute to my concern for listening's relation to power. While it is clear that *listening to* others is key to nurturing dialogue and understanding within the arenas of power and politics, *listening out for* forms the basis for extending precisely the limits of recognition and representation, participation and involvement.

Following such views, listening emerges as essential to supporting political process—in fact, it can be argued that listening is what defines political process, especially in relation to democracy. This finds articulation in what Andrew Dobson emphasizes as "re-politicization" in the context of democratic procedure. Such a view is founded on understanding the ways in which governments, or political bodies, may undermine political process by limiting the degree to which public opinion may influence decision-making, or when procedural formats work at directing or prescribing a given outcome, thereby excluding

---

[29] Gideon Calder, quoted in Dobson, *Listening for Democracy*, 37. See also Gideon Calder, "Listening, Democracy and the Environment," *In-Spire Journal of Law, Politics and Societies*, vol. 4, no. 2 (2009): 26–41.

Listening-against 141

a range of alternative viewpoints. These forms of "de-politicization" come to reduce engaging with a greater public sphere. For Dobson, arguing for listening in such contexts operates to "re-politicize" particular issues or situations.[30] As he outlines, "de-politicitization is an act (or a succession of acts) of closure" against which listening works, for listening is "the performance of opening out and opening up."[31] Developing listening practices in the context of political process enhances the capacity for dialogue; it supports understanding across difference, fostering empathy and open-mindedness, as well as allowing for the suspension of judgment and entrenched views. The *opening out* and *opening up* that listening conducts is crucial for fulfilling the democratic promise of responsive government. This finds expression when Kuik Shiao-Yin, a former Member of Parliament in Singapore, writes: "We can avoid unnecessarily adversarial relationships with our dissenters if we choose to be slow to speak and quick to listen for the truths our naysayers are offering."[32]

⸺

In considering the political affordances of listening, and what I'm concerned to highlight by way of the mode of *listening-against*, listening can be positioned as a *diplomatic force*. As Calder argues, processes of dialogical encounter and work entail the necessity to *listen to* others, which greatly aids in building trust, acknowledging difference and finding compromise. Calder extends this fundamental ground listening provides through the concept of *listening out for*, a mode of listening that challenges existing power structures and political borders by affording the marginalized or underrepresented the possibility of entry, or by interrupting a given status quo. In following these perspectives, I'm led to understand such modes of listening through the notion of *listening-against*. By posing the idea of listening-against, I'm concerned to position listening within the context of political struggle as what not only sets the conditions for dialogical process but does so in an effort to enact change. Listening-against may be a form of aggressive listening, an urgent listening, a listening that not only builds trust and supports understanding but works at interrupting so as to better fight for what's right. I sense this already in the concept of *listening out for*, which suggests that a given status quo needs to be challenged; that what exists within an established set of discourses, policies, or laws requires debate

---

[30] Dobson, *Listening for Democracy*, 196.
[31] Ibid.
[32] Kuik Shiao-Yin, *The Power of a People* (Singapore: Epigram Books, 2019), 19.

and broader reflection, so as to keep open to difference and dissent. Importantly, in supporting a deeper political process, *listening out for* moves the lines often demarcating dominant power, giving room for the hearing of dissenting views, as well as demands for change. This helps shift the responsibility from the margin to the center, to suggest that it is imperative not only that the marginalized speak up but that the center learns to listen better.

Alongside listening's ability to open out and open up, fostering political processes of dialogue and deliberation, listening may also work at saying *no*—it may function to intervene within particular struggles, to *listen-against* an existing set of rules, codes, arrangements. If listening impacts and influences the procedures of political work by opening, allowing for what Mary F. Scudder highlights as the "uptake" or fair consideration of differing views,[33] it may also contribute to acts of refusal—it may be an act of refusal in itself. Re-politicization, as founded on listening-against, is an act that complicates and staggers the smooth operations of dominant power; it re-introduces process, as the very thing that supports dialogue, which, as Dobson suggests, can be defined as "structured disagreement."[34] Being open to dissenting views, to my ear, names an *interruptive* process or frictional state, where entrenched opinions may ease, or be shattered, where ideological lines may break or bend, where the borders of certain power structures may be breached. In this sense, listening may figure much-needed scenes of empathy, of nonjudgmental attention, of caring dialogue and fair consideration, but in doing so, it productively destabilizes a given order (as well as potentially one's own position). These are critical acts that raise the volume on political participation.

↜

This is the diplomatic force I sense in listening, and which finds a range of methodological articulations as well as grounded enactments. For instance, the Center for Peace and Conflict Studies in Cambodia has been working for many years on educating peace leaders that can assist in intervening in the region's multiple conflict zones. This includes a focus on mediation, facilitation, and negotiation practices that can strengthen peace-building. As part of the Center's ongoing research and organizing, a range of studies into listening as a methodology has been developed, leading to underscoring listening as fundamental to conflict

---

[33] Mary F. Scudder, *Beyond Empathy and Inclusion: The Challenge of Listening in Democratic Deliberation* (Oxford: Oxford University Press, 2023).
[34] Dobson, *Listening for Democracy*, 107.

resolution and peace-building. One such research study identifies listening as necessary in ensuring the full participation of local communities targeted for aid by various nongovernmental agencies. Undertaking a "listening project" gives room so that "authentic voices of local communities can be heard by political and military actors, strategists, donors, and non-governmental and international agencies. In conflict transformation and peace building, even a small shift can be significant in making real the human plight, and in reconnecting the broken relationships or the disrupted communication between groups or communities in conflict."[35] Underpinning this focus is an understanding of how communities affected by conflict are often mistrustful of official organizations and agencies who purport to act in their best interests; moreover, individuals within such communities may not feel at ease to truly speak their minds, they may feel insecure, threatened or uncertain, and may distort or withhold facts. Following these perspectives, finding ways of building trust and communication entails creating "relaxed and open" conditions that may best facilitate dialogue, as well as leveling the field through the integration of local community members in the facilitation process itself.

In identifying listening as an important part of peace work, the Center has developed listening methodologies and practices, which are centered around creating dialogical encounters and sessions with local communities, agencies, and government leaders affected or implicated within a given conflict. Such sessions are facilitated through "field listeners" who understand the context, language, customs, and struggles of local communities, and are tasked with deepening the level of conversation and exchange between the organizing facilitator and the community, which should include a diversity of community members so as to achieve a balanced overview of the situation.[36] Through defining "guiding questions" together and building dialogue sustained over time, a listening project can help ensure "participation of all members in a society in the decision-making process" so as to "build ownership and legitimacy."[37] Furthermore, listening helps deepen conflict analysis, as it "seeks to capture

---

[35] Soth Plai Ngarm, "Listening Methodology: Application of a Peacebuilding Research," (Siem Reap City, Cambodia: Center for Peace and Conflict Studies, 2022), 4.

[36] The project The Listening Zones of NGOs further highlights listening's role in facilitating peace work. In particular, the project sought to understand the importance of language within situations of conflict resolution practices. See the project website: https://www.reading.ac.uk/languages-cultu res/research/listening-zones-of-ngos (accessed July 2024).

[37] Ngarm, "Listening Methodology," 8.

the voices of people at the grassroots level." Through listening, "we can learn how policies, peace processes, and / or conflict affect people at this level" which "helps us understand the relationship between top-level and grassroots and the relationship dynamics" and "provides for a holistic understanding at all levels."[38]

〜

The listening projects and practices developed by the Center for Peace and Conflict Studies are helpful in recognizing listening's role in addressing conflict and contributing to a political process. Listening intervenes in ways that help ensure diplomatic solutions, and that impact greatly on the communicative processes by which peace-building is undertaken. Alongside such perspectives, it is important to consider the limitations of listening as well—or in what ways listening is strained, particularly when confronting those who refuse to listen, or when encountering views with which one disagrees.

In their book, *Rhetorical Listening in Action*, Krista Ratcliffe and Kyle Jensen offer important approaches to further understanding listening as key to communication. In particular, the authors pose the ever-challenging question: how is it possible to truly listen to those one disagrees with? Underpinning the concept of "rhetorical listening" is recognition as to a lack on the part of educational programs (in the United States, which is the author's main focus) to include lessons on listening: whereas a focus on reading, writing, and speaking is supported, listening (as a rhetorical art) is fundamentally absent. If one is to enhance the capacity for living alongside those one may disagree with, across neighbors and nations, bringing greater attention to listening is desperately needed. As the authors highlight, while "difficult-to-listen-to situations" are often not considered rhetorical problems—as rhetorical problems are considered to be problems in communication, in how one writes or speaks—such situations do call out for rhetorical action. "*Rhetorical problems may be defined in two ways: first, as situations in which speakers/writers must express their ideas, feelings, values, and beliefs in ways that their audiences can actually hear them, especially across differences; and second, as situations in which listeners/audiences must open themselves to actually hear ideas, feelings, values, and beliefs, even those with which they disagree.*"[39] By establishing a more pronounced focus on listening as part of rhetorical problems, Ratcliffe

---

[38] Ibid., 18.

[39] Krista Ratcliffe and Kyle Jensen, *Rhetorical Listening in Action: A Concept-Tactic Approach* (Anderson, SC: Parlor Press, 2022), 1.

and Jensen chart a set of "concept-tactics"; these are aimed at contending with difficult-to-listen-to situations, suggesting a means to act as "rhetorical listeners." This includes the necessity for people to "recognize the situatedness and the constructedness of their belief systems and cultural systems" and how they are mediated through language and discourse.[40] By acknowledging such aspects, one may find greater insight into the possibilities and limitations of not only one's own but also other's belief systems and how they come to influence views and opinions. To be a *rhetorical listener* is therefore to promote greater understanding of self and others as situated within particular frames of reference, which can enhance ways of working through or with disagreement.

At its core, rhetorical listening is aimed at fostering a "listening mindset," as what can aid in civic dialogue and cohabiting the political arenas that necessitate communicative capacities. This approach to listening is based on recognizing difficult-to-listen-to situations as rhetorical problems or situations whose challenges require "rhetorical strategies." These are concepts that afford paths toward building more nuanced forms of communication, particularly in support of diplomatic processes of negotiation, or of setting the tone for a more affirmative form of debate. Rather than approach political discourse, for example, as a scene where "winner takes all," a rhetorical listening approach enters such situations with the intent of arriving at "win-win" solutions. This is a radically alternate mindset, one that directs political discourse and debate along a more cooperative path in which participants feel as if "their stakes have been heard, considered, and factored, however possible, into decisions."[41] This necessitates a willingness to listen, to acknowledge one's own cultural logics and situated understanding onto existing problems, as well as accountability, and to remain curious and critical about arguments and counterarguments.[42] As Ratcliffe and Jensen suggest, "rhetorical listening offers listeners one means to engage competing perspectives and, in many cases, to engender respect among reasonable people who disagree."[43] These arguments are grounded in acknowledging the too-often polarizing effects of disagreement that reduce complex realities to oversimplified opinions and solutions. For the authors, listening functions as one important

40 Ibid., 7.
41 Ibid., 21.
42 Ibid., 24.
43 Ibid., 25.

avenue for contending with and participating in the multifaceted movements of power.

〜

The ability to create positive communicative conditions and experiences needs to further incorporate a more pronounced appreciation for affect and emotion. While rhetorical listening highlights the situatedness and constructedness of viewpoints, and the cultural logics shaping how one may see certain problems and issues, much of the ways in which communicational exchanges occur exist on the level of affect and emotion: situatedness is dynamically embodied, and agreement and disagreement are deeply felt. And as I've been detailing throughout the previous chapters, a great deal of listening's power is found in its capacity to bridge somatic and linguistic, emotional and cognitive, inner and outer worlds. It is along these lines that negotiations with power, and the work of civic dialogue and diplomacy, must bring into consideration the dimension of felt experience.

Addressing the place or presence of affect and emotion within political process and communicativeness is central to the project of Deep Democracy. Deep Democracy is a group facilitation method aimed at accessing and expressing the inherent intelligence and wisdom found within a given group. It works at encouraging dissenting voices, supporting the creative potential intrinsic to situations of conflict where majority and minority voices and views are embraced as equally contributing to finding solutions. In this regard, it views decision-making as a process in which diverse opinions and concerns are understood to benefit the group—what is termed "the gift" of a given conflict. Such a perspective encourages one to recognize a dissenting view as an opportunity for personal and community growth. It therefore works at facilitating an open and generous atmosphere to make use of the collective skills and resources of a given group. "By taking the group's process as a teacher, everyone becomes a learner and leader."[44]

〜

Developed by the psychotherapist and founder of process-oriented psychology Arnold Mindell, Deep Democracy incorporates a focus on the emotional, psychological experiences or backgrounds of individuals, seeking to bring to the surface the feelings that are often suppressed when confronting

---

[44] Mindell, *The Deep Democracy of Open Forums*, 5.

uneven power relations in which some voices dominate. This includes an acknowledgment of history and memory, and how these are fundamentally shaping emotional, psychological worlds—or what Ratcliffe and Jensen term "ecologies of memory."[45] Ecologies of memory echo with Mindell's idea of "the dreaming background" operative within any organization or group. As Mindell argues, organizations are *living systems* constituted equally by formal procedures and emotional worlds, rules of conduct and spirited desires, abstract principles and suppressed communication. Within any given assembly, community, or meeting, finding ways of working together can only be fully realized if processes include engaging with the dreaming background, to grant space for noticing "the feelings, dreaming, and social power" present within any given debate. Accordingly, "we need a … deeper democracy, based on awareness of what is happening inside ourselves and others."[46] For Mindell, too often power is cast as central to political process, whereas awareness should be the goal.

Importantly, methods of Deep Democracy work toward participatory forms of leadership, where issues are co-resolved. This finds a point of reference in what Ratcliffe and Jensen term "listening metonymically."[47] As a listening position or exercise, listening metonymically is performed by noting an "identity category" of another person, for example, that someone may be an actor, a mother, a liberal democrat. By *eavesdropping* onto that category, a listener may gain fuller insight into another's opinion or concern, and the ways in which identity (and membership within a larger cultural group) impacts onto the logics of viewpoint. Importantly, listening metonymically is about encountering views that may be unfamiliar, and that often come to represent a particular cultural logic or experience far from one's own. Furthermore, it allows one to appreciate how persons are never simply constituted by one identity, but are rather intersectional, inhabiting a range of identity categories, each of which contributes to one's viewpoint or concern. Listening metonymically is therefore an exercise in listening below the surface, to attend to the dreaming backgrounds as well as cultural logics, to better appreciate and gain awareness as to the complexity of individuals (including oneself).

⌁

---

[45] Ratcliffe and Jensen, *Rhetorical Listening in Action*, 78.
[46] Mindell, *The Deep Democracy of Open Forums*, 14.
[47] Ratcliffe and Jensen, *Rhetorical Listening in Action*, 47.

Underscoring listening as a diplomatic force is anchored in recognizing the role listening plays in political process, in the working through of conflict, and how central it is to peace-building. From deep democracy and rhetorical situations to public cultures and the re-politicization of urgent issues, listening influences how communities and societies find ways of living together. Such a force of listening, as what enhances dialogical process and ways to overcome or hold conflict, is positioned here as fundamental to the working through of politics and power. Importantly, listening as a diplomatic force captures a sense for how listening moves across scales, from the nurturing of intimacy and empathy among families, friends, and relations in general, to supporting community work, the social bonds and encounters in which listening aids in facilitating acknowledgment of others; and further, to the macropolitical struggles and scenes whose vocalized debates and deliberations necessitate an equally impassioned, considered form of listening. While each of these examples suggest different experiences, different concerns, and expectations, they all impart a sense for the importance of listening in bettering the world.

Restorative Circles, Feminist Policies

Listening as power, as what may work in the service of governmental control as well as in the resistant acts that seek to empower people, *to scratch against dominant grooves*, comes to necessitate a more pronounced acknowledgment in terms of developing practices across institutional and noninstitutional settings, even rituals through which listening cultures are strengthened. What kind of place does listening hold within our lives and communities? How is listening given room, for attending to the inner dimensions of thought and feeling, as well as the shared inner work needed for deepening democracy? Is listening afforded time and space within political procedures and cultures, of both dominant systems and those of resistance? To listen-against is to demand greater listening; it is to wield a diplomatic force, a rhetorical action, a scratch onto prevailing structures so as to keep attuned to the lives of people.

⌒

It is my concern to pose these lines of questioning, mapping initiatives and practices that accentuate listening's place within political process. This entails a move that works at keeping close to the lives of people, but that also becomes suggestive for rethinking conventions of what constitutes the political and enactments of justice-making. If listening is the very thing that underpins re-politicization—challenging an existing status quo, or ensuring the unfolding of process—what kind of impact might listening have structurally? Or, what type of political culture does listening engender, prompt, incite? As Ratcliffe and Jensen, along with Arnold Mindell, suggest, building a listening mindset is fundamentally transformative in terms of finding ways of addressing or holding disagreement; it supports approaching conflict as a gift, and the circulation of diverse views as the basis for more nuanced understanding and growth.

To follow these concerns, I'm interested to highlight the work of restorative circles, and the overall field of restorative justice, which can be appreciated as an intervention onto dominant approaches to conflict. Restorative circles have a range of applications and importantly help facilitate conflict resolution within a given community; they are focused on fostering communication in situations of breakdown, and where emotional, psychological, and physical harm is experienced. Bringing group members together in a circle, to engage in a restorative process, is deeply effective in overcoming conflict. Importantly, restorative circles are used proactively, in order to create safe and respectful environments that encourage active participation and ways of speaking *with* rather than *to* each other; and circles are also applied retroactively, in order to address conflicts within communities, or experiences of harm and crime, and work at restoring social well-being.

Key to restorative circles is the role of the facilitator, or "circle keepers."[48] Circle keepers are needed so as to bring together those involved or affected by dispute, or harmed through another's actions. This requires creating supportive conditions in order that those involved feel safe to speak and share their experiences, which includes often saying and hearing difficult things. This is further facilitated through the use of a "talking piece," which is an object that is passed around the circle, and which assures that each person speaks and is equally heard, one at a time, as participants are not allowed to speak until handed the piece. Importantly, circles may be enlarged to integrate a broad range of participants, including those who have been harmed and those who have caused harm, as well as family and community members. This may further include more official participants, such as teachers, justice officers, and civic leaders. In doing so, circles play an important role in recognizing how conflicts are not always limited

---

[48] Howard Zehr, *The Little Book of Restorative Justice* (New York: Good Books, 2015), 64–5.

to those directly involved, but can be seen to arise out of structural problems or issues within a given community. Howard Zehr, a key advocate for restorative practices, emphasizes this crucial aspect, acknowledging how persons, families as well as communities may be injured by crime, for example, and they may also be complicit in its perpetration. In this regard, restorative practices seek to balance "concern for all" in justice processes.[49]

Throughout the work of restorative circles, and restorative practices more generally, listening is emphasized as an essential component. As Berit Follestad and Nina Wroldsen highlight, circles give time and space for learning from each other about how each experiences a given situation; it is often about addressing expectations and disappointments, and about deep needs as well, and in doing so, circles help empower those involved, to feel open and safe, and to truly encounter each other through a more horizontal structure.[50] Restorative listening is a listening that contributes to nurturing "nonviolent communication,"[51] which, for Follestad and Wroldsen, helps shift from statements of blame and accusation— of finding fault and working at punishment—to a more inclusive dialogue, where participants' perspectives are given equal value. This entails building trust as well as identifying strategies for meeting needs. Through such processes, and ways of listening and speaking, individuals have a far greater chance of achieving a healthier sense of belonging as well as resolution of conflict.[52] This echoes back to methods of Deep Democracy, recognizing how conflicts present us with opportunities, or *gifts*, through which individual and collective growth can be experienced. Importantly, Follestad and Wroldsen advocate for the integration of circles on a structural level, in particular, within the environment of schools. Implementing circles as a routine within a given educational program can do much to promote "greater psychosocial health, diminish the growth of negative behaviour, exclusion and bullying, and reduce the incidence of conflict, violence, racism and students being subjected to radicalisation."[53]

૮~૨

---

[49] Ibid., 42.

[50] Berit Follestad and Nina Wroldsen, *Using Restorative Circles in Schools: How to Build Strong Learning Communities and Foster Student Wellbeing* (London: Jessica Kingsley, 2019).

[51] Berit Follestad and Nina Wroldsen's reference to "nonviolent communication" stems from the work of Marshall Rosenberg who has developed methods of nonviolent communication beginning in the 1960s and 1970s. For more, see Marshall B. Rosenberg, *Nonviolent Communication: A Language of Life* (Encinitas, CA: Puddle Dancer Press, 2003).

[52] Follestad and Wroldsen, *Using Restorative Circles in Schools*, 32–3.

[53] Ibid., 48.

Expressions of restorative practices, as practices that challenge established systems—as found within educational environments and criminal justice systems—can be further considered through the work of the Center for Feminist Foreign Policy (CFFP). As an organization, CFFP advocates for feminist foreign policy, which has emerged as a strategic intervention on the culture of foreign policy worldwide. First adopted in Sweden in 2014, feminist foreign policy acts as a governing set of principles for foreign policymaking based on emphasizing gender equality, and by placing the individual, as opposed to the state, at the center of how we understand security. In doing so, feminist foreign policy asks: How to work on behalf of security for those most vulnerable and at risk? It further undermines understanding security as a question of military defense and the weaponization of borders. Feminist foreign policy places emphasis instead on peace-building by putting women into positions where foreign policy decisions are made. Such a move is based upon research which shows that where women are in charge there is a profoundly better chance for finding peaceful solutions to conflict.[54] This has been further articulated with the passing of the United Nations Security Council Resolution 135 in 2020, on Women, Peace and Security, bringing greater traction to feminist foreign policy as an intervention onto dominant political cultures. Anna Provan, from CFFP, underscores such a perspective when she emphatically states that "there will be no peace without feminism."[55]

The Center for Feminist Foreign Policy seeks to map and manifest an alternative approach and understanding of defense and diplomacy. In doing so, their work challenges a culture of foreign policymaking by drawing upon feminist practices and ethics, often shaped by a more *personalized* and *egalitarian* understanding of the political, which entails a greater focus on listening. As Manuela Zechner suggests in her research into caring collectives in the context of social movements in Spain (prefiguring and emerging around the 15M Movement in 2011) and the "feminization" of politics these movements articulate, feminism works at drawing the political, and its processes, closer to *the body*, closer to questions of care and caring practices, and which include a more pronounced sense for interdependency and feelings of shared responsibility.[56] Of particular

---

[54] See Kristina Lunz, *The Future of Foreign Policy Is Feminist* (Cambridge: Polity Press, 2023).
[55] Anna Provan, "Centre for Feminist Foreign Policy," *Free Berlin* no. 9 (April 2021): 11.
[56] Manuela Zechner, *Commoning Care and Collective Power* (Vienna: transversal texts, 2021).

interest are the neighborhood initiatives led by single mothers aimed at building support structures for childcare, leading to self-organized platforms. "Their ethos is that parents, pedagogues and children work together and constitute strong care network or *tribú*—recognizing that modern urban parenting is a very individualizing and precarious matter that requires the invention of new support structures."[57] Zechner is particularly concerned to emphasize how the "micropolitical" dimensions of personal experiences, concerns, and feelings are crucial for building grassroots movements in ways that connect institutional and noninstitutional settings. Working across government offices, educational and healthcare environments, along with neighborhood schools, the homes of friends and community members, the mothers' networks shift questions of care in ways that affirm their own agency—to bring "the political down to the embodied level,"[58] and to build greater collective and common power. Moreover, they "reflect on ways of being affected, situated and response-able in relation to different problems or policies,"[59] so as to figure greater connection between work and life, personal experience and governmental structures. These are embodied, rhythmic connections that underpin localized support networks, bridging the micropolitical dimensions of affect, emotion, of taking care and caring together, with the civic structures, city offices, and political administrations. Such rhythmic alignments enable ways of enacting change, bringing the political down to the embodied level. And they entail *listening to* as well as *listening out for* those that may struggle to find footing within local environments, to work at modulating or recalibrating the structures, or defining new ones, by which individuals and communities may thrive.

↩

From the practices of restorative circles that aim to give room for equal say, and that shift focus toward collective repair rather than individual punishment, to feminist foreign policymaking that challenges the "militarized conception of state security," focusing instead on "feminist security"[60] (which entails a rethinking of the nation state as a patriarchal, imperialist structure) and putting people first, especially those most at risk, what constitutes established conventions of political power is put into question.

---

[57] Ibid., 86.
[58] Ibid., 82.
[59] Ibid.
[60] Lunz, *The Future of Foreign Policy Is Feminist*, 29.

Extending from Zechner's thinking, listening as a diplomatic force, as a restorative practice, as a feminist positionality, may contribute to working at greater *synchronization* between sites and scenes of care and politics, home and institutions, in which micropolitical expressions of embodied feeling and shared urgencies find their way into working macropolitically. This is centered on recognizing listening as an attentional work that spans personal and political worlds. As I'm arguing throughout *Poetics of Listening*, listening is emphasized as what contributes to aligning inner life and social-political contexts, that nurtures the capacity to recognize and build (if not fight for) connections across temporal and spatial scales, from the intimate to the global, the fleeting to the enduring. It furthermore enacts forms of self-care by sensing when life and work, home and society, fall out of balance, are misaligned or unjustly positioned in relation to each. To bring *into sync* first necessitates recognition of the constituent parts of a potential whole; to sense the harmonic order or rhythmic connection toward which one may work, and that at times demands greater collective calling or mobilization. To work at feminist foreign policy is one such mobilization, one that delivers challenge to dominant approaches and cultures surrounding foreign relations which, as Kristina Lunz argues, are too often defined by a politics of national securitization and defense.[61] This is echoed by Pavitra Sundar who argues that to "listen with a feminist ear" is to "sound out alternative temporal, spatial, and relational possibilities."[62] This entails listening-against the grain and in defiance of dominant structures and habits.[63] It is a situated, reflexive, and restorative listening that works at *bringing the political down to the embodied level* so as to keep societal structures and political policies *in sync* with individual lives.

Negative Listening

The potentiality of listening to impact and support processes of negotiation, diplomacy, political work, and the facilitation of restorative practices comes to affirm understandings of listening as contributing to individual and collective

---

[61] Ibid.
[62] Pavitra Sundar, *Listening with a Feminist Ear: Soundwork in Bombay Cinema* (Ann Arbor: University of Michigan Press, 2023), 7.
[63] Ibid., 6.

agency. As I'm emphasizing, listening is profoundly agentive, spanning across all types of movements, assemblies and debates—it is mobilized against systems and structures whose irresponsiveness to the cries of people is seen as *turning a deaf ear*. As Andrew Dobson argues, governments and institutions of power are democratic in so far as they enter into dialogical exchange with people. Yet, what of situations marked by absence, by a pervasive neglect, by political violence, situations in which power works at killing? What of instances in which history is left unfinished, populations erased, when negotiations or diplomacy fail, to leave behind nothing but ruins? How to attend to the aftermath, where the left behind pieces call out for attention, for investigation, for truth-telling? These are situations defined by the breakdown of dialogue and political process, and whose intensities challenge or overwhelm the capacity to do the work of listening—where does listening go in such situations?

↫

The anthropologist Yael Navaro develops the concept of "negative methodology" as a way to contend with the realities of disappearance and loss, of the missing.[64] In particular, she seeks to address the remains of political violence, the fragments and the ruins—*what happens when we are left with ruins?* As she notes, acts of (anthropological) research and the project of finding truth often proceed by trying to put the pieces back together; to fill in the gaps, the silences of broken communities, in an attempt to solve the problem (often through gestures of reconstruction) of unfinished history. In contrast to this "positivist" method, she calls for a "negative methodology." Negative methodology is a counter-methodology, one that does not aim to give voice to the voiceless, but rather holds the tension between history and truth, between the leftover and the need to know; negative methodology wields a refusal to complete the narrative, to capture history within a totalizing representation, instead, it keeps within the gaps, asking us to attend *by way* of the emptiness, the shards, the absent—a research approach that "stays in the fissures, rifts, enigmas, and hollows of knowledge production."[65] These are gestures and positions that draw out "the ethnographic research imaginary," suggesting parallel routes to that of "evidentiary knowledge making."[66]

---

[64]   Yael Navaro, "The Aftermath of Mass Violence: A Negative Methodology," *Annual Review of Anthropology*, vol. 49 (2020): 161–73.
[65]   Ibid., 162.
[66]   Ibid.

Listening-against 155

Negative methodology is marked by what Yael Navaro terms a "methodological pessimism."[67] Such a pessimism is positioned as generative of sensing, researching, and attending to the aftermath of political violence in ways that specifically allow for *not-knowing*, or that prompt a research positionality marked by frustration, lack, when sites may resist the researcher's desire to find out, to finally hold and thereby make present that which is terribly absent. The methodological pessimism posed by Navaro is therefore one that may effectively interrupt assumptions and expectations, turning one toward the jagged reality in which truth may never be found. Such a position may lead research practices, and the ethnographic imaginary, toward a consideration of not so much what is visible, evident, present, but what is absent—and importantly, what has been made absent or emptied out—and which calls for other forms of study.

This is not to suggest that evidentiary work, the capturing of facts, and the telling of what happened are less valuable—these are intensely needed. One may think of innumerable scenes of political violence in which living with ruins is unbearable, and where gaining truth is radically transformative; yet, negative methodology offers an important perspective, suggesting counterintuitive routes and techniques.

↩

One particular example Navaro cites is that of Saidiya Hartman, whose work on slave histories comes to challenge how it is that one may grasp the truth as to missing individuals, communities, cultures. Hartman addresses the cultural and epistemic violence perpetrated by the Atlantic slave trade—whose historical records are marked by absence, voids, by erased identities—a violence which "resides precisely in all the stories that we cannot know and that will never be recovered."[68] Rather than write a "coherent narrative," Hartman proceeds by way of the "incommensurability" between a commitment to history and what the archive does not provide, between the irretrievability of slave history and the drive toward narrative. Consequently, her work proceeds by way of a "narrative restraint" whose performance lends to a reconceptualization of knowledge production.

Concerns for how to give narrative to that which resists knowing finds further articulation in the poetic work *Zong!* by M. NourbeSe Philip, a work that equally attempts to address the violence of slavery. *Zong!* is a series of poems referencing

---

[67] Ibid., 164.
[68] Saidiya Hartman, quoted in Navaro, 164.

156   *Poetics of Listening*

an incident that occurred in the eighteenth century aboard an English slave ship; having set sail from the west coast of Africa for Jamaica, the ship *Zong* was severely delayed due to navigational errors. The delay led some of the "cargo of African slaves" to die of illness and lack of water; it further provoked the captain and crew to "throw 150 slaves overboard" in order to "preserve" the rest of the cargo, subsequently enabling the ship's owners to collect insurance on "lost property."[69] The incident led to a court case in which the insurers were obliged to pay the ship's owners for the loss. Philip's approach to addressing the violence of slavery, and the particular brutality of the *Zong* case, is to write by way of the legal documents, court case summary, and the insurance claim. These function as the basis for Philip's poems due to the fact that, as the author highlights, "the only reason why we have a record is because of insurance—a record of property."[70] The insurance document and legal texts are understood to both contain *and* mask the story of the *Zong* incident, and in doing so, they come to exacerbate the violent withdrawal of knowledge as to the identities of slaves: the slave has no name, rather, the documents state an "inventory of property," which leads Philip to suggest that *silence is its own language*. It is a language that must be written somehow, and which directs the author toward a particular strategy, one that moves from the loss of the name, legally held under as "lost property," toward an occupation of that absence—"to lock myself into this particular and peculiar discursive landscape in the belief that the story" of these murdered people "is locked in this text."[71]

Zong! is a writing that performs its own restriction, its own confinement; it pins itself down within the legal records, to pick apart the left-behind documents, selecting verbs and nouns from their lines in an act that parallels the way slaves were selected. These are *murderous gestures* enacted onto the documents, a cutting, a pulling apart, resulting in "semantic mayhem" from out of which signs of life may appear, giving outline to the "untold story that tells itself by not telling."[72] These are negative strategies that unsteadily mark the page with broken words and deep silences, flayed sentences and gagged meanings, and that stagger the author in her attempts: "The poems resist my attempt at meaning or coherence and, at times, I too approach the irrationality and confusion, if not

---

[69]   M. NourbeSe Philip, *Zong!* (Middleton, CT: Wesleyan University Press, 2008).
[70]   Ibid., 191.
[71]   Ibid.
[72]   Ibid., 194.

the madness, of a system that could enable, encourage even, a man to drown 150 people as a way to maximize profit."[73] Philip's unsettled and unsettling work arranges for an altogether different form of writing, one akin to Hartman's *narrative restraint*: to formulate a means, a path, a madness so as to *tell without telling*.

⌒

Hartman's and Philip's approaches to engaging with histories of slavery draw forward forms of writing or textualization that may help return to the discussion on rhetorical situations (elaborated through the work of Krista Ratcliffe and Kyle Jensen). As Ratcliffe and Jensen highlight, rhetorical situations—as situations marked by the urgencies of communication, of speaking, listening, writing, and narrating—are often underpinned by "unstated hauntings."[74] These are hauntings that carry within them an unfinished relation to history, where memories of people and places (and their erasures) call out for ways of telling, honoring, restoring, and that come to impact onto how we may communicate about often difficult issues. Rhetorical listening is positioned as a path for better acknowledging the sedimented layers of rhetorical situations, and the ways in which one may *write more carefully*, bringing attention or holding a relation to the unstated hauntings nested within given places, histories, communities. As Hartman and Philip both reveal, writing so as to memorialize what or who has gone missing demands a deep tussle with existing as well as withdrawn languages, archives, records, and histories. From narrative restraint to semantic mayhem, writing as listeners opens paths toward encountering the voices of the lost.

Writing comes to listen-against the archive, figuring techniques that cut across time and place, to find ways of living with histories of violence. As Ramon Amaro argues, the Black technical object, as the objectification of Black subjects by way of dominant systems, may cast back upon the system an image, a noise, a writing whose unrecognizability becomes the very means by which to rework a given logic. As with hip-hop's art of bricolage, Philip's poetic work not only stands as a cultural object but also introduces a technique, one of semantic mayhem. Such technique figures a textual performative that works at *telling what cannot be told*. The paradoxical, dissonant textual body of *Zong!* does much to short-circuit the historical record, drawing from its words, its legal code, a

---

[73] Ibid., 195.
[74] Ratcliffe and Jensen, *Rhetorical Listening in Action*, 79.

Black technical object whose facelessness (as the withdrawn identities of the African men, women, and children who perished) pushes against the given law of computation and the smooth procedures of the system at work.

༄

Following Navaro, and the poems of Philip, I may return to questions of power, and in what ways listening supports political processes, especially in fostering deeper attention to injustice. As Calder and Dobson highlight, in order for listening to do its political work, one must move from a position of *listening to* to that of *listening out for*—where listening out for moves people and power from the articulated presence of the audible, to that which is inaudible and unheard. As Navaro and Philip both demonstrate, when faced with the complexities of unfinished history it becomes imperative to orient toward the silences, the gaps, the withdrawn. These are realities that stagger the work of listening, that put listening into crisis, suggesting the necessity to integrate within its affirmative movements a degree of pessimism—*to listen-against listening itself.*

In following these negative strategies and methodologies, I'm led to pose the concept of *negative listening*, as a listening that may assist in approaching the inaudible and the unheard on their own terms; that delays listening as what *tries* to hear and, in doing so, may too easily fill in the gaps. Instead, a negative listening is positioned as what keeps one close to a more nuanced form of listening, an uncertain, pessimistic listening, especially in terms of recognizing how the inaudible may resound in the negative. A negative listening is listening in broken times, to listen by way of the ruins, the remains, and what they (with)hold; a listening adept at holding a relation to absence, attuning to traces left behind, and which can figure itself in the fissures, the silences, the voids. Negative listening moves among the fragments, to pick up stray frequencies, those which hover under or above hearing range, the vibrational murmur or deep humming that carries the dead. These are ways of listening that listen-against official narratives, to gather from the pieces a range of echoes carried over from those gone missing. Negative listening is shadowy work, supporting modes of dark navigation, especially when confronting erasures and a lack of documents, a blind trajectory into the madness Philip speaks of, and through which one may come to witness that which cannot be witnessed.

Negative listening, as I'm concerned to emphasize, is a form of listening that does not necessarily search for answers, to finally hear the voiceless or the missing; rather, it calls for staying in the gaps—to inhabit the difficult reality of the inaudible and the unheard. A listening that may travel into the waters, the unmarked graves, the emptied grounds of violence, in ways that re-politicize that which may come to pass as official history. These are listenings that attend to jagged stories, stolen breaths, denied voices; listenings that are urgently needed, and that contribute not only to the ongoing writing of history, but also to the understanding of listening's role in struggles for justice—to extend the limits of listenability toward that which is missing or ruined.

Negative listening is conceptualized as what may contribute to the methodological figures of rhetorical listening, of restorative circles, and what it means to be a field listener in situations of conflict; a negative listening that follows the traces, that acknowledges the gaps present within any public world or community, that also refuses to gloss over the cracks, the rough edges, the remains that silently call out. Here, listening may interrupt itself in its desire for fulfillment, for capture—to recognize the limits of listening, and how listening may overpower others or steer away from the messy reality of disagreement in favor of resolution. Listening, by way of a methodological pessimism, can stagger itself, forcing one to stay with the gaps, the broken circle, those instances when communities may never be restored. These are difficult listenings, and yet, they are crucial, leading one to attend to the debris; to find strategies for going on, ever-more carefully, attuning one's listening to the shards.

Following these perspectives, I'm led to think *political listening* by way of a poetic position. Such a position is understood as emerging by way of the potential found in a range of methodologies, from restorative to negative, from deep to restrained, from scratched to self-actualized; these methodologies that aid in conceptualizing ways of empowering people in working through social and historical, epistemic and rhetorical challenges. While poetics may be perceived as out of place when contending with political violence, I'm encouraged to highlight its significance—for poetics, to my mind, gives traction to a listening approach adept at attuning precisely to the present absent, the immaterial material, the audible inaudible informing any political process; that opens a capacity for noticing the dreaming background of an organized assembly while giving recognition to articulated demands; that helps in acknowledging and nurturing caring networks, that aids in bringing the political down so as to synchronize personal lives and civic institutions; that knows of the unstated hauntings informing any constituent body; a listening approach that respects the borders of others, that recognizes the urgencies around protection, while keeping an ear attuned to the cry for allies.

Furthermore, poetics names the potentiality of writing *otherwise*, about history, loss, place and people, to figure a rhetoric, a discourse, that may rework the rules of meaning and, importantly, the structure of a prevailing logic—a poetics that, as Philip's highlights, allows for pulling at the legal document, the archive, to deploy a certain "semantic mayhem" so as to give room to the vibrational depths, the shadowy domain, the fragments of history, all of which cut against rational traditions. This is a form of epistemic justice that violates the held-in-place logic of presence/absence, heard/unheard, living/dead, opening up to that which challenges reason; and which, as Philip's does, tears at the order of the law (and the archival-machinic code) so as to follow the unhearable, to face the faceless, keeping hold of the remains and where they may lead.

Listening as Emergent Strategy

Listening works at specificity, providing an extremely important means for attending to the diversity of a social world. It helps deepen acknowledgment of the different views and experiences, concerns and values, held by individuals and communities. It does this by also affording ways of moving over lines often separating subject and object, human and more-than-human, us and them. It is not to say that listening automatically results in the overcoming of crisis, or in agreement and the resolution of conflict. Rather, the affirmative influence of listening is expressed in its capacity to enhance a process of care and consideration, affording room for a plurality of views; from the present to the absent, the background to the foreground, listening supplies a means for an integrative, global view and understanding, and which influences the scene of political struggle by inserting an interval, a pause, a patient work, that suggests paths forward. In its diplomatic force, its feminist rhythms of connection, its rhetorical capacity to address the complexities of history and the gray zones of meaning, listening works at creating possibilities.

The listening I'm emphasizing is a listening positioned to *make a change*; listening as an "emergent strategy" following adrienne maree brown.[75]

---

[75] adrienne maree brown, *Emergent Strategy: Shaping Change, Changing Worlds* (Chico, CA: AK press, 2017).

Emergent strategies are strategies "for building complex patterns and systems of change through relatively small interactions" and that come from "movements intentionally practicing [an] adaptive, relational way of being, on our own and with others."[76] These are strategies that follow examples set by the natural world, by the ever-changing, interdependent web of relations whose rhythms express *an adaptive, relational way of being*. Such ecological patterns and movements give lesson as to how one may live as well as shape change, following the profound energy and creative dynamism of emergence. For brown, emergence is a model for how one may participate in a greater pattern of connections, to recognize oneself and one's actions as contributing to the ongoing aliveness of an ecosystem, and from which strategies can be nurtured for how we may "intentionally change in ways that grow our capacity to embody the just and liberated worlds we long for."[77] These are strategies following the generative flow and flowering of emergence, for "emergence emphasizes critical connections over critical mass, building authentic relationships, listening with all the senses of the body and mind."[78]

It is along these emergent lines that I sense in listening a diplomatic force that takes guidance from a relational way of being. The diplomatic force of listening supports ways of attending to difference, acknowledging contrasting views as well as uneven power; it incites a move beyond often entrenched configurations of self and other, us and them, a listening supportive of critical connections and that works at building authentic relationships; a listening that gives room to the dreaming background present within any formal operation of governance. The power of such listening echoes with Leonard Waks's concept of "apophatic listening," as the capacity to suspend *a priori* meanings, judgments and expectations, so as to truly encounter and contend with unfamiliar views within a dialogical process.[79] Apophatic listening returns us to Deep Democracy's notion of the *gift of conflict*, as what affords opportunities for growth, for an enriched psychosocial world, for knowing otherwise by way of the experiences and views of others.

◠

---

[76] Ibid., 2.

[77] Ibid., 3.

[78] Ibid.

[79] See Dobson on Leonard Waks, *Listening for Democracy*, 67–8. See also Leonard Waks, "Listening and Questioning: The Apophatic/Cataphatic Distinction Revisited," *Learning Inquiry*, vol. 1, no. 2 (August 2007):153–61.

This is not to forget, or overlook, the structural challenges and violences that shape zones of conflict as well as spaces where listening is afforded. As brown reminds, community work and social movements are riddled with tension, conflict, disagreement, with internal fights as well as negotiations with greater structures and systems of power. Emergent strategies, as brown highlights, are strategies that require resilience, shared labor, that are founded on vulnerability, taking responsibility and being responsive, and that acknowledge conflict as part of process. Therefore, they come to necessitate a great deal of emotional, affective, and physical awareness, and are built upon an intensified understanding of interdependency and what obligates us to each other.

In her article "We Are Divided," Isabelle Stengers offers a critical questioning of capitalism and its impact on the planet. Her argument is centered around recognizing the degree to which capitalism, as an overarching governing ideology and system, institutionalizes an "operational logic" that degrades our capacity to participate and care for the interdependency underpinning life. Stengers elaborates a critical opposition by posing diplomacy as a path toward reclaiming interdependency as a guiding formulation. It is the "diplomatic arts" that afford ways of working together, of finding agreement or compromise on divisive issues, and that function as the foundation for cooperation. Fundamental to the diplomatic arts is the relation to what Stengers underscores as "obligation"—or, that which obligates us to each other. "To be obligated is to know one is indebted to something other than oneself for what one is."[80] This integrates recognition as to the interdependent realities shaping relationships, communities, and environments—that the capacity for life and its flourishing is beholden to an intensely interwoven ecology of relations and practices, not to mention material sources and resources. Extending this toward greater political arenas, obligation can function to help guarantee a level of cooperation, because it is founded on recognizing the degree to which all those involved benefit from a shared world. Such cooperative possibilities are put into motion by way of the diplomatic arts, not only because they help nurture ways of working together, of reaching agreement and compromise; importantly, "the art of the diplomat requires hesitation."[81] Hesitation, as Stengers highlights, helps foster a process of consideration, especially as to proposed agreements, treaties or laws; by pausing to consider, one also tables the motion before a group of peers or experts,

---

[80] Isabelle Stengers, "We Are Divided," *e-flux journal* #114 (12/2020): 1.
[81] Ibid.

allowing for questioning and debate. In short, the diplomat moves between nations, communities, and agencies, presenting a given motion or agreement as an "object of collective consultation."[82]

The art of consultation central to diplomacy is precisely what has gone missing within current systems of capitalistic power Stengers argues. For capitalism "unravels relationships of interdependence," replacing them instead with "chains of dependence," which become unsustainable configurations. These developments crucially undermine the capacity to *feel interdependency* as what grounds us, and that calls us into a greater sense for what obligates us to each other. These are feelings that must be "reactivated" and which may further support the "reassertion" of the importance of the diplomat as the one who conveys "not models or arguments but activators of the imagination, incentives to expand the scope of the possible reinvention of new ways to formulate problems."[83]

In mapping the importance of the diplomat, Stengers seeks to challenge the ongoingness of capitalistic violence as it degrades and destroys the planet; and furthermore, how it has contributed to installing an ideological-material foundation that turns us away from feelings of interdependency. While hesitation and delay may at times be the very things standing in the way of halting violence and war, I follow Stengers' arguments as what may enhance understanding listening's role within political process, for listening is central to feeling interdependency as well as ensuring a considered process of consultation. Listening itself may be conceived as an act of hesitation, a hesitant position that staggers the often singular pace and direction of concerted action. Listening, as I've tried to highlight, and which I sense additionally in Stengers's idea of the diplomat, is action *otherwise*—articulating agency as a form of radical receptivity, as the ability to hold time and space for things to be said and life stories to be heard; listening as a gesture that engenders paths of connection and cooperation, that opens up and opens out—and in doing so, figures an interval, one that affords greater sensitivity for all that's at stake, that brings the political down to an embodied level, to better feel the interdependent realities and how we may act in accordance, as protectors of a shared world.

‿

The emergent strategies highlighted by brown, and the feelings of interdependency underpinning what Stengers identifies as the diplomatic arts,

---

[82] Ibid., 2.
[83] Ibid., 4.

must include, following the negative methodology of Navaro, a sensitivity for the "unstated hauntings" and "silenced histories" that influence the movements of politics and public struggles. Relationships of interdependence, as manifesting a diplomatic art, are relationships that connect across the living *and* the dead, the visible *and* the invisible; these are "activators of imagination" that draw from the knowledges and languages buried in the soil, or lost to the oceans, and whose persistent resonances can aid in finding "new ways to formulate problems," especially in terms of contending with the ongoingness of political violence with its *necropolitical* features.[84] What I'm keen to suggest is that what constitutes arenas of power are always tensed by the marginalized as well as the missing or killed. To listen-against is not only to interrupt existing hegemonic orders so as to give room for the previously unheard. It is additionally to *destitute* what counts as dominant power by turning attention to the disappeared, the ruined, the lost; the faceless, voiceless absences that make a claim onto relationships of interdependence; and that may help in bringing the political down to the embodied level.

Is not listening the capacity to attune equally to the present *and* the absent, to the voiced articulations of persons *and* the unsounded traces of the missing? Listening as what knows by way of a radical receptivity the silent dimensions always contouring time and place, voice and meaning? These are poetic capacities through which we may know without knowing, hear without hearing, speak without speaking, and that keeps one close to feelings of interdependency in all their breadth. And which must contain a listening out for what the dead say, for they are crucial in formulating a future to come.

The diplomatic arts, as what enables a process of consultation, must be understood to traffic not only in the agreements and disagreements passing among the living, but in the nebulous, shadowy, dreaming backgrounds full of lost souls and disappeared persons that forever reside in the folds of the present. And which participate in the interdependent journeys defining the human story. It is along these lines that I sense the urgency to turn our (political) listening to the negative worlds such backgrounds and absences define, and which pull at my body, the social body, the body politic, and the bodies yet to come. For what they provide is a crucial anchor, keeping us close to a past not yet memorialized, a past whose remains help orient the work of emergent strategies, for navigating

---

[84] For more on the necropolitical, see Achille Mbembe, *Necropolitics* (Durham, NC: Duke University Press, 2019).

the troubles and honoring our and others' vulnerabilities. These negative worlds echo with what Julietta Singh terms "the ghost archives."[85] Archives which contain only pieces of a larger story, and which are brought to life, or held in place, by the wishing and desiring to understand more, to listen for "everything that remains right there, but just out of reach."[86] These are ghostly, negative listenings that attend to the ongoingness of a past that is far from over. Such listenings refigure dominant (Western) temporal orders defined as linear, as future- and goal-oriented, where pasts are pushed under or back, to be left behind. As I've been concerned to emphasize, listening enables ways of inhabiting multiple temporal configurations, where all that is carried within a body, a person, a community reverberates in the present. These are the inner voices, the intergenerational stories, the dreaming and remembering that shimmer across the sensible. And that contribute with deep force to our social and political worlds.

⌒

Returning to Philip and Hartman, and their focus on the irretrievable identities of slaves, I'm led to wonder and even sense that when turning to such impossible writing, such impossible research, it may not be that the dead and the missing need us to recover some grain of truth, to follow their traces beyond historical record and knowledge; rather, it might be that these are relationships in which we are just as dependent upon their irretrievable identities, those stories of lost and killed others—they may, in fact, come to rescue the living, pulling us into the horror as well as the humanity of ourselves. Such a negative form of knowledge is precisely what contributes to the art of consultation, to help weigh and weigh again decision-making. Behind the diplomat, standing just behind, are those persons whose haunting absence productively clouds the independent position, giving us the courage to hesitate, to listen, to take counsel from *everything that remains right there, but just out of reach.*

The Power of Listening

In reflecting upon listening as a question of power, I've been interested to demonstrate listening's contribution to political processes, showing how it aids in deepening democracy and fostering peace-building. From listening to others,

---

[85] Julietta Singh, *No Archive Will Restore You* (Goleta, CA: 3Ecologies Books/Immediations, 2018).
[86] Ibid., 96.

166   *Poetics of Listening*

so as to work through pressing issues, to listening out for the unheard in ways that challenge established policies and approaches, listening figures as part of the call for political action, underpinning the work of change. While voice and speaking are often positioned as the driving forces of politics, listening is vital for enhancing how it is expressions of dissent or rage, demand or need, are taken on board and given fair consideration. Listening shows the degree to which governments or institutional establishments are responsive—to listen is to not only demonstrate concern, it is to show a willingness to change as well. As Dobson poses, "listening is, at one and the same time, an expression of power and a means of redistributing it."[87] This extends to practices that work at reconfiguring the dynamics of conflict and related enactments of diplomacy. Restorative circles and feminist policies seek to challenge the dominant (patriarchal, militarized) structures that understand conflict as a question of defense, and even punishment, rather than restoration. These are practices and positions that can aid in the diplomatic arts which, as Isabelle Stengers argues, contribute to renewing feelings of interdependency. Across these different arenas, listening is an active force, where it not only allows for considered dialogue and the building of trust but also deepens democracy by supporting the necessary inner work essential to the project of politics. To gain awareness of the cultural logics, the dreaming backgrounds, the absences and unfinished histories always standing behind articulated viewpoints and the actions of others, not to mention the macropolitical movements of nation-states, is a fundamental part of how listening contributes.

↬

Within the analysis of political listening I'm developing, from the negative to the emergent to the apophatic, *feelings of interdependency* are given greater traction. If listening furthers one's ability to attend to inner and outer worlds, fostering greater relational understanding by way of a certain radical receptivity, it can be appreciated to help with the reactivation of the diplomatic arts Stengers finds missing today. As I elaborate in Chapter 3, listening affords keeping close to the world of feelings; it is what brings awareness by way of the felt sense, an empathic, experiential knowing that allows for working through the affective currents passing across and through bodies. These are aspects that can be brought into engaging feelings of interdependency as part of the diplomatic arts. Listening

---

[87]   Dobson, *Listening for Democracy*, 58.

may insert a gap or interval onto the ongoingness of things; it is the necessary break or art of pause within dialogue that allows for more considered exchange, shifting the pace of debate with an intensity of concern. These are aspects that support the diplomatic arts, as an art of consultation and a weighing of decision-making. And that work at bringing the political down to an embodied level—to wield a language of connection, keeping individual lives and governmental structures *in sync*.

Moreover, these are dynamics that manifest the power of listening, as what intervenes with consideration, that conditions the movements of dialogue with a patient work, that affords the making of new social, historical narratives from leftover fragments. From the shadowy to the spectral, the watery to the cosmic, listening is adept at recognizing, sensing, acknowledging, even communing with what otherwise may go unremarked or be forgotten. It may discern singularities, it may work at specificity and situatedness, but it also captures correspondences, sympathies, affinities across bodies, meanings and worlds. It evokes a holistic view, a language of connection, recognizing each part along with an ever-shifting whole: *it attends to who speaks as well as who is absent*. It may be along the lines of listening-against that listening can do much in navigating impasse, rupture, broken harmony and to attend to the gaps, the remains, so as to aid in the emergent work needed to shape change.

$\backsim$

Returning to my opening reflections on Jacques Attali's analysis of noise and power, techniques of listening afford ways of surveilling populations, noting articulations of outspoken dissent, probing the movements of data to identify any questionable signals and signs, and which may even work at instilling a general fear as to who or what may be listening. In contrast, as Dobson argues, listening is profoundly political in so far as it gives indication as to the *responsiveness* of government toward its people: listening is central to the processes by which marginalized or dispossessed communities may gain entry into the constituted arenas of power, signaling the degree to which dominant power may bend. Listening, in this regard, can be cast as a power in itself: it both supports forms of control, management, domination as well as the work of conflict resolution, restorative process, deep democracy.

In considering these perspectives, finding ways of nurturing listening cultures in support of the power of people, especially those at risk and who need to be heard, emerges as essential. To be heard, to demand to be listened to, to listen out for those voices or views that reside outside dominant culture, can be appreciated to give weight to the need for listening practices. If listening is fundamental to the dynamics of power and politics, it behooves us to conceive of more pronounced structures of listening—what Jim Macnamara calls "architectures of listening"[88]—so as to enhance listening cultures across society. These are architectures as techniques and practices in themselves, that function not simply as physical spaces and environments, but more importantly, as structured moments, policies, and strategies in which listening is brought to the fore on an organizational level. Such proposals seek to integrate listening more overtly as part of institutional structures and public procedures in ways that enhance collaborative engagement and the "reinvigoration of the public sphere."[89] If listening, or listening-against, underpins the move toward re-politicization, which is generally a call for a more robust consideration of diverse voices and views, developing the means for building listening cultures seems strikingly crucial. These are initiatives and perspectives that contribute to fostering a *listening citizenry*. Being a listening citizen supports not only the ability to perform as a political subject within an established arena of power, it furthermore helps in keeping attuned to the power of listening itself.

---

[88] Jim Macnamara, *Creating an 'Architecture of Listening' in Organizations: The Basis of Engagement, Trust, Healthy Democracy, Social Equity, and Business Sustainability* (Sydney, NSW: University of Technology Sydney, 2015).

[89] Ibid., 8.

5

Listening-across: Ecological Thinking, Biopoetics, and Planetary Practices

In examining research and literature on ecological thinking and environmental crisis, I'm interested in the degree to which listening is at times positioned as what may enable fuller consideration of the more-than-human, where listening forms a pathway of radical connection that extends across species and matters—and further, how listening influences planetary practices. This appears, for example, in Anna Tsing's critical call for an "art of noticing," which is underscored as the basis for a research methodology sensitive to the intensely dissonant weave or "patchiness" of human and more-than-human coexistence.[1] Importantly, for Tsing the art of noticing is founded on the capacity to attune to the "polyphony" of globalized life, including the particular sites and scenes of precarious struggle constituted by multiple forces, practices, species, and lives. These are sites of "disturbed ecologies" and ruination, where capitalist production, migration flows, community resilience, violence, greed, and individual survival entwine, to forge ever-uncertain ways of living and enduring—what Tsing highlights as forms of collaborative survival in precarious times.[2] Tracking disturbed ecologies is to immerse our knowledge practices in a cacophonous world of "contaminated diversity" and "encounter-based collaboration"; it is to demand an "open imagination" as to our current global realities, the messy stories and histories that resist gestures of "summing up." As Tsing argues, it is imperative that we start to listen, for "it is in listening to that cacophony of troubled stories that we might encounter our best hopes for precarious survival."[3]

---

[1] Anna Lowenhaupt Tsing, *The Mushroom at the End of the World: On the Possibility of Life in Capitalist Ruins* (Princeton: Princeton University Press, 2015).

[2] Ibid.

[3] Ibid., 34.

Additionally, Cormac Cullinan poses listening as a means for recognizing the rhythms of planetary systems, the natural cycles and dynamic movements that are expressive of biodiverse living—or what Cullinan emphasizes as the "Earth Community." "If we want to participate fully in the dances of the Earth Community we need to listen carefully for the beat and adjust our rhythm and timing accordingly."[4] By way of listening, as the author suggests, one may better align with the living laws and holistic systems governing nature.

As I've been concerned to propose, the relational awareness prompted by listening is not only transformative on the level of personal experience; rather, listening opens onto ways of knowing. From processes of self-reflection and inner voicing to the dialogical work performed in learning from others, from somatic well-being and knowledge of the body to the political struggles in which it becomes essential to *listen out for* the marginalized, listening generates epistemic possibilities. Accordingly, I'm concerned to emphasize an ecological model of listening to better appreciate the affordances listening offers in terms of gaining a planetary perspective. Finding ways of bringing human-centered systems of governance in line with natural laws for Cullinan takes guidance by way of listening's ability to sense beyond the human, fostering *feelings of interdependency*. If listening *exposes* us to others, to make one susceptible to the impingement of an outside, while acting to bridge the often tense separations defining communities by nurturing affinities, it necessarily accents a deep relation to place, environment, land—what Susan Raffo describes as *the ground under our feet*.[5] And which Cullinan also emphasizes in his call for a paradigm shift in systems of governance: "This relationship between human and land is fundamental. It is a relationship that shapes the minds and hearts of individuals and the identity of nations. Changing how we understand and recognize this relationship is at the heart of shifting to a new governance paradigm."[6]

The expanded orientation prompted by listening gives traction to attending to the nature of a given environment and to work through one's place within such an environment. Importantly, this is not only on the level of sensing, rather, listening impacts and influences what it means to be in place. If listening connects, it also threads; if listening opens, it also nurtures. And if listening

---

[4] Cormac Cullinan, *Wild Law: A Manifesto for Earth Justice*, second edition (Cambridge: Green Books, 2011), 137.

[5] Susan Raffo, *Liberated to the Bone: Histories, Bodies, Futures* (Chico, CA: AK Press, 2022), 12.

[6] Cullinan, *Wild Law*, 142.

closes, it does so in ways that limit the exposure of oneself to a given environment. Such views find elaboration in Yves Citton's critical work on attention. For Citton, it becomes imperative within today's attentional economies to *take back* attention as an ecological capacity and force.[7] As part of this view, Citton highlights the importance of fostering "reflexive attention" so as to support ways of questioning how attention is directed and framed—to contend with dominant lines of orientation. This is founded on recognizing how attention is profoundly influenced by others—attention is *steered* by way of all we may encounter within a given environment, from familial, social values and languages to systems of representation and the structures around which meanings are circulated and instrumentalized in ways that shape our attentional capacities. For Citton, attention is a political question that has intensified within the context of an information society with its expansive technologies. To engage the politics of attention, Citton calls for a shift from the economy to the *ecology of attention*, where attention is not paid but given, and through which we may engage attention as a joint endeavor. Through such a shift, the ecology of attention may support changing the dynamics of attention from transaction to transformation, from exchange to engagement, from information to intimacy, accentuating the relational value of attention. As Simone Weil poses, "attention is the rarest and purest form of generosity."[8]

From reflexive to joint attention, the ecology of attention speaks toward the ways in which I'm approaching a poetics of listening, and in this chapter can assist in detailing listening's influence on fostering planetary practices. Part of such work includes engaging with questions of epistemology, and the legacies of settler-colonialism and related knowledge regimes founded on traditions of Western science. To work at an ecology of attention, as what can nurture transformation, engagement, and intimacy, it becomes essential to address epistemic injustices, to carve out new attentional times and spaces by which to enrich a shared world. These are specifically aimed at challenging the drift toward "cognitive consonance" as what lessens experiences of difference, undermining the capacity to inhabit a *world of many worlds*. In contrast, what is needed are labs of experimentation in which multiple knowledges and languages can coinhabit a given space, opening onto experiencing the *dissonant* coexistence of multiple

---

[7] Yves Citton, *The Ecology of Attention* (Cambridge: Polity Press, 2019).
[8] Simone Weil, letter to Joë Bousquet, 13 April 1942, in Simone Pétrement, *Simone Weil: A Life* (New York: Pantheon Books, 1976).

ways of sensing and responding, practicing and relating. This is furthered in Anna Tsing's *The Mushroom at the End of the World*, in which the author works at an *art of noticing*—an art supportive of configuring a narrative of multiple strands, voices, views, and living things. Tsing's is a storying whose attentional performance guides readers into the polyphony she identifies as defining of planetary life and whose dissonant ordering breathes as a complex assemblage of people and place, creatures and matters.

⌐

In what way does listening impart paths toward recognition not only of human others, but the planetary lives and living systems that surround? Is listening equally a tool for nurturing reflexive attention and the joint experimentation essential for gaining awareness as to the planetary presences that constitute the very matters and processes that make life possible? To give room for the dissonances by which to know of difference and to share in the polyphony of multiple worlds? These are questions I'm concerned to follow, finding in listening—with its poetic ground and sky, its art of noticing—a means for not only attending to self and other but also the matters and energies of which one is profoundly a part. To *listen-across* is to gain knowledge as to the worlds within the world that define the nature of our coexistence with others. Such ecological listening works at upsetting an anthropocentric worldview, to help highlight the fact that humans are not the only ones listening. There are many others doing listening, and doing it in ways that far exceed the shape and scale of human listening. These are listenings that do much to highlight the human as *other*, as one of many, and from which it becomes possible to understand oneself as a modest guest of this planetary world. As Gary Snyder outlines in *The Practice of the Wild*, becoming aware of one's own position as a guest of nature is to feel by way of all the eyes and ears that follow, from out of the bustling woods and living waters, one's human presence.[9]

The lessons learned by way of the natural world, that support acknowledging the sacred bonds that pass across all living things, become the basis for an "etiquette of freedom" as Snyder poses. It is to "acknowledge that each of us at the table will eventually be part of the meal,"[10] a view which is not simply pragmatic, but which can reinforce a feeling for biological, planetary coexistence.

---

[9] Gary Snyder, *The Practice of the Wild: Essays* (Berkeley: Counterpoint, 2020).
[10] Ibid., 20.

Biophonic Vitality, Sounded Creations

In his book, *The Great Animal Orchestra*, audio recordist Bernie Krause suggests that natural soundscapes, with their complex range of sonorities, speak to us as fellow creatures; the sounds of wild life, in fact, stand as the ground from which all music and language emerge, lending to the existence of a single "sonorant family."

> This is the tuning of the great animal orchestra, a revelation of the acoustic harmony of the wild, the planet's deeply connected expression of natural sounds and rhythm. It is the baseline for what we hear in today's remaining wild places, and it is likely that the origins of every piece of music we enjoy and word we speak come, at some point, from this collective voice.[11]

Suggested in Krause's environmental work is an understanding of sound as expressive of life itself. Through the capacity to sound—from underwater clicks and tones to forest chirps and shouts—animal life attracts, threatens, connects, and calls, maintaining itself amid a greater *biophony*. This extends to questions of territory, where the ability for species to signal to each other is key. As Krause observes, the "orchestra" of the natural soundscape is one in which species carve out their own "acoustic niche" within a spectrum of frequencies. A healthy biome will therefore consist of a "dense and diverse" soundscape, where each species or "voice" comes to occupy a given bandwidth within a broader acoustic sphere. Soundscapes are thus organized, orchestral, and are heard as processes in which natural ecological systems find balance. Accordingly, through an analysis of recorded soundscapes over time, Krause argues that it becomes observable when a given biome is undergoing change, especially when affected by human intervention. As he highlights, "biophonies from stressed, endangered, or altered biomes tend to show little organizational structure."[12]

Krause provides an entry into the sound world as a vitalist, planetary ecology full of natural intelligence, and whose compositional complexity expresses a living system dense with polyphony. This is further elaborated in David George Haskell's *Sounds Wild and Broken*. Listening to the world around, from metropolises boiling with human noise to vast forests teeming with an array of

---

[11] Bernie Krause, *The Great Animal Orchestra: Finding the Origins of Music in the World's Wild Places* (New York: Back Bay Books, 2013), 10.

[12] Ibid., 80.

species, Haskell maps sound as *generative and creative*—from "waves in ancient plasma, the songs of crickets and whales" through to "the babble of young sparrows and humans, the tones of human breath in mammoth ivory," all of which highlight sounds not only as events but as creators.[13] From the slow emergence of the universe, with its oscillating vibrations of energy, to the sounding of voice and song, and the musics that figure as spiritual connectors to the world around, sound is emphasized as fundamental to planetary life, from the microbial to the cosmological. For Haskell, it therefore becomes imperative that humans learn to listen to the incredible range of planetary voices, for sound teaches us about the ephemeral nature of life itself; it locates us in the ongoingness of its passing, the fleeting animation defining each moment, thereby keeping us sensitive to existence in all its power and vulnerability.

⤸

Practices of environmental audio recording find a point of elaborated reference in the field of sound art. Bringing attention to the world around—from urban territories to natural ecosystems, along with all the entangled and enmeshed junctures between—a great deal of sound artworks are driven by a fascination with existing environments, as well as in creating environments in which sound can be experienced through diverse manifestations. These are works that find in sound a vital materiality, a matter constitutive of and constituted by living worlds, and that further aspire to *narratives of creation*: that seek to *sound out* emergent worlds, giving animation to what is there and also what might be.

Following upon the creative force of sound, works of sound art often harness, amplify, and rhythm into being a living system, one that seeds and grows experiential situations of listening grounded in relations to place. These include the recording of a vast range of sites, as well as other ways of collecting and presenting sound. Such modes of work echo Snyder's practice of the wild, in terms of finding ways of attuning to the "living mind" of a planetary consciousness, where one's sense of self is felt as environmentally shaped, as touched by and participant within a greater weave of natural intelligence. By way of such an expanded perspective, sound is posited as a vitalist force that lends to an ecological position; from the vibrational to the resonant, the rhythmic to the echoic, sound opens onto ways of honoring existing ecologies as well as generating new paths of connection.

---

[13] David George Haskell, *Sounds Wild and Broken* (London: Faber & Faber, 2022), 177.

Ariel Bustamante, an artist from Chile currently living and working in Bolivia, emphasizes the ways in which sound offers opportunities or vocabularies for elaborating an environmental sensitivity. In recent years, this has led the artist more fully toward listening as a practice in itself, especially in terms of its capacity to afford ways of noticing natural forces.

> Not that long ago, I lived alone in the Atacama desert for almost one year. In this uninhabited area, I spent infinite hours listening to the winds, walking behind them, searching for patterns and forms. After a while, they seemed to become something else than just physical phenomena, at that point they appeared to have their own desires and preoccupations, and a strong urge to talk and be touched.[14]

The experiences Bustamante encountered in the desert led the artist into a deeper relational practice, one finding guidance from the land, the desert, and the wind. Learning to *walk with the wind*, for Bustamante, was to learn of the sacred forces to which one's own presence is held, and that impart their messages, their gifts and stories, as paths to be followed.

In collaboration with writer and musician German Lazaro from the Uru-Chipaya Indigenous community in Bolivia, and held as part of *The Listening Biennial* in 2023, Bustamante organized a *Thami paxs̀*, an intimate gathering for *knowing the winds*. As the collaborators outline, the gathering took guidance from *Soqo Pawlu*, a wind-person that circulates across the shared deserts of Bolivia and Chile, managing the air currents across the region. By offering an intimate space, one supported through the affectionate sharing of touch and voice, participants were invited to follow the wind, *Soqo Pawlu*, deepening contact with the movement of its currents. Bustamante and Lazaro craft a listening practice for sensing and honoring the winds that continually pass through the environment and ourselves, that carry the voices of memories and other species, and that ferry messages sent from across the deserts. These are currents that open us to "alternative routes to cross different types of borders," from national to racial, geographic to disciplinary—routes that expose us to trans-human, trans-species coexistence.[15]

---

[14] Ariel Bustamante, statement made as part of his participation in the artist residency program at Schloss Solitude, Stuttgart, Germany. See https://www.akademie-solitude.de/en/person/ariel-bustamante/ (accessed July 2024).

[15] Ariel Bustamante and German Lazaro, artist statement as part of *The Listening Biennial* 2023. See https://listeningbiennial.net/biennial-editions/second-edition (accessed July 2024).

176 *Poetics of Listening*

Bustamante's creative approach can be appreciated as participating within a greater culture of listening practices, in which sound is positioned as an extensive material, energetic basis for connecting across worlds, one that is never simply audible, but rather opens onto an affective, experiential dimension. This includes a deep engagement with places and people, with diverse environments and the diversity of living forms—and where listening becomes a channel, a connector, a methodology for conversing, communing, or walking with earth beings. These are gestures and techniques that accentuate the inherently vitalist nature of sound, and that follow ways of knowing shaped by listening, giving way to *narratives of creation*—to sing with the winds of the earth.

↜

Importantly, sound not only affords processes of survival, in terms of staying alert as to the movements of predators within an environment, or keeping attuned to the tonalities of place and community; but it also enables spiritual connection and the articulation of belief. To hear the voices of a greater living world, from animal calls to the nuanced movements of water and wind, is central to receiving divine messages as well as staying connected to the sacred. This is carried in the metaphoric, material relation to sound as an energetic, vitalist force that passes across physical and metaphysical worlds, whose concrete yet ephemeral qualities open a potent channel for spiritual transmission and ancestral connection. To receive and transmit messages, to create music and song, to pray and give thanks, all express ways by which sacred bonds are honored, and which position sound as an energetic carrier of the mystical as well as participant within models of the universe. Echoing David George Haskell's concern for sound as an energetic foundation to planetary matters, the philosophical notion of the "music of the spheres" also speaks to sound's primary positioning, and how "harmonic tunings" act as an organizational structure spanning from the cosmic to the molecular. Listening, as Joachim Ernst-Berendt emphasizes, is therefore our most "vital sense" in that it functions as a "gateway" to comprehending the universe.[16]

---

[16] Joachim Ernst-Berendt, *The Third Ear: On Listening to the World* (New York: Owl Book, 1992), 36. Ernst-Berendt's celebratory view of sound as the basis of natural formation, as vitality itself that spawns the growth and organization of the planet, and that affords a sense for the multidimensional qualities of experience, echoes with a greater scientific, philosophical history stemming from Pythagoras and the notion of the harmony of the planets. Pythagorian philosophy argues for an understanding of universal harmony based on ratios, where consonance is derived through

In *Braiding Sweetgrass*, Potawatomi botanist, writer, and educator Robin Wall Kimmerer reflects upon the lines separating Western science and Indigenous understandings of the earth. This includes a pronounced difference when it comes to sensing natural environments, in which the latter recognizes and honors these as full of living things, from animals to trees, lands to waters. Seeing and hearing, touching and tasting, moving and smelling all come to act as a fundamental ground of knowledge and connection, one shaped by a profound understanding of nature as sentient. Kimmerer invites readers into a rich fabric of interconnectedness, one that is resonant and conversant. "In the old times, our elders say, the trees talked to each other. They'd stand in their own council and craft a plan. But scientists decided long ago that plants were deaf and mute, locked in isolation without communication."[17] The communicative capacity of plants signals but one area in which the natural world comes to life, especially in ways that challenge traditions of Western science (and dominant views onto nature as mute).[18]

Through emphasizing the sentience of nature, Kimmerer raises ethical, political questions; she engages ecological struggles and environmental issues with a sense for nurturing care for the richly interwoven ways in which humans are embedded in planetary relations. For Kimmerer, such recognition of the living planet must move science toward a deeper appreciation for the sacredness of life itself. "How, in our modern world, can we find our way to understand the earth as a gift again, to make our relation with the world sacred again?"[19] In response, the author provides a tapestry of stories, meditations, and thoughtful anecdotes, all of which speak toward a life attuned to the sacredness of the earth. This includes a relation to ceremony, where gestures of thanks and acknowledgment, as well as practices of care that contribute to a reciprocity of gift-giving, articulate

---

distance and interval, and the measurement of points along a string. Moving from observations of planetary orbits to the scales of musical harmony, Pythagorian thought is based on finding connection between music and a universal system of proportion and balance. Music, in fact, becomes the fundamental arena through which natural order is expressed as a harmonic whole.

[17] Robin Wall Kimmerer, *Braiding Sweetgrass: Indigenous Wisdom, Scientific Knowledge and the Teachings of Plants* (London: Penguin Books, 2020), 19.

[18] For an insightful consideration of bioacoustic research on the communicativeness of plants and its relation to creative sound art practices, see David Vélez, "Listening with plants: Contesting Coloniality in Sonic Art Collaboration with Vegetal Life," paper presented at *Soundings: Assemblies of Listenings and Voices across the Souths* (Berlin, August 2022).

[19] Kimmerer, *Braiding Sweetgrass*, 31.

178   *Poetics of Listening*

greater responsiveness and responsibility. Ceremony names a form of attention that keeps one awake to the living nature surrounding, and that enacts forms of planetary housekeeping.

Participating in the entangled nature of living things, and caring for what one takes from the earth and gives in return, finds support in one's capacity to listen. "To be native to a place we must learn to speak its language," begins Kimmerer's engagement with being at home in the world, with finding home through participation in its languages. Learning the language of places is founded on the capacity to listen, where understanding is based on attending to what is there, to how a given place is expressive of a greater web of relations. Importantly, listening allows for acknowledging the limits of oneself, to search for guidance from the environment—as a listener, one becomes observant, attentive, a modest guest, and which lends to more responsive ways of *doing science*. "Science and traditional knowledge may ask different questions and speak different languages, but they may converge when they both truly listen to the plants."[20]

Listening-across acts as a step toward learning the languages of places; it emerges as an ongoing education in how to recognize the complex web of life while also nurturing ways of participating, to honor and also celebrate the gifts of nature: to figure an ethics, a ceremonial responsibility, to invent ways of receiving and giving back. It is by way of these reflections, and the call for taking back attention from the economies that quicken the pace on environmental devastation, that I'm moved to appreciate listening as *ceremonial*. If, as Anna Tsing highlights, listening opens onto ways of attending to the polyphony of planetary relations, to learn the languages of places, from the trees to the winds, and to find ways of contributing to the web of life with its complex entanglements, it seems important to foster a view onto listening as *gift-giving*—as a practice of reciprocity. This finds further expression in moments where listening in silence becomes a way of honoring the dead. From the capacity to care for the self and others, to feel oneself interdependently bound to communities and living worlds, as well as the ground under our feet, listening is a gesture we need to honor in fuller ways.

[20]   Ibid., 165.

Worlds within a World, the Epistemological Work of Listening

To *listen-across* is to approach the complexities inherent to a planetary reality. And which lends to supporting *ecologies of practices* attuned to the enmeshed natures of coexisting worlds, with their unpredictable intersections and junctures, and which are constitutive of multiple knowings that entangle in dissonant and consonant ways. The formulation of *ecologies* along such lines—ecologies of practices, of multiple worlds, of interspecies relations—is key to approaching environmental ruination and related histories of settler-colonialism that stand behind the ongoingness of global violence by dominant powers. As Lorraine Code convincingly argues, ecological thinking is fundamental to working against the universalizing, "monolithic" narratives of progress.[21] These are narratives that greatly reduce and oversimplify—that are at odds with the thick relationality and troubled stories Anna Tsing works at noticing.

The call for a planetary paradigm is one that gains traction by way of ecological thinking. This entails engaging with a decoloniality informed by Indigenous cultures and "epistemologies of the South" which, as Boaventura de Sousa Santos argues, contribute opportunities for both unlearning and learning (particularly within a European context). These are epistemologies informed by histories of colonial conquest and rule, by an intersection of appropriated knowledges of the "Global North" and those of Indigenous communities, and which carry lessons in how to navigate the "disturbed ecologies" of neocolonial, capitalistic realities. Epistemologies of the South are paths by which European culture may further work at taking stock of its own prejudices, giving account as to debts needing to be paid. This includes acknowledging the deep history of resistances within Europe itself—those individuals, communities, schools, and movements that work by way of the margins *within*, becoming a "south" across different contexts and sites spanning the "north." These are epistemologies and practices that can contribute to moving toward a "post-abyssal democracy." "In my view it is rather the time for a post-colonial, post-imperial conversation between

---

[21] Lorraine Code, *Ecological Thinking: The Politics of Epistemic Location* (Oxford: Oxford University Press, 2006), 55.

Europe and the vast non-European world."[22] Such forms of conversation are urgently called for to address current challenges spanning the globe and that can contribute to reworking institutions of democracy by integrating lessons from the "metaphorical" as well as "real" souths.[23]

The call for new conversations and new democratic configurations work at shifting the attention economies and knowledge regimes shaped by settler-colonialism, to foster an "intercultural democracy" suited to a globalized planet.[24] The mutual learning called for between north and south is positioned so as to *democratize democracy*, explicitly affording ways of enhancing the "demodiversity" Santos sees as a resource inherent to the contemporary global condition.

Amitav Ghosh calls for similar forms of alteration. In *The Nutmeg's Curse*, the author highlights the ways in which particular legacies of European philosophical and religious thinking contributed greatly to installing an economic paradigm central to settler-colonialism (emerging in the sixteenth century) in which matter, or nature, is cast as inert and therefore available for extraction, terraforming, and overproduction.[25] This was to have devastating consequences in terms of fueling a greater mechanism of imperial conquest which continues today.[26] Ecological thinking, in contrast, figures a worldview that honors the animistic, sentient qualities of the earth, and that works at decolonizing the legacies of settler-colonialism, and related knowledge regimes, which position nature as a resource. Epistemologies of the South are thus aids in challenging mechanistic approaches and thinking, helping to mount what Ghosh terms a "vitalist politics" in preparation for a post-European world to come.[27]

---

[22] Boaventura de Sousa Santos, "A New Vision of Europe: Learning from the Global South," in *Demodiversity: Towards Post-Abyssal Democracies*, ed. Boaventura de Sousa Santos and José Manuel Mendes (New York: Routledge, 2021), 34.

[23] Ibid., 34.

[24] Ibid., 19.

[25] Amitav Ghosh, *The Nutmeg's Curse: Parables for a Planet in Crisis* (London: John Murray, 2022).

[26] In reflecting upon the greater historical, philosophical backdrop to today's multiple crises, Amitav Ghosh notes:

> This metaphysic, fundamentally an ideology of conquest, would eventually become hegemonic in the West, and is now shared by the entire global elite: within its parameters the idea that a volcano can produce meaning, or that the nutmeg can be a protagonist in history, can never be anything other than a delusion or "primitive superstition." To envisage the world in this way was a crucial step toward making an inert Nature a reality. Ghosh, *The Nutmeg's Curse*, 39.

[27] The perspective of a "vitalist politics" that Amitav Ghosh articulates as key to working at planetarity as a way of life is founded on recognizing the web of life constituting our "mutual dependence."

Listening-across 181

‿

In considering current environmental, political urgencies, I'm concerned to explore listening as generative of ecological thinking and which may contribute to a vitalist politics. Central to this is to follow Mario Blaser and Marisol de la Cadena's argument as to the necessity to honor multiple worlds, belief systems, and discourses, particularly on the part of dominant knowledge practices. To do so it becomes imperative to recognize the tendency for knowledge practices to reinforce themselves, to produce knowledge in ways that "reinstate" their methodologies and worldviews.[28] In defining and demarcating a given body of knowledge, knowledge practices may come to *displace* that which is not recognizable as legitimate ways of knowing, undermining the capacity to recognize the given cultures shaped and expressed through such knowing. Practices of knowledge purport methods of doing, of sensing and storying, which position a given object or field of study, housing it within particular discursive frames that are reflective of a larger belief system. Blaser and de la Cadena work at decolonizing modern knowledge practices and their entrenched legacies, demanding a break, an opening by which heterogeneity may resound more fully—and through which knowledge-makers can be more open to being surprised and interrupted by their own studies.[29] In the context of ecological thinking, this may be exemplified by shifting a view onto nature from one of object to that of subject, where the land is *living*.

Such views and acts find traction by way of a "grammar of animacy," which, as Robin Wall Kimmerer argues, specifically redresses the shortcomings of scientific objectivity. She writes: "Science can be a language of distance which reduces a being to its working parts; it is a language of objects. The language scientists speak, however precise, is based on a profound error in grammar, an omission, a grave loss, in translation from the native languages" inherent to the natural world.[30] In contrast, a grammar of animacy is one shaped by recognition of the "unseen energies that animate everything" and where words become gestures of evocation, respect, reciprocity. Knowledge practices from within a framework

---

He writes: "A necessary first step toward finding solutions is to find a common idiom and a shared story—a narrative of humility in which humans acknowledge their mutual dependence not just on each other, but on 'all our relatives.'" Ghosh, *The Nutmeg's Curse*, 242.

[28] Mario Blaser and Marisol de la Cadena, "Pluriverse: Proposals for a World of Many Worlds," in *A World of Many Worlds*, ed. Mario Blaser and Marisol de la Cadena (Durham, NC: Duke University Press, 2018), 6.

[29] Ibid., 8.

[30] Kimmerer, *Braiding Sweetgrass*, 49.

182 *Poetics of Listening*

of animacy become ritualized, ceremonial, meaningful in terms of contributing to an ecology of relations. This is a direction, a methodological commitment, that grounds itself in community. As Shawn Wilson argues, Indigenous research practices are founded on "relational accountability" in which knowledge production is guided by respecting and enhancing the communities to which one is a part.[31] And which entails a relation to land and more-than-human others.

↜

It is along these lines that transdisciplinary, transcultural meeting points and dialogical encounters and processes gain relevance, where knowledge practices and research methodologies may encounter each other, to figure a robust ecology of attention so as to incite us "toward a disposition to be attentive to practices that make worlds even if they do not satisfy our demand (the demand of modern epistemology) to prove their reality (as they do not leave historical evidence, let alone scientific)."[32] These are the conversations and un/learning processes Santos identifies as necessary for realizing a more equitable future.

Mario Blaser and Marisol de la Cadena's critical engagement with knowledge practices contributes to the issue of epistemic justice by arguing for *pluriversality*—as a configuration of practices that proceed in ways that honor and celebrate a *world of many worlds*. This takes guidance by way of Indigenous cultures and practices, along with ethnographic fieldwork methods, all of which come to anchor epistemic approaches to the specificities of place and the traditions and belief systems by which communities thrive. *The ground carries knowledge, and it becomes the basis by which knowing endures; these are the situated knowledges we may also come to carry, and that carry us.* Acknowledging and working *by way of the ground* better enables an ethical research practice, where one comes to recognize the conventions and habits by which knowledge is produced and that are carried in one's given form of practice. To keep to the ground is to know of one's epistemological home and community, while also finding ways of attending to the ground of others: to sense when that ground resists one's own entry. To be *out of place* can form the basis for feeling one's own body as uprooted, as *misfitting* within a given way of doing things, and to step evermore lightly because

---

[31] Shawn Wilson, *Research Is Ceremony: Indigenous Research Methods* (Halifax: Fernwood Publishing, 2008), 99.

[32] Blaser and de la Cadena, "Pluriverse," 4.

of it. Fieldwork is work done to feel the ground, and it is to work at remaining sensitive to the steps one brings onto that ground.

༄

In considering the question of ethical knowledge practices, I'm led to appreciate how listening may contribute. Listening is a deeply holistic form of attention that supports ways of knowing across self and others, and furthermore, is textured by the particularities of place; listening is grounding as it affords engaging with the immediate, remaining sensitive to the fullness of the moment and all it contains. Moreover it is generative of an environmental position in terms of its capacity for recognizing the near *and* the far, human *and* more-than-human, at one and the same time. And it participates in crafting ways of connecting oneself with surrounding environments—by keeping alert as to the balance of things, to the *soundness* of a given place. Listening forms the basis for intensifying relations in ways that also extend how relationality may be conceived and lived—it can be appreciated to encourage an emergent process, where contact and conversation are living processes, and where one's own voice and views are informed, inflected, unsettled by others. This includes accenting knowing as always partial, as bound to curiosity, a receptivity that staggers final statements, keeping one open to difference as underpinning a world of many worlds.

It is by way of these views that listening, or *listening-across*, is posed as a capacity, a subject position by which to better participate in the thick relationality defining a planetary reality—a means by which to cultivate relational accountability. To remain sensitive to one's own methodologies, the knowledge productions one follows and generates, in ways that can enhance the demodiversity Santos calls for.

Listening grounds me, attends to the roots, the entanglements and complexity of situations, while exposing myself to the rich, jagged diversity of others, to sense feelings of interdependency as shared biologies, matters, so as to know of my body as a materiality spanning across planetary things and beings. By way of such polyphonic realities and imaginaries, I gain a deeper sense for my own limited view, as well as the joy and care found in following others.

༄

Throughout *Poetics of Listening*, listening is positioned as a gesture, a capacity that affords entry onto the embodied materialities constitutive of personal, interpersonal, social, and political worlds. This finds extension within the context of ecological, planetary thinking. As I've been concerned to highlight, listening aids in feeling oneself as a planetary subject or *guest*, opening a means for honoring and participating in the animate rhythms of coexistence. Furthermore, by way of sounded listening practices such realities and experiences lend to the crafting of narratives of creation, as gestures of reciprocity. How might these practices and narratives be carried into epistemic models of inquiry? And where recognition of a world of many worlds features as a guiding ethical concern?

These are questions and perspectives that find articulation in the work of Anastasia (A) Khodyreva, a researcher and writer focusing on creative, ecofeminist methodologies and alternative worldings. Fundamental to this is an emphasis on collaborative, collective work, researching and writing together, and keeping close to a mode of inquiry shaped by listening, so as to remain sensitive to the enmeshed agencies co-constituting a given scene of research.

In the narrative document "Attempts at Spectral Listening," Khodyreva furthers such approaches by sensing the influencing ground of the Seili Island off the coast of Finland.[33] In collaboration with curator Taru Elfving, along with "co-listeners" Yvonne Billimore, Jaana Laakkonen, Anu Pasanen, Nina Vurdelja, and Kari Yli-Annala, Khodyreva documents a field study undertaken on the island in 2023 (in partnership with The Listening Biennial). Importantly, the field study was centered on the concept of "spectral listening," which acted as an embodied method by which to walk, sense and attune to the island environmentally, historically, politically. Listening, in effect, was mobilized as a research method, a path by which to constitute and stay with ways of noticing (echoing Anna Tsing). As Khodyreva and their colleagues elaborate,

> to notice might be to intentionally be attentive to oneself situated in dynamics of ever-nascent relations with human and non-human others and one's fluctuating agency in a specific context. To notice is a full-bodied project of being in a specific material, physical, bodily, affective, geopolitical, cultural, historical and socio-environmental spacetime. To notice is to put one's imaginaries to check and trace their effects in co-forming a milieu: imaginaries are never abstractions but consequential political matterings.[34]

---

[33] Anastasia (A) Khodyreva with Taru Elfving, Yvonne Billimore, Jaana Laakkonen, Anu Pasanen, Nina Vurdelja, and Kari Yli-Annala, "Attempts at Spectral Listening," published on *The Listening Biennial* website. See https://listeningbiennial.net/discourses/attempts-in-spectral-listening (accessed July 2024).

[34] Ibid.

By way of such felt processes, *spectral listening* emerges as a possible method by which to extend understandings of embodied practice, where noticing works at attuning to the less-than-visible and underrepresented—it is envisioned as a listening that may attend to the ever-shifting ground of place and people, the textured depths and sediments of a given milieu. This includes attending to what it means to walk and sense, to search and research the island, alone and with others—a listening that may help recognize all that is "submerged" or obfuscated and which gives indication as to the *islands within the island*. These *spectral islands* are the ghosts of former expeditions and colonizations, when the island functioned as a leper colony in the seventeenth century, and later as a mental asylum, where the "sick" were off-shored, invisibilized—ghosts that are no less present, material, if one is able to "hear-notice" their enduring presence: "The unruly presence of the souls enclosed in the asylums can be, however, heard-noticed if one is skilled in reading the landscapes." Such hearing-noticings are those that attune environmentally—to read by way of a situated attentiveness to things. In doing so, "one comes across the plants used as sedatives, stumbles upon apple trees, black currant and raspberry bushes nurtured and harvested by the exiled to sustain their bodies and souls and to add to their herring-heavy ration."[35]

$\backsim$

The hearing-noticing and listening-storying Spectral Listening offers are ones that search for ways of knowing, which remain deeply committed to crafting knowledge practices sensitive to an epistemic politics—a form of collaborative, collective noticing that attends to what is there, that proceeds cautiously, and that recognizes its own limitations.

> I wonder if spectral listening means staying in the troubled loop, persistently in search of ways of listening "better," listening for nuance and resistance. Listening as aligning different—in our group, feminist, chronically sick, migrant, economically precarious, gender nonconforming—knowledges. Listening as an agile state of searchy commitment to synesthetic resistance from one's situated position reaching out to other bodies-in-search.[36]

Attending and attuning to an ecological sensitivity, Spectral Listening articulates an emergent mode of inquiry, one that is situated and embodied; a modality

---

[35] Ibid.
[36] Ibid.

that can be appreciated to stagger the epistemological drive toward mastery or tidy completion. Importantly, as Lorraine Code argues, the point is not to "eschew mastery" or control outright, but rather, to "develop ways of articulating and enacting both, so as to shift the emphasis away from presumptions of entitlement and toward assuming the responsibilities and precautionary policies integral to democratically negotiated power and authority."[37] Such views find expression in creative-critical practices that foreground *following* rather than *mastering* a given object of research, that proceed in ways sensitive to the habits and habitats of oneself and others, and that remain open to a diverse range of epistemic sources.[38] These are *partial* gestures and positionalities that figure a range of explorative and experimental outcomes—a listening-writing that follows, attunes, treads lightly, and that knows by way of a sensitivity for the limits of one's own understanding. Taking tender steps across the island, Spectral Listening exemplifies what Code highlights as the "politics of epistemic location," which orients knowledge practices by way of ecological thinking.

Founded on understandings of situated knowledge, Code works at elaborating an ethico-political position where situation is *"constitutive of* enactments of subjectivity" and which lend to recognition of the *thick relationality* always already underpinning objects of research.[39] Extending from Donna Haraway and the broader field of ecofeminism, Code's ecological thinking offers a deeply nuanced "frame for reconfiguring knowledge, sociality, and subjectivity and for reexamining the potential of epistemic and ethico-political practices to produce habitats where people can live well together and respectfully with and within the physical/natural world."[40] Through such an undertaking, ecological thinking performs a crucial interruption onto knowledge regimes founded upon universalist tendencies and methods of objectification and which undervalue the belief systems and material conditions inherent to, or overlaid onto, a given field of research and the cultures of others.

↶

Following Lorraine Code, and the ecofeminist methods of attunement put into motion by Khodyreva and Spectral Listening, it is my concern to position listening more fully as a contribution to ecological thinking. From

---

[37] Code, *Ecological Thinking*, 32.
[38] For more on following as a method, see Katve-Kaisa Konturri, *Ways of Following: Art, Materiality, Collaboration* (London: Open Humanities Press, 2018).
[39] Code, *Ecological Thinking*, 19.
[40] Ibid.

listening practices that follow and learn from the wind, that assist in knowing one's listening as one limited form—a listening among a spectrum of other listenings—to the methodologies founded on hearing-noticing, which help in reading the landscape, sensing the influencing fact of an ethnographic imaginary, and that write themselves as listening stories, listening emerges as an important capacity to enhancing ecological thinking and planetary practices. Such epistemological work figures, as Gemma Corradi Fiumara argues, in a counter-history to what we know as the enlightened, modern subject. As Fiumara poses, Western philosophy is a conflicted project shaped by a tension between *logos* as the basis or expression of reason, in terms of a rational speaking subject, and *logos* as more inclusive of listening. While speaking has come to represent, through its expressive character, the fact of a rational subject, as an index of thought itself, listening has been relegated a substantially reduced role. Extending from the writings of Martin Heidegger on questions of language, Fiumara identifies how dominant conceptualizations of *logos* (and logic) suppress the fuller meanings, as found in the original Greek verb *legein* which, as Heidegger notes, carries original meanings connected to "laying down," "collecting," or "preserving." As Fiumara highlights, *legein* suggests a richer movement to the noun *logos*, one that carries a pronounced relation to listening—as *the bringing together of things, the collecting of many*—within its definition. Through her philosophical inquiry, Fiumara aims at recuperating the rather forgotten or suppressed art of listening. This entails a commitment to "retrieve subordinate, minor dimensions" of human understanding, to pick up the "lesser elements" central to what it means to think and speak as well as perform as a reasoning subject.[41]

Essential to Fiumara's attempt to restore listening to *logos* is to open a critical path for countering dominant understandings or approaches that tend to value speaking over listening. Such a logic forms a fundamental structure to particular Western systems with their emphasis on production and progress at the expense of gathering and preserving. Within such a prevailing framework, life itself is positioned upon a line of "personal development," where achievements come to signal progression and betterment. Success is celebrated by way of the capacity to innovate rather than preserve, to stand tall rather than lay down, to break new

---

[41] Gemma Corradi Fiumara, *The Other Side of Language: A Philosophy of Listening* (London: Routledge, 1990), 3–4.

ground rather than care for its current existence. Performances of speech are subsequently located within a logic that requires the demonstration of individual exceptionalism, articulated by way of the "capacity for ordering and explaining, detached from any propensity to receive and listen."[42]

Steven Connor furthers such critical thinking in his article "The Modern Auditory I" in which he charts an auditory influence spanning Western modernity.[43] While established narratives emphasize a predominantly "ocularcentric" paradigm, where the capacity for scientific observation, analysis, and dissection—as well as "ordering and explaining"—contribute to modern knowledge regimes, in which matter or nature is cast as inert, as available to a controlling gaze, Connor instead traces a counternarrative founded on the auditory. From auditory technologies to modern literary, artistic works that channel the unconscious with all its internal noises, and from telephony and radiophony that spirit transmitted forms of culture, to the new noises of industry and war that would bombard the modern self, sound is shown as deeply present and influential within a seemingly ocularcentric modern culture.

Considering modernity as an arena of intensified sound, Connor further addresses the ways in which a great deal of postmodern thinking, from Luce Irigaray and Jean-Francois Lyotard to Jacques Lacan and Emmanuel Levinas, gives priority to the aural, displacing the "unity of the subject" by way of a mode of hearing. This is founded on what Connor highlights as the "weak object" of sound, for sound is radically diffuse, it doesn't hold together; rather, it figures a world of vapors, ephemeral passings, vibratory tremblings, and temporary agitations. This is a world full of noise, resonance, animation, a world in which the "auditory I" is figured as participant, dissolute, as vulnerable and exposed.

Importantly, for Connor, the auditory presents itself as a key experience and metaphor for enabling an orientation toward a less autonomously conceived subject, an auditory self that is an "attentive rather than investigatory self, which takes part in the world rather than taking aim at it."[44] As he further elaborates, "the self defined in terms of hearing rather than sight is a self imaged not as a point, but as a membrane; not as a picture, but as a channel through which voices,

---

[42] Ibid., 10.
[43] Steven Connor, "The Modern 'Auditory I,'" in *Rewriting the Self: Histories from the Renaissance to the Present*, ed. Roy Porter (London: Routledge, 1997).
[44] Ibid., 219.

noises and musics travel."[45] The auditory thus emerges as interruptive to the psychic-social centering of the self with its propensity for action, independence, and mastery.

↩

The modern auditory I is offered as an indication of a nascent, underrepresented—or, as Fiumara emphasizes, *suppressed*—ground in which sound and listening generate a different ontological and epistemological pathway. Connor's auditory model is suggestive for knowledge practices sensitive to others, that expose themselves to their own situated vulnerabilities, all of which emerge as assets: the weakness of an auditory position is equally its strength, for such weakness, such dissolute positionality, is what keeps one grounded in the nature of a given study, the environment in which one is situated, not to mention one's own limited view. In doing so, listening is fundamental to the ongoing project of epistemic justice—to weaken the conceptualization of an autonomous subject and the call for exceptional research. Moreover, it may greatly assist in the processes of unlearning/learning Santos highlights as crucial for "European society" today. As Fiumara argues, retrieving listening as a vital contributor to *logos* is essential for reworking knowledge practices, for listening requires that we learn to "dwell with, abide by, whatever we try to know"—that we "aim at coexistence-with, rather than knowledge-of."[46] A position that is ultimately more "ecological than logical."[47]

Self-organized Study as Ecology of Learning

Following these perspectives, I'm interested to think further as to listening's role in ecological thinking and the crafting of planetary practices. As expressed in works of sound art, listening is emphasized as enabling of an environmental position, one attuned to the living textures and ecosystems of given places. This includes the figuring of a *weak logic*, in which audiences are invited into experimental states of listening, often with a view toward enhancing interconnectedness. Such experiences are suggestive for listening's role in ecological thinking and ethical knowledge practices. How to work at the mutual learning Santos calls for, as key to

---

[45] Ibid., 207.
[46] Fiumara, *The Other Side of Language*, 15.
[47] Ibid., 16.

190 *Poetics of Listening*

shaping a planetary world, a demodiversity? If, within the context of knowledge practices, it becomes crucial to orient methodologies and discursive structures so as to honor a world of many worlds, in what ways can new approaches be explored, made available?

Contending with the issue of epistemic justice, and current challenges around environmental devastation, a range of self-organized schools and learning situations have proliferated in recent years, most of which gesture toward reworking knowledge practices. Often taking place within or in relation to contemporary art institutions and communities, these initiatives work at creating opportunities for people to come together in ways that are rare to find in more formalized educational programs. As such, they indicate new educational and epistemological desires and urgencies, in terms of moving outside conventional institutional structures with their established routines. In contrast, a great deal of these alternative initiatives express a wish or need for transdisciplinary meeting points and experimental formats. Often integrating a multiplicity of issues, discursive languages, and knowledge practices, situations are developed so as to give room for emergent expressions and understandings. And importantly, where knowing *and* feeling, studying *and* practicing, are fully integrated. Through such approaches, learning processes are expressed in ways that are not only about knowledge production; rather, at stake within such situations is the prefiguring or rehearsing of more holistic forms of living.

Central to many of these educational, learning initiatives is an engagement with current realities of the globalized planet, where disciplinary borders, individualized competition, and academic mechanisms, such as peer review, seem to fall short in terms of decolonizing knowledge practices. This is exacerbated by the ongoing cuts to the humanities across American-European higher education and the intensification of an overbearing managerial structuring in which students and staff are increasingly called upon to perform in ever-productive ways. As Wendy Brown argues,

> when neoliberalization is complete, when all academic knowledge, and indeed, all university activity is valued according to its capacity to augment human, corporate or finance capital, the humanities, if they exist at all, will be barely recognizable. At this point, it is not only medieval English poetry, Sanskrit, and political philosophy that disappears from the curriculum, but thinking, teaching, and learning that pertains to questions of what, apart from capital accumulation and appreciation, planetary life might be about or worth. This

is the disappearance of the humanities, to be sure, but also of an educated citizenry and hence, of the soul and sinew of democracy.[48]

It is clear that in tension with formalized education, interests in creative collaboration, hybrid knowledge experience, and embodied and situated practices are working at reorganizing epistemological regimes and communities. Moreover, contemporary art has increasingly shifted toward a focus on "research-based" practices. Even within the context of exhibition-making it is common today to encounter a range of educational, social, and performative programming with the aim of generating new knowledge. I take such practices or turns as profoundly ecological in their scope in terms of giving manifestation to the need for creating new ways of living on a shared planet, which include new ways of challenging dominant systems that cut against a pluriversal approach. In short, what these tendencies reveal is a general turn toward configuring diverse practices which can help in cultivating the tools, experiences, and knowledges relevant for a planetary world.

⚰

I may turn to the Tree School initiated by Decolonizing Architecture Art Research (DAAR) (Sandi Hilal and Alessandro Petti) as one such example of an alternative learning initiative geared toward ecological thinking. DAAR has been working since the early 2000s, bringing focus to the issue of decolonizing knowledge practices originally within the context of Palestine through their Campus in Camps project. Recognizing a lack of discussion on the topic of decolonization in the region, in particular in relation to architecture, DAAR formed Campus in Camps as a way to put into question the spatial politics shaping camp-life, as well as how architecture is deployed as a form of colonization. Importantly, Campus in Camps sought ways to learn from life in the camps, to follow the embedded knowledges and practices established by those residing in the camps since their establishment following 1948. As DAAR highlights, the refugees of the camps "have managed to create different concepts of what a 'neighbor' is and what 'being together' means and to build collectivity beyond the state,"[49]

---

[48] Wendy Brown, "Neoliberalized Knowledge," *History of the Present*, vol. 1, no. 1 (Summer 2011): 123–4.

[49] Sandi Hilal and Alessandro Petti (DAAR), "Tree Schools: In Conversation with WHW," in *Artistic Ecologies: New Compasses and Tools*, ed. Pablo Martínez, Emily Pethick, What, How & For Whom/ WHW (London: Sternberg Press, 2022), 57.

192 *Poetics of Listening*

examples which can contribute essential knowledge to other communities and contexts equally subjected to forms of political-colonial violence.

Extending from this initial work, the Tree School has become a mobile framework for bringing people together since its inception in 2014. Shaped by an ethos of conviviality and "the joy of learning together,"[50] the School is expressive of the greater sweep of initiatives I'm interested to follow, explicitly working at emergent forms of learning:

> While at a Tree School, our life becomes an important source of knowledge. It's not about books or quoting philosophers. The Tree School is the opposite of what we learned to do in traditional schools. Instead, we look at who we are, who our parents and grandparents were, how we go about our daily lives. The trees and other nature that surround us remind us that being together as human beings and exchanging and sharing knowledge—thinking together—is already enough to have a school. To build a school, we need nothing more than the shade of a tree and people willing to be together and learn together. This creates one of the best learning environments, because everyone is there because they want to be there and to learn from each other. Because we understand that the lives of the other people around us are an important source of knowledge. At a Tree School, people value each other and exchange ideas.[51]

The Tree School is centered on an emergent approach, where forms of study are anchored in what people bring with them, seeking ways to give room for addressing what is happening in their lives and communities; there is no set program or curriculum established beforehand; rather the School is about inviting participants to collectively direct and organize the flow of exchange, employing a more horizontal structure. It also has a flexible time frame, lasting days or months, or even years, depending on the situation. Such flexibility and responsiveness is key to its approach, which is further expressed in DAAR's resistance to setting out an exact methodology; instead, they provide what they term "ingredients" operative within the making of a Tree School. These include rituals, conversations, dislocation, unlearning, unpredictability, *Al-Atabeh* (Arabic for designating the space connecting the entrance of a house with its surroundings), cooking, and *ritrovo* (Italian, meaning "getting together with the joy of being together as friends"). These are ingredients that give way to a learning situation profoundly aligned with ecological thinking. And which include being

---

[50] Ibid., 54.
[51] Ibid., 61.

located under or in relation to trees. The tree forms a symbolic, material, and ecological center for the Tree School, where each gathering manifests under the shade of a tree, or around an engagement with a particular species. This is a gesture that draws upon the ways in which trees extend across cultures to symbolize knowledge, from the sacred to the academic, the communal to the solitary.[52] Within the context of the School, being close to trees signals an ecologically oriented knowledge practice, in which gathering in nature supports ways of learning across human and more-than-human worlds. As Code argues, attending to the politics of epistemic location is necessary in decolonizing knowledge practices. "In standard educational settings, knowledge rarely has anything to do with your everyday life. With the Tree School, we believe that the learning needs to adapt to the situations and needs of the learners—to actually be very close to the knowledge grounded in people's experiences."[53]

⌣

DAAR's work speaks toward the urgencies underlying current sociopolitical, ecological crises, which are increasingly riddled with a complex knowledge economy, where facts, data, and reporting are susceptible to constant manipulation. While such an economy, with its related expanse of cognitive labors, may support a general proliferation of a "common intelligence," it equally spawns uncertainty and skepticism as to the reliability of information. Amitav Ghosh highlights this by pointing out that while environmental crisis is clearly a pressing issue, supported by innumerable reports and leading experts, it is still put into question by many governments and officials, as well as approached with skepticism across popular media.[54] From the crisis of education to the ecological crisis, these serve as an influencing backdrop to the intensification of self-organized, alternative schools and learning situations taking place across the globe. All of which can be said to work at constituting an ecology of attention in support of a planetary way of being. From the Common Ecologies school and Solar dos Abacaxis to The School of Mutants and the Empathic Pedagogies Network, many self-organized initiatives are seeking ways to form collective experiences that integrate discursive, environmental, and somatic practices, and that aim at nurturing ways of learning from each other.

⌣

[52] See Wangari Maathai, *The World We Once Lived In* (London: Penguin Books, 2021).
[53] Hilal and Petti (DAAR), "Tree Schools," 72.
[54] Ghosh, *The Nutmeg's Curse,* 235.

I find in the proliferation of self-organized schools and learning initiatives a hopeful turn, as they give greatly to the unlearning/learning Santos calls for, as well as configuring structures by which to coinhabit a world of many worlds. I also detect within such initiatives a deep relation to a listening practice. As DAAR suggests through the Tree School, emergent forms of learning together are founded on the capacity to speak and hear each other, to give room for sharing "our experiences with one another, and, through that, to create collectivity."[55] This extends across many such learning situations and educational initiatives, where giving time and space for hearing each other, for finding ways of defining and inhabiting an epistemic location full of multiple discourses and practices, as well as more-than-human others, necessitates a deeply active form of listening.

In my own practice, I have also been part of developing different educational initiatives, which has led more recently to establishing The Listening Academy. Launched in 2021, as part of the first edition of The Listening Biennial, the Academy focuses on creating situations in which listening can be researched, discussed, and practiced from a diversity of perspectives. This includes connecting across a range of disciplines, understanding listening as both general and specialized, and as centered on people's lives as well as inviting greater theoretical, methodological elaboration. Parallel to the Tree School, The Listening Academy also aims at horizontal approaches. Often facilitated through invited scholars, artists, and organizers—and taking place at a range of locations across the world—discussions, activities, and material testings are guided collectively, shaped by participants and the flow of exchange over an extended duration. This allows for the building of friendships and collaborations, and the spreading of care and attention that underpins listening in general. In this way, The Listening Academy inquires into listening as a topic while creating situations founded on enacting listening itself. Through such work, I understand The Listening Academy as a contribution to the greater culture of self-organized learning, which can bring a more concentrated concern for listening.

༄

It is along these lines that I come to understand The Listening Academy, along with other current alternative learning situations, in relation to Citton's concept of *the ecology of attention*. As Citton underscores, attentional capitalism today is predicated on an "ontology of visibility" in which wealth or prestige accrues

---

[55] Hilal and Petti (DAAR), "Tree Schools," 72.

by way of gaining appearance. In short, the more one is perceived by others, the more one exists and is valued.[56] Such an ontological-economic configuration is entangled with the technical capabilities to move data with ease, which positions personal, social connections as currencies within the data-stream of profit.

The ontology of visibility that Citton identifies as central to an economy of attention becomes the basis for an overarching critical concern. Against the prevailing logic of such an economy, one that instrumentalizes and exhausts attention, Citton sets out to *take back* attention. Through a series of insightful analyses, he works at defining an "ecosophical" framework (following Félix Guattari's arguments in *Three Ecologies*), which articulates a transversal perspective crossing social, ecological, and mental axes so as to better capture the far-reaching consequences of an attentional economy, for "whether the things that are most dear to us blossom or are crushed depends on this."[57] To work at greater critical understanding of what's at stake in the instrumentalization of attention today, Citton calls for the creation of "aesthetic labs" in order to enliven, as well as challenge, the dynamics of attention. Such labs are conceived as experiments in "dissonance" where attentional patterns are enhanced or unsettled by encountering a diversity of voices and views, knowledges and practices.

Alternative schools and learning initiatives can be appreciated to function as aesthetic labs, where the exposure to diverse views, practices, languages, and experiences is central—as well as taking the time for slower forms of reflection and research that can unfold outside the obligation for tangible outcome. Through such experimental platforms, disciplinary borders are put on hold and established languages are stretched by way of more emergent strategies and collective becomings. These are labs of dissonance that foster an ecology of attention and that afford ways of cohabiting a world of many worlds.

Sounding a Livable Life

In his work on climate crisis and the Anthropocene, Andreas Weber argues that a great deal of contemporary urgencies are grounded in a broader "global crisis

---

[56] Citton, *The Ecology of Attention*, 46.
[57] Ibid., 23.

of sense-making" that impedes the ability to build sustainable practices.[58] Such a crisis contributes to what Weber further identifies as a pervasive *culture of death* defining Western society (and beyond), whereby the vitality of the natural world—and the capacity for humans to feel alive, to honor *aliveness* as what flows and connects across bodies and living worlds—is undermined or made purely instrumental within a greater socioeconomic order. Weber's critical project of aliveness—or what he terms *enlivenment*—is aimed at a radical shift in support of a culture of life, understanding that life is what makes of material existence a meaningful experience. Life names the metabolic, generative, poetic interconnectedness by which bodies seek fuller contact with other bodies. Life is the flourishing of shared sensual existence, giving way to an embodied expressivity or flowering—what Weber highlights as "the beauty of living things."[59] As he further specifies, "the world is matter desiring to come into contact with other matter, and it creates meaning to the degree to which this desire is realized or not."[60] Such meaningfulness of life, as the realization of itself as contact, as collective flourishing and the celebration of interdependent vitality, functions as the rightful guide for the making of human societies. As Weber suggests, by way of reflections on Indigenous cultures as well as histories of European commons, systems of economy need not be modeled on continual growth and the optimization of trading goods; rather, participating in the natural state of a given ecosystem is fundamental, which includes developing practices of reciprocity, as well as contributing in ways that support or enhance the general "fertility" of a given environment—not so as to overproduce but to honor the beauty of living things.[61] "Human householding," as Weber notes, may function in ways that retain a metabolic balance with what the earth offers.

For Weber, this natural order of life, as the vitality of shared aliveness, is thoroughly challenged by an "ideology of death" shaping a great deal of current socioeconomic systems that approach the natural world as *dead matter* and which are built upon histories of colonial-capitalistic violence. This finds an important point of reference in Achille Mbembe's conceptualization of necropolitics.[62] As

---

[58] Andreas Weber, *Enlivenment: Toward a Poetics for the Anthropocene* (Cambridge, MA: MIT Press, 2019), 20.

[59] Ibid., 99.

[60] Ibid., 8.

[61] Ibid., 91.

[62] Achille Mbembe, *Necropolitics* (Durham, NC: Duke University Press, 2019).

Mbembe argues, contemporary political power has increasingly shifted by way of the normalization of war, violence, and conflict, articulating itself through its capacity for dictating who lives and dies. "Necropower" becomes the new prevailing logic, overturning histories of liberal democracy and the concepts of equality and the sovereign good; contemporary necropower, instead, installs war as the new form of politics.[63] This is a reality marked by the proliferation of the "living dead"—persons no longer sovereign over their own bodies but subjugated to the dictates of a given power.

Mbembe's thinking speaks toward the culture of death which Weber identifies as pervasive today, whose violence extends to that of the natural world. Mbembe attends to necropolitics as a system that affects human as well as more-than-human lives, that is expressive of a greater history of colonial violence and extractivist methods, devastating planetary ecosystems while making life itself expendable. In response, Mbembe calls for a "planetary curriculum." This is a curriculum which "implies salvaging whatever remains of reason as a shared human faculty"—to rework configurations and conceptualizations of reason, especially critical of new mechanisms of computation and algorithmic power which do much to perpetuate systems of domination. At the center of a planetary curriculum is to question in what ways life can be repaired.[64]

⟿

Andreas Weber's project of enlivenment is aimed at challenging the deeply entrenched ideology of death which, as I've been pursuing in this chapter, is an extension of a greater historical trajectory shaped by settler-colonialism and the drive of imperialism. It is increasingly urgent, as Weber argues, to fight for "policies of life," which can foster a more meaningful relation with life itself, with the aliveness that is the sensual, generative, breathing force of planetary coexistence. This includes, for example, conceiving of "enlivenment economies" founded on principles and practices of commoning and that express a "natural anticapitalism" based on ecological thinking and reciprocity. These are policies, practices, and ways of thinking that keep close to the vitality of embodied experience, giving expression to a *biopoetics*.[65]

---

[63] Ibid., 66.
[64] Sindre Bangstad and Torbjørn Tumyr Nilsen, "Thoughts on the Planetary: An Interview with Achille Mbembe," in *Radical Sympathy*, ed. Brandon LaBelle (Berlin: Errant Bodies Press, 2022), 86.
[65] Weber, *Enlivenment*, 77, 162.

198   *Poetics of Listening*

Biopoetics, for Weber, names the reality of being a feeling body situated within a world of animate interconnectedness; it is the very state of living things through which experience becomes meaningful, as fundamentally "part and parcel of our everyday world of social communication, linked to our exchanges and interactions, to laughter and consternation, to the needs of our flesh."[66] A "poetics for the Anthropocene," as Weber calls it, is one that can politically act to "reclaim our right to feel our needs authentically as embodied beings needing connection."[67] Biopoetics is deeply aligned with a grammar of animacy as it underpins the felt intimacy of a shared world, giving way to a knowledge of connection which, in light of ongoing environmental crises, opens a path toward reclaiming aliveness—for enhancing a culture of life. This includes reclaiming a natural relation to dying—to make death meaningful against the necropolitical logic that reduces the poetic significance of death as a part of living things. "We can only value aliveness if we admit its intimate connection with dying."[68] These are deeply transformative positions within today's environment, as they seek to collect and gather, to hold and preserve, to wield a grammar of animacy as part of articulating a vitalist position and politics—a new form of reason: to cultivate what Weber terms "poetic precision" so as to truly acknowledge and participate in a living cosmos.[69]

↩

Weber's philosophy of enlivenment offers meaningful input into articulating ecological thinking and related practices. It suggests a positive positioning of life that is never strictly a human affair; rather, life must be conceived as a vitalist force, a biopoetical ecology that extends across human and more-than-human others. In what ways can the biopoetic, as the foundation of enlivenment, contribute to thinking further about sound, listening, and the orchestral qualities of nature? Are there links to be made between potential "policies of enlivenment" and the world of environmental sound?

Returning to Bernie Krause, and the importance he grants to the sounds of natural environments, I'm led to find in experiences of sound a path for elaborating ecological thinking. This can be appreciated by considering how sound is often positioned as an index of life itself—how it signals by way of

---

[66]   Ibid., 78.
[67]   Ibid., 35.
[68]   Ibid., 163.
[69]   Ibid., 152.

its animate force the living existence of *something*, a being, a creature, a living organism. While there are critical perspectives to raise, elaborated through, for example, a consideration of deafness, and how the non-sounded, or seemingly mute, can be cast as inert, as less-than-human, in the case of Krause and the framework of ecological listening I'm considering, underscoring the world as a living, sounding orchestra opens the potentiality of *noticing* a broader web of relations. Raising the volume on environmental worlds, Krause orients noticing toward a planetary perspective. From the biophonic, as sounds produced by animals and organisms, to the anthropophonic, and the world of man-made sounds, and further, to the geophonic constituted by the sounds of earth beings, such as rivers and winds, Krause's identification of the different strata or spheres of acoustic information must be appreciated not only as objective classification. Rather, these are biopoetical, anthropoetical, and geopoetical pathways by which to feel the sonorous, animate energies of living worlds— to know by way of hearing-noticing the material entanglements and spectral foldings constituting the web of life. And which come to suggest ways of not only noticing the orchestral world around but also participating in its culture of life. Such participation, as Kimmerer notes, is about learning the languages of places so as to commune more fully with the gifts of wood and water, soil and sun, flower and grass. These are paths that move from noticing and observing, to reciprocating, to collecting, and to preserving in gestures that lend to ways of becoming indigenous to place.[70]

Listening-across the frequencies of given environments may help appreciate the sounding of life-worlds as a component of planetary coexistence, where vitality is signaled by way of the vibratory animation of things. And which calls us into forms of *sounding-with*: in the human languages and songs, myths and stories that "call out to our neighbors," keeping us involved in the web of life.[71] And in doing so, lend to countering the "crisis of sensing" Weber identifies as central to political, environmental challenges today. This is not to essentialize sound as the basis for life—to concretize a dominant acoustic order onto what counts as the living. Rather, it is to contribute to the assembly of knowledges, practices, and metaphoric seedings that may assist in directing human societies and systems toward a more robust and nuanced planetary rhythm. David George Haskell suggests as much in his biological account of sound-sensing and how

---

[70] Kimmerer, *Braiding Sweetgrass*, 210.
[71] Ibid., 209.

it operates across living creatures. As Haskell outlines, sound-sensing, and the capacity to hear, has its roots in the evolution of *cilia*: the hair-like appendages that first enabled single-cell microbes to move. Furthermore, cilia function as antennae affording ways of sensing the environment, to feel the vibratory animation of a given medium (of air, of water, of the gelatinous mass of a given bacteria) as it is poked and shivered, pushed and modulated by the movement of other living things nearby. That these cilia would come to figure as the hair-like elements as part of the inner ear and the hearing sense of humans (as well as other animals) for Haskell points toward an important aspect of hearing in terms of its relation to vibration and movement, to sensing the living. "Our language divides sensations of 'sound,' 'body motion,' and 'balance,' but they all emerge from hair cells in interconnected fluid-filled canals in our inner ears."[72] Sound-sensing is therefore positioned as part of a greater capacity to move as a body within an environment, in which the ear assists in orientation, balance, and proprioception. From the receptive to the active, sound-sensing is fully embedded within the animate verve of a given life-ecology.

It is along these lines that I may underscore sound as a framework for engaging life and in what ways it functions as animate force lending to narratives of creation. As part of such a framework, I may pose the idea of an *acoustic politics* as a contribution to Weber's project of enlivenment, a politics by which to contend with the ideologies of death that silence a great deal of animal species, that decimate the living land with all its stories and animating songs, and that position human lives as expendable.

Giving focus to an acoustic politics, and the sounding of life-worlds, may come to enrich understandings not only of what counts as biological life but also how individual agency and the enactments of hearing and being heard are essential to political life. As I elaborate in Chapter 4, the capacity to hear and be heard can be appreciated as vital to political process, forming a foundation by which social equality is measured: from the right to speak to the right to be heard, understandings of justice are greatly informed by an *acoustic imaginary*.[73] Such views prompt a deeper appreciation for the ways in which voice, in all

---

[72] Haskell, *Sounds Wild and Broken*, 15.
[73] For an analysis of sound's relation to justice, see James E. K. Parker, *Acoustic Jurisprudence: Listening to the Trial of Simon Bikindi* (Oxford: Oxford University Press, 2015), and Brandon LaBelle, *Acoustic Justice: Listening, Performativity, and the Work of Reorientation* (New York: Bloomsbury Academic, 2021).

its breadth—from the articulations of language to the sonorous qualities of utterance, and further, to the signing and non-auditory expressions that equally *speak*—is essential to capturing social support as well as political recognition.

The urgency underpinning hearing and being heard can be found across a range of situations in which struggles for biological survival are equally struggles for political recognition. As Didier Fassin chronicles, refugees fleeing zones of conflict mostly confront a difficult and debilitating process of securing residency in European states, which highlights the tension between biological survival and political recognition. An "ethics of life,"[74] as Fassin asserts, pivots across a threshold between the biological and the political. While saving lives underpins gestures of humanitarian aid, the necessity to recognize the political claims of persons is equally vital, where certain lives are acknowledged as having physical, biological as well as political agency. For example, the case of hunger striking in the context of the Northern Ireland conflict draws out this critical view. As Bobby Sands and other members of the Irish Republican Army argued, putting their bodies in danger was a political act. Or additionally, in the case of Iranian migrants who, stranded on the border between Greece and Macedonia in 2015, sewed their lips shut in protest.[75] As Fassin argues, such examples force into view how political survival *exceeds* biological survival, calling into question what counts as life itself.[76]

Fighting for political rights is grounded in the capacity to be heard, where being silenced or removed, mistreated or violated, draw out acts of resistance. Within such situations it becomes necessary to speak *otherwise*, to pull at established structures shaping "norms of intelligibility."[77] These are views that within the context of planetary practices are extended through the concept of the rights of nature. The rights of nature as a project argues for natural bodies or earth beings, from rivers to forests to mountains, to be recognized as sentient, as *having voice*: these are earth beings whose sacred grounds and stories function as carriers of spiritual ancestry. To give recognition as to the sentience of earth beings is to *politicize* nature, granting voice to the seemingly inanimate.

---

[74] Didier Fassin, *Life: A Critical User's Manual* (Cambridge: Polity Press, 2019), 79.
[75] "Migrant Crisis: 'Iranians' Sew Lips Shut in Border Protest," November 23, 2015. See https://www.bbc.com/news/world-europe-34903677# (accessed July 2024).
[76] Fassin, *Life*, 85.
[77] Leah Bassel, *The Politics of Listening: Possibilities and Challenges for Democratic Life* (London: Palgrave, 2017), 26.

202   *Poetics of Listening*

A number of creative projects can be appreciated as working at manifesting systems that may give greater representation to the breadth of species populating a given region. Such projects, by reimagining human structures of governance, can be seen to contribute to reorienting the frame by which justice is often heard to proceed. For example, The Parliament of Organisms Democracy, developed by a group of artists, researchers, and activists in Berlin, aims at establishing a democratic system that represents all living species within a given state or territory.[78] To do so, the Parliament is structured around seven representational categories, or parliamentary groups, including mollusks and worms; arthropods; trees, shrubs, climbers; herbs, grasses, perennials; fungi, mosses, lichens; vertebrates; bacteria, single-celled organisms, and viruses; and integrating what the group terms neobiota, or newly established species. Each of the parliamentary groups consists of humans who are tasked with representing them through participation in parliamentary assemblies and sessions. These have taken place since 2018 when the project was founded and are mostly situated in Germany and Austria.

Central to the running of the project is the establishment of a constitution, which is based on a Universal Declaration of Organisms' Rights.[79] Outlining a series of ten articles, the declaration sets out a framework of basic rights with the goal that "no living being can be denied the right to a free and species-appropriate life." Furthermore, establishing species rights supports "the preparation of a political solution" that will include all species. As such, "The Basic Organisms' Rights are supposed to become the foundation of a democratic/representational system with all organisms being equally heard." From the right to free movement, and the prohibition of all forms of slavery, to the right to recognition and procreation, the Parliament attempts to reorient human systems of governance toward a planetary perspective. This includes, as part of its prefigurative performances, the displacing of hearing and being heard outside of human sociality; while humans come to stand in for other species, from flora to fauna, viral to emergent, the project invites us to retune understandings of voice as centered on human subjectivity. This includes shifting notions of representational democracy, and the sense of citizenship as being for humans

---

[78] For more on the project, see the related website: https://organismendemokratie.org/en/how/parliament/ (accessed July 2024).
[79] The Universal Declaration of Organisms' Rights can be found here: https://organismendemokratie.org/en/constitution/ (accessed July 2024).

only. The performativity of citizenship, in this context, is enacted not only in the service of social equality for humans but also for the sake of other species. To represent the rights of other species, through a democratic process, requires perceiving the world through an altogether different set of eyes, ears, antennae, membranes, webs.

The Parliament of Organisms Democracy is a dramaturgical staging that invites a creative rethinking of the structures and systems through which government is enacted. This is partially founded on wielding a grammar of animacy and the recognition of the "life that passes through all things."[80] Moreover, a grammar of animacy affords ways of addressing things that emphasize a deep bond or thick relationality between oneself and others, from human friends to earth beings. And which is already found in the mimetic attributes of language itself. Kimmerer notes as she works at learning her native Potawatomi language: "With the beautiful clusters of consonants of *zh* and *mb* and *shwe* and *kwe* and *mshk*, our language sounds like wind in the pines and water over rocks, sounds our ears may have been more delicately attuned to in the past, but no longer. To learn again, you really have to listen."[81] These are perspectives that underpin attempts to constitute new systems of governance which honor the agency of earth beings and planetary others. And that support a "democracy of species, not a tyranny of one."[82]

Projects such as the Parliament of Organisms Democracy come to enact a form of politics shaped by a grammar of animacy, where assumptions around what counts as voice, along with the operations of hearing and being heard central to rights and recognition, are displaced, reoriented by way of a planetary view. Within such a context, broader understandings of livability—in which the right to life is not strictly centered on human beings—come to form an ethical, political ground influencing processes of governance and the operations of law. Shifting the frame of address so as to hear beyond the human is to work at an ecological construct of justice-making. This is certainly not without its challenges and pitfalls. One might equally argue that the language of rights is explicitly based upon a human system whose application to planetary others wields a certain violence, perpetuating a political framework that can never do

[80] Kimmerer, *Braiding Sweetgrass*, 55.
[81] Ibid., 53.
[82] Ibid., 58.

justice to the radically different forms of life so defining of the planet. These are tensions and challenges to be integrated into any such performative reworking of law and government.

Planetary Gardening and the Will to Listen

I've been focusing on listening as an ecological methodology and position, one that may support a paradigm of life. This includes the ways in which a pluriversal approach to knowledge practices can take guidance from listening as an art of noticing. As Anna Tsing highlights, fostering the capacity for noticing the troubled stories constituting the globalized planet today is crucial, allowing for recognizing and engaging with unlikely forms of collaborative survival. Digging into the patchiness of our precarious times, with their disturbed ecologies and polyphonic human/more-than-human coexistences, Tsing offers routes toward a different kind of storytelling, one that stems from a radical receptivity. This finds further expression in the research approach of the Spectral Listening group, whose "technique" of hearing-noticing is *discovered* as they listen-walk the island of Seili. As they note, the island itself becomes a guide, a partner, a mutually co-constitutive actant. I've been exploring the particular modality of listening-across as a means for elaborating such forms of noticing, as what can contribute to keeping one close to situated research and practice. These are approaches increasingly taken up within self-organized learning situations and educational initiatives, which seek to upset disciplinary borders and dominant knowledge practices in favor of a pluriversal position. The horizontal, emergent approach these initiatives come to articulate reflect the urgencies around cultivating a new form of reason—a planetary curriculum. Listening is cast as a subject position, a methodology that may hear-notice the entanglements of human and more-than-human worlds, to contribute to unlearning/learning ways of feeling the ground, to notice and follow the messiness of planetary interconnectedness, and which calls out for other practices of law and governance, politics and economy. If listening gives way to an ecological sensitivity, a thick relationality, it may radically aid in cultivating a planetary way of being.

Listening practices can become grounds by which to trouble the will to mastery and a related logic of human exceptionalism. These are no easy undertakings or routes—it could be said that listening, as that suppressed faculty, has long been held under by systems that demand an objective knowledge as the carrier of truth, as well as the articulations of a self in control of its own path—obliged to stake out one's own ground. To take back attention as Yves Citton argues, and to fight for policies of enlivenment in support of the beauty of living things, is to work against systems that have and continue to devastate the planet. Moreover, listening is not without its own burdens and challenges: listening is never free from the particularity of a cultural logic, or personal bias, it too may wield a colonizing force, an oppressive intent, a hostile work. These are struggles and tensions that are carried in the listening one may do, make, give, or learn. It can be further said that, as part of the unlearning/learning Santos calls for, lessons in unlearning and learning listening are needed.

∽

In what ways is it possible to shift focus toward a vitalist position, a vitalist politics? How to arrive at forms of thinking supportive of *biopoetical aliveness*? And how might practices of listening help orient human activity so as to open onto the thick relationality defining life with others, not to mention the patchiness of planetary coexistence? To contribute to policies of life and the enlivenment of socioeconomic systems? From listening to trees and winds and islands, following their deep lessons and currents, to speaking as if a mollusk in the crafting of new parliamentary formations, or in the sacred enactments of reciprocity made by way of grammars of animacy, practices emerge that seek ways of embodying Gary Snyder's "etiquette of freedom," as one attuned to a planetary way of being.

The possibility of a planetary approach or etiquette finds additional manifestation in the work and thinking of Gilles Clément. A gardener, educator, and planetary thinker, Clément maps what he terms "third landscape."[83] Third landscape designates the rewilded zones found in interstitial cracks, left-behind and abandoned territories, and that operates as pockets of emergent nature; it is neither a place completely defined by nature nor controlled by humans. Third landscape is, instead, that interstice abandoned but not yet fully reclaimed, and where something new may take hold. Such zones Clément underscores as places of *biological invention*.[84]

---

[83] For more on Gilles Clément and his concept of third landscape, see Gilles Clément, *"The Planetary Garden" and Other Writings* (Philadelphia: University of Pennsylvania Press, 2015).

[84] See the insightful overview of Clément's thinking, developed in the context of Scuola del Terzo Luogo in the city of Lecce, Italy: https://urbanimagination.cargo.site/Third-landscape (accessed July 2024).

206 *Poetics of Listening*

Importantly, these are zones marked by *indecision*, where everything is not completely chaotic, but which is not yet organized or planned as well. As such, they come to offer a conceptualization of design that moves beyond a dualistic positioning between nature and culture. Thirdness, instead, suggests a scene of interspecies connection and contagion, a sort of "frontier" in which an ecological situation may flourish.

Clément sees in third landscape the possibility of a new "planetary garden" situated somewhere between "the forest and the zoo," providing a certain encounter and synergy across human and more-than-human others; it is a symbiotic or biopoetic relationship founded on mutual exchange, in which humans undertake to "act as little as possible to allow the greatest possible diversity."[85] These are the "third natures" that Anna Tsing also describes in *The Mushroom at the End of the World* which, as the author poses, are defined by "what manages to live despite capitalism"[86] and, importantly, suggest a challenge to dominant conceptualizations of linear progress. Third natures, in contrast, speak toward the "open-ended assemblages of entangled ways of life" that figure across "many kinds of temporal rhythms."[87]

I follow Tsing's third natures and Clément's third landscape as expressive of a planetary way of being, where the emergent dynamics inherent to living things are given ground. Moreover, Clément's call for *indecision* as a principle may assist in elaborating a planetary practice, as it cuts against dominant views of the productive (Western) subject set on mastering nature. Within the context of a self aligned with mastery, to be indecisive is to fail or falter at being properly self-sufficient.[88] Decisiveness is expressive of the "epistemized self" Steven Connor identifies as central to enlightenment thinking, in which the will to know emerges in tandem with scientific rationality and the framing of nature as "passive" and "separate."[89]

---

[85] Ibid.

[86] Tsing, *The Mushroom at the End of the World*, viii.

[87] Ibid.

[88] The quandary of indecisiveness is certainly expressed as the key existential crisis in Shakespeare's *Hamlet*, particularly through the figure of the ghost-father. The ghost-father's demand that Hamlet avenge his death by taking the life of Claudius leads Hamlet into a state of indecision: in effect, the question of life and death, of right and wrong, is put to the test, as Hamlet grapples with his indecisiveness. Hamlet's encounters with the ghost-father, and the subsequent crisis that ensues, is suggestive for how indecision *haunts* subjectivity; it is at the heart of a Western paradigm in which decisiveness and taking action are valued (grounded in the historical context of the emergence of modern capitalism).

[89] Connor, "The Modern 'Auditory I'," 203.

While decisiveness may certainly be needed in terms of enacting change, and engaging with current crises, it may also overlook or overwhelm the inherent intelligence of living things—as well as the forms of collaborative survival which take hold as open-ended assemblages of diverse actants. Indecision, as Clément suggests, makes a vital contribution to keeping the ground fertile for biological invention, for biopoetical emergence, affording more generative ways of "working with." This is clearly a challenge to hegemonic views that understand nature as passive and separate, and decisiveness as a sign of knowing what to do. Rather, indecision is positioned as what gives way to "careful observation" of natural habitats, which for Clément allows for finding ways of acting in collaboration with living things.[90]

Clément's third landscape or planetary garden is a biopoetical story that tells of possible ways of cohabiting disturbed ecologies—to recognize the emergent assemblages that gesture toward collaborative survival today. To my ear, such a story also engenders a certain approach toward knowledge practices attuned to noticing the ground under the feet—to take up a position of the careful observer, a listening-walker. In considering Clément's model of the planetary garden, as one founded on indecision, I'm tempted to hear in such an approach an emphasis on thinking rather than knowing. Following Hannah Arendt's arguments in *The Life of the Mind*, the *will to know* may be understood to obfuscate the contemplative act of thinking which opens onto more meditative processes.[91] In contrast to a will to know, which underpins a model of science, thinking is aligned with art, and as Arendt underscores is conducive to reflection; shifting from the search for truth, thinking instead searches for meaning and opens onto curiosity, awareness, *listening*. While knowing is useful, its ability to bring meaning to our experiences is limited. It is by way of thinking, and its connection to art (which is cast as useless), that meaningful connections with the world are to be found, nurtured, lived. Thinking tends toward wisdom rather than truth.[92]

It is by way of such perspectives that planetary gardening may be seen to figure a relation to knowledge practices aligned with thinking and that center themselves around contemplation, and being a careful observer. This suggests an approach that gives way to the cultivation of reflection, experience, and

---

[90] Clément, *"The Planetary Garden" and Other Writings*, 47.
[91] Hannah Arendt, *The Life of the Mind* (New York: Harcourt, 1978).
[92] Ibid., 15.

208 *Poetics of Listening*

the nurturing of meaningful connections. And which I sense as reflective of listening—an art of noticing that is more along the lines of gathering, collecting, and preserving, as opposed to controlling, producing, and progressing underpinning dominant practices.

↬

Moving along these rather indecisive lines, lines that are never straight but meander by way of thinking, a listening-writing that stays attuned to the ground in order to keep meaningful, to keep useless, I want to close these reflections with a poetic image. In contrast to a will to know shaping dominant practices, I'm urged to follow the idea of a *will to listen* as a counternarrative, a counterparadigm: a will to listen as what may come to aid in elaborating ecological thinking in all its situated, pluriversal wisdom. And which may help intervene within systems that work at mastering nature in the name of progress.

This finds further support in Arendt's reference to thinking as a capacity that may *ground* a life of action. Following her work *Eichmann in Jerusalem: A Report on the Banality of Evil*, which focuses on the trial of Adolf Eichmann, a Nazi official and central organizer of the Holocaust, Arendt speculatively posits the question: Could the activity of thinking be among the conditions that make one abstain from acts of evil-doing, or even "condition against it"? Eichmann's *thoughtlessness*, Arendt reflects, may account for his horrific actions. These are perspectives that return to philosophical traditions which position contemplation over action, in which "thinking aims at and ends in contemplation, and contemplation is not an activity but a passivity."[93] Accordingly, the passivity of thinking, as what gives way to contemplation and, by extension, art and wisdom, keeps one close to the ground of a living world; it positions one as a careful observer, a modest guest, and aligns readily with a grammar of animacy (art and wisdom are grounded in the recognition that all matter is alive). These are perspectives greatly attuned to a poetics of listening. In following Arendt's propositions, I'm tempted to contour the idea of "passivity" with "receptivity," recognizing in thinking a listening approach—a way of receiving that holds, gathers, attends, cares, that is active *in its ability to observe and work-with*. Noticing, thinking, listening—as what supports learning the lessons of the ground, that follows the land and the wind as sources of meaning, and that tends toward an ecology of attention—come to suggest that underpinning a planetary way of being is the indecisive art of contemplation.

[93] Ibid., 6.

Postface: The Will to Listen

I have been pursuing a range of perspectives on the topic of listening, aiming to trace its many sides and dimensions, as well as to delve into the transformative work it conducts. This has included reflecting upon the ways in which listening contributes to a care of the self and a care of others, giving way to self-knowledge and ethical know-how; how it supports bodily awareness, contributing to how we may attend to the hurt and vitality of our bodies—to listen for *the story of your body*. In addition, I've tried to identify listening's role in struggles for recognition, how it fosters community and practices of reciprocity, and how it participates in political work and enacting change—to intervene within situations of conflict and violence. To listen functions as a methodology for peace-building, restorative processes, for truth-telling and its reconciliatory potential. Listening, in short, *as* medicine. This has included a concern for coexistence and a planetary way of being, and how listening invites an ecological orientation. Listening opens us to others in ways that challenge human exceptionalism. In doing so, I find in listening a critical means for challenging dominant systems that do much to damage environments and lives, and which affords greater acknowledgment and sensitivity for a world of many worlds—a position reflective of a *will to listen*.

As my interest has been to follow listening as it influences and shapes individual lives and the life of social, political, and planetary worlds, I have moved across a range of literatures, disciplines, and studies, from sociology, anthropology, political theory to sound studies, neuroscience, literature, and ecology; from musicology, meditation, psychoanalysis to somatic therapies, nursing, poetry, and Indigenous studies, as well as art and education. This is reflective of a listening approach, in terms of gathering and collecting, giving room and finding connections, listening to and listening out for a multiplicity of voices and views. And by recognizing how listening is supportive of life in all its meaningfulness. Even as listening can be positioned and performed as part of mechanisms of control, from surveillance techniques to more abusive systems of political silencing, it is quite clearly giving something vital to our deepest needs. Yet, listening does also produce anxiety—at times, in certain environments, one may need to not listen in order to survive, to deal with the noise or the silence of a given situation. One may also grow anxious as one waits for a verdict, a decision, and one can also be greatly harmed by what listening reveals, makes available, induces, or imposes. There are a great many risks in listening—it can also be exhausting, especially if one is taking in stories of trauma, or tending to pain, or having to endure situations of violence or discriminatory speech. As I've tried to suggest, these are aspects of listening which are important to consider. And which are equally treated, challenged and worked through by listening itself—listening may hurt, but it also heals; it may lend to acts of control and abuse, and it may just as easily support and set free. Knowing when not to listen is expressive of listening.

These different sides to listening are fundamental to its story, its poetics: it is often oscillating between too much and too little, between pleasure and pain, between giving and taking; listening may lead to something I may not want to find or know, and it may give way to feelings of well-being, anchoring oneself in ways that are transformative, restorative. This tension or dynamic finds a particular articulation when turning to the broader definitions of the word "listen": to listen is to "pay attention" to a given sound as well as "to give heed" or "to obey"; in "paying attention" one is also expected to react, to follow. This is present in the expression "listen up," or even "you're not listening to me" which suggests one needs to abide, to turn but to also *give way* to another's needs or expectations. Listening suggests a following, a giving over of oneself, which oscillates between obedience and generosity, control and collaboration, and in doing so, is suggestive for a less polarizing understanding and position. In giving heed, for instance, one also gives room, allowing for things to be said and feelings to be acknowledged; in following one also learns, discovers, attunes in more nuanced ways; in paying attention one also supports, fosters empathy and trust. Obedience may also be about following one's feelings, being guided by what feels right, attending to what oneself or others need. To abide may also lead to acting in the service of a greater good, to feel a sense of duty for the well-being of others or for certain causes. These perspectives lend to thinking otherwise as to what constitutes agency. Listening as obeyance, as following, as giving heed emerges as the basis for mutual care, and an approach to agency grounded in radical receptivity—a form of hosting.[1] Moreover, listening

---

[1] Lisbeth Lipari, *Listening, Thinking, Being: Toward an Ethics of Attunement* (University Park: Pennsylvania State University Press, 2014), 102.

can be appreciated as a sensibility given to abide by the wisdom of the body which, as Silvia Federici shows, forms the basis for a connection with the earth, living in accordance with its natural laws and rhythms. These are understandings that lend to a vitalist position, finding in listening a means for seeing *the life in things*, and which expresses itself in the ability to give attention to the environment and its voices, so as to learn its languages—to abide by its grammar of animacy.

Following these perspectives has led to posing listening as poetic, as what inclines toward things in a sympathetic manner—that wields a language of connection—affording ways of knowing by way of the inside. Poetics proceeds by way of an art of noticing, which is a listening art—it is, as the poet Esther Vincent notes, a devotional form of attention.[2] Poetics is a way of feeling that moves across seen and unseen worlds, that knows of the pains and pleasures, the social struggles and joyous births. And that aids in finding the words when faced with challenging realities. From the stories of self and other, friends and strangers, of memories kept and passed down, and the stories of communities and social worlds, those that lift-up or call for change, and that give way to histories of families and nations, to the narratives found in books, records, documents, some archived and others withdrawn, erased or lost—as well as all the stories yet to be told, or the ones that honor the earth, found in songs of the wind, the roots—poetics is a knowledge of how things fit together. How to listen to all these stories, to listen in ways that pick up, hold, care for? That finds ways of noticing as well as questioning, that close around particular perspectives only to keep open as well? And that may allow us to pause, at times, letting go of all they hold so as to tell a different story, one of silence, of breath, of knowing when to listen differently, feeling when it's time to also end the story, to close the paragraph, to put it to rest.

---

[2] Esther Vincent, from an interview: https://singaporeunbound.org/blog/2021/8/31/art-is-esther-vincent (accessed July 2024).

Bibliography

Amaro, Ramon. *The Black Technical Object: On Machine Learning and the Aspiration of Black Being*. London: Sternberg Press, 2022.

Anzaldúa, Gloria. *Borderlands/La Frontera: The New Mestiza*. San Francisco: Aunt Lute Books, 2012.

Anzaldúa, Gloria. *Interviews/Entrevistas*, edited by AnaLouise Keating. New York: Routledge, 2000.

Attali, Jacques. *Noise: The Political Economy of Music*. Minneapolis: University of Minnesota Press, 1985.

Bachelard, Gaston. *The Poetics of Reverie: Childhood, Language, and the Cosmos*. Boston: Beacon Press, 1971.

Baker, Willa Blythe. *The Wakeful Body: Somatic Mindfulness as a Path to Freedom*. Boulder, CO: Shambhala, 2021.

Bangstad, Sindre, and Torbjørn Tumyr Nilsen. "Thoughts on the Planetary: An Interview with Achille Mbembe." In *Radical Sympathy*, edited by Brandon LaBelle, 71–96. Berlin: Errant Bodies Press, 2022.

Bassel, Leah. *The Politics of Listening: Possibilities and Challenges for Democratic Life*. London: Palgrave, 2017.

Becker, Judith. *Deep Listeners: Music, Emotion, and Trancing*. Bloomington: Indiana University Press, 2004.

Benjamin, Jessica. *Beyond Doer and Done To: Recognition Theory, Intersubjectivity and the Third*. New York: Routledge, 2018.

Bennett, Jane. *Influx and Efflux: Writing Up with Walt Whitman*. Durham, NC: Duke University Press, 2020.

Bennett, Jane. *The Enchantment of Modern Life: Attachments, Crossings, and Ethics*. Princeton: Princeton University Press, 2001.

Berardi, Franco "Bifo." *The Uprising: On Poetry and Finance*. Los Angeles: semiotext(e), 2012.

Bhabha, Homi K. *The Location of Culture*. London: Routledge, 1994.

Bickford, Susan. *The Dissonance of Democracy: Listening, Conflict, and Citizenship*. Ithaca, NY: Cornell University Press, 1996.

Black Audio Film Collective, *Mothership Connection* (Directed by John Akomfrah, 1995).

Blaser, Mario, and Marisol de la Cadena. "Pluriverse: Proposals for a World of Many Worlds." In *A World of Many Worlds*, edited by Mario Blaser and Marisol de la Cadena, 1–22. Durham, NC: Duke University Press, 2018.

Bohm, David. *On Dialogue*. London: Routledge, 1996.

brown, adrienne maree. *Emergent Strategy: Shaping Change, Changing Worlds*. Chico, CA: AK Press, 2017.

Brown, Wendy. "Neoliberalized Knowledge." *History of the Present*, vol. 1, no. 1 (Summer 2011): 113–29.

Burton, Mary Ingouville. *The Truth and Reconciliation Commission*. Auckland Park: Jacana Media, 2021.

Calder, Gideon. "Listening, Democracy and the Environment." *In-Spire Journal of Law, Politics and Societies*, vol. 4, no. 2 (2009): 26–41.

Casarino, Cesare, and Antonio Negri. *In Praise of the Common: A Conversation on Philosophy and Politics*. Minneapolis: University of Minnesota Press, 2008.

Cha, Theresa Hak Kyung. *Dictée*. Berkeley: Third Woman Press, 1995.

Citton, Yves. *The Ecology of Attention*. Cambridge: Polity Press, 2019.

Cixous, Hélène. "The Laugh of the Medusa." *Signs*, vol. 1, no. 4 (Summer 1976): 875–93.

Clément, Catherine. *Syncope: The Philosophy of Rapture*. Minneapolis: University of Minnesota Press, 1994.

Clément, Gilles. *"The Planetary Garden" and Other Writings*. Philadelphia: University of Pennsylvania Press, 2015.

Code, Lorraine. *Ecological Thinking: The Politics of Epistemic Location*. Oxford: Oxford University Press, 2006.

Connor, Steven. "The Modern 'Auditory I.'" In *Rewriting The Self: Histories from the Renaissance to the Present*, edited by Roy Porter, 203–23. London: Routledge, 1997.

Connor, Steven. "Writing the White Voice." A talk given at the Sound, Silence and the Arts Symposium, Nanyang Technological University, Singapore, February 28, 2009. Accessed July 23, 2024. http://stevenconnor.com/whitevoice.html.

Coulthard, Glen Sean. *Red Skin, White Masks: Rejecting the Colonial Politics of Recognition*. Minneapolis: University of Minnesota Press, 2014.

Cullinan, Cormac. *Wild Law: A Manifesto for Earth Justice*, second edition. Cambridge: Green Books, 2011.

Damasio, Antonio. *Feeling and Knowing: Making Minds Conscious*. New York: Pantheon Books, 2023.

Dana, Deb. *Anchored: How to Befriend Your Nervous System Using Polyvagal Theory*. Boulder, CO: Sounds True, 2021.

Daughtry, J. Martin. *Listening to War: Sound, Music, Trauma and Survival in Wartime Iraq*. Oxford: Oxford University Press, 2015.

Davis, Megan, and George Williams. *Everything You Need to Know about the Voice*. Sydney: UNSW Press, 2023.

Davis, Megan. "Self-Determination and the Right to Be Heard." In *A Rightful Place: A Road Map to Recognition*, edited by Shireen Morris, 119–46. Carlton, VIC: Black, 2017.

Bibliography

de Quincey, Tess. "Body Weather—Dance in Practice." Accessed July 20, 2024. https://dequinceyco.net/archive/articles/.

de Quincey, Tess. "Thinking through Dance—Dancing through Thought." Sydney Seminar for the Arts and Philosophy: Ideas in Movement—about Dance, May 22, 2005. Accessed July 20, 2024. https://dequinceyco.net/archive/articles/.

Dobson, Andrew. *Listening for Democracy: Recognition, Representation, Reconciliation.* Oxford: Oxford University Press, 2014.

Dragičević, Nina. *Auditory Poverty and Its Discontents.* Berlin: Errant Bodies Press, 2024.

Dreher, Tanja, and Anshuman A. Mondal (eds.). *Ethical Responsiveness and the Politics of Difference.* London: Palgrave Macmillan, 2018.

Ernst-Berendt, Joachim. *The Third Ear: On Listening to the World.* New York: Owl Book, 1992.

Fanon, Frantz. *Black Skin, White Masks.* New York: Grove Press, 2008.

Farinati, Lucia, and Claudia Firth. *The Force of Listening.* Berlin: Errant Bodies Press, 2017.

Farmer, Frank. *After the Public Turn: Composition, Counterpublics, and the Citizen Bricoleur.* Boulder, CO: Utah State University Press, 2013.

Fassin, Didier. *Life: A Critical User's Manual.* Cambridge: Polity Press, 2019.

Federici, Silvia. *Beyond the Periphery of the Skin: Rethinking, Remaking, and Reclaiming the Body in Contemporary Capitalism.* Oakland: PM Press, 2020.

Fiumara, Gemma Corradi. *The Metaphoric Process: Connections between Language and Life.* London: Routledge, 1995.

Fiumara, Gemma Corradi. *The Other Side of Language: A Philosophy of Listening.* London: Routledge, 1990.

Follestad, Berit, and Nina Wroldsen. *Using Restorative Circles in Schools: How to Build Strong Learning Communities and Foster Student Wellbeing.* London: Jessica Kingsley, 2019.

Foucault, Michel. "The Hermeneutic of the Subject." In *Ethics: Subjectivity and Truth*, edited by Paul Rabinow, 93–106. London: Penguin, 2000.

Foucault, Michel. *Politics, Philosophy, Culture: Interviews and Other Writings of Michel Foucault.* New York: Routledge, 1990.

Foucault, Michel. "Technologies of the Self." In *Ethics: Subjectivity and Truth*, edited by Paul Rabinow, 223–51. London: Penguin, 2000.

Freeman, Damien and Nicola Hunter. "When Two Rivers Become One." In *A Rightful Place: A Road Map to Recognition*, edited by Shireen Morris, 173–94. Carlton, VIC: Black, 2017.

Freud, Sigmund. "A Note on the Unconscious in Psychoanalysis." In *The Complete Psychological Works of Sigmund Freud*, vol. 12, edited by James Strachey, 260–6. London: Penguin Books, 2001.

Freud, Sigmund. *Civilization and Its Discontents.* London: Penguin Classics, 2002.

Ghosh, Amitav. *The Nutmeg's Curse: Parables for a Planet in Crisis*. London: John Murray, 2022.

Gilman-Opalsky, Richard. *The Communism of Love: An Inquiry into the Poverty of Exchange Value*. Chico, CA: AK Press, 2020.

Glenn, Cheryl. *Unspoken: A Rhetoric of Silence*. Carbondale: Southern Illinois University Press, 2004.

Gobodo-Madikizela, Pumla. *A Human Being Died That Night: A South African Woman Confronts the Legacy of Apartheid*. Boston: Mariner Books, 2004.

Griffin, Fred L. *Creative Listening and the Psychoanalytic Process: Sensibility, Engagement and Envisioning*. London: Routledge, 2016.

Hanisch, Carol. "The Personal Is Political." In *Notes from the Second Year: Radical Feminism*, edited by Shulamith Firestone and Anne Koedt, 76–7. New York: Notes from the Second Year, 1970.

Harjo, Joy. *Catching the Light*. New Haven: Yale University Press, 2022.

Harjo, Joy. *Poet Warrior: A Memoir*. New York: W. W. Norton, 2021.

Hartman, Saidiya. *Wayward Lives, Beautiful Experiments: Intimate Histories of Riotous Black Girls, Troublesome Women and Queer Radicals*. London: Serpent's Tail, 2021.

Haskell, David George. *Sounds Wild and Broken*. London: Faber & Faber, 2022.

Hilal, Sandi, and Alessandro Petti (DAAR). "Tree Schools: In Conversation with WHW." In *Artistic Ecologies: New Compasses and Tools*, edited by Pablo Martínez, Emily Pethick, and What, How & For Whom/WHW, 54–91. London: Sternberg Press, 2022.

Honneth, Axel. *The Struggle for Recognition: The Moral Grammar of Social Conflicts*. Cambridge: Polity Press, 1996.

hooks, bell. "Love as the Practice of Freedom." In *Outlaw Culture: Resisting Representations*, 243–50. New York: Routledge, 1994.

Irigaray, Luce. *The Way of Love*. London: Continuum, 2004.

Kagan, Paula N. "Feeling Listened To: A Lived Experience of Humanbecoming." *Nursing Science Quarterly*, vol. 21, no. 1 (January 2008): 59–67.

Khodyreva, Anastasia (A), with Taru Elfving, Yvonne Billimore, Jaana Laakkonen, Anu Pasanen, Nina Vurdelja, and Kari Yli-Annala. "Attempts at Spectral Listening." *The Listening Biennial* website, accessed July 23, 2024. https://listeningbiennial.net/dis courses/attempts-in-spectral-listening.

Kimmerer, Robin Wall. *Braiding Sweetgrass: Indigenous Wisdom, Scientific Knowledge and the Teachings of Plants*. London: Penguin Books, 2020.

Konturri, Katve-Kaisa. *Ways of Following: Art, Materiality, Collaboration*. London: Open Humanities Press, 2018.

Koskinen, Camilla A-L, and Unni Ä. Lindström. "An Envisioning about the Caring in Listening." *Scandinavian Journal of Caring Sciences*, vol, 29, no. 3 (September 2015): 548–54.

Krasny, Elke. "On Care and Citizenship: Performing Healing (in) the Museum." *Passepartout—New Infrastructures*, no. 40 (2020): 3–28.

Krause, Bernie. *The Great Animal Orchestra: Finding the Origins of Music in the World's Wild Places*. New York: Back Bay Books, 2013.

Köttering, Martin, and Sabine Boshamer (eds.). *The Controversy over Documenta Fifteen: Background, Interpretation, and Analysis*. Hamburg: Materialverlag HFBK, 2023.

LaBelle, Brandon. *Acoustic Justice: Listening, Performativity, and the Work of Reorientation*. New York: Bloomsbury Academic, 2021.

Lacan, Jacques. *Écrits: The First Complete Edition in English*. New York: W. W. Norton, 2007.

Laub, Dori. "Bearing Witness, or the Vicissitudes of Listening," in *Testimony: Crises of Witnessing in Literature, Psychoanalysis, and History*, edited by Shoshana Felman and Dori Laub, 57–74. New York: Routledge, 1992.

Lipari, Lisbeth. *Listening, Thinking, Being: Toward an Ethics of Attunement*. University Park: Pennsylvania State University Press, 2014.

Lispector, Clarice. *Água Viva*. New York: New Directions, 2012.

Lloyd, Justine. "The Listening Cure." *Continuum: Journal of Media and Cultural Studies*, vol. 23, no. 4 (August 2009): 477–87.

Longmire, Warren C. "Odd Futures: How Hip Hop Defined Post-Modernism." In *Black Quantum Futurism: Theory and Practice*, vol. 1, edited by Rasheedah Phillips, 61–72. Philadelphia: Afrofuturist Affair/House of Future Sciences, 2015.

López, María del Rosario Acosta. "From Aesthetics as Critique to Grammars of Listening: On Reconfiguring Sensibility as a Political Task." *Journal of World Philosophies* 6 (Summer 2021): 139–56.

Lunz, Kristina. *The Future of Foreign Policy is Feminist*. Cambridge: Polity Press, 2023.

Maathai, Wangari. *The World We Once Lived In*. London: Penguin Books, 2021.

Macnamara, Jim. *Creating an 'Architecture of Listening' in Organizations: The Basis of Engagement, Trust, Healthy Democracy, Social Equity, and Business Sustainability*. Sydney, NSW: University of Technology Sydney, 2015.

Marya, Rupa, and Raj Patel. *Inflamed: Deep Medicine and the Anatomy of Injustice*. London: Penguin Books, 2022.

Mayor (Mayo), Thomas. *Finding the Heart of the Nation: The Journey of the Uluru Statement from the Heart Continues*. Richmond, Victoria: Hardie Grant Explore, 2022.

Mbembe, Achille. *Necropolitics*. Durham, NC: Duke University Press, 2019.

Mead, George Herbert. *Mind, Self and Society: The Definitive Edition*. Chicago: University of Chicago Press, 2015.

Mindell, Arnold. *The Deep Democracy of Open Forums: Political Steps to Conflict Prevention and Resolution for the Family, Workplace, and World*. Charlottesville, VA: Hampton Roads, 2002.

Mlodinow, Leonard. *Emotional: The New Thinking about Feelings*. London: Penguin Books, 2023.

Moten, Fred. "Hesitant Sociology: Blackness and Poetry," filmed spring 2016, University of Chicago, accessed July 23, 2024. https://www.youtube.com/watch?v=J5Zw uq898AY

Nancy, Jean-Luc. *Listening*. New York: Fordham University Press, 2007.

Navaro, Yael. "The Aftermath of Mass Violence: A Negative Methodology." *Annual Review of Anthropology*, vol. 49 (2020): 161–73.

Ngarm, Soth Plai. *Listening Methodology: Application of a Peacebuilding Research*. Siem Reap City, Cambodia: Center for Peace and Conflict Studies, 2022.

Oliveros, Pauline. *Quantum Listening*. London: Ignota Books, 2021.

O'Neil, Cathy. *Weapons of Math Destruction: How Big Data Increases Inequality and Threatens Democracy*. London: Penguin Books, 2017.

Papaeti, Anna. "On Music, Torture and Detention: Reflections on Issues of Research and Discipline." *Transposition*, Hors-série 2 (2020): 1–18.

Parker, James E. K. *Acoustic Jurisprudence: Listening to the Trial of Simon Bikindi*. Oxford: Oxford University Press, 2015.

Parker, James E. K., and Sean Dockray. "'All Possible Sounds': Speech, Music, and the Emergence of Machine Listening." *Sound Studies*, vol. 9, no. 2 (2023): 253–81.

Parks, Elizabeth S. *The Ethics of Listening: Creating Space for Sustainable Dialogue*. Lanham: Lexington Books, 2019.

Pearson, Noel. "A Rightful Place." In *A Rightful Place: A Road Map to Recognition*, edited by Shireen Morris, 5–117. Carlton, VIC: Black, 2017.

Pétrement, Simone. *Simone Weil: A Life*. New York: Pantheon Books, 1976.

Philip, M. NourbeSe. *Zong!* Middleton, CT: Wesleyan University Press, 2008.

Provan, Anna. "Centre for Feminist Foreign Policy." *Free Berlin*, no. 9 (April 2021): 8–13.

Raffo, Susan. *Liberated to the Bone: Histories, Bodies, Futures*. Chico, CA: AK Press, 2022.

Rancière, Jacques. *The Politics of Aesthetics: The Distribution of the Sensible*. New York: Bloomsbury, 2013.

Ratcliffe, Krista, and Kyle Jensen. *Rhetorical Listening in Action: A Concept-Tactic Approach*. Anderson, SC: Parlor Press, 2022.

Reik, Theodor. *Listening with the Third Ear: The Inner Experience of a Psychoanalyst*. New York: Farrar, Straus, 1949.

Robinson, Dylan. *Hungry Listening: Resonant Theory for Indigenous Sound Studies*. Minneapolis: University of Minnesota Press, 2020.

Rosenberg, Marshall B. *Nonviolent Communication: A Language of Life*. Encinitas, CA: Puddle Dancer Press, 2003.

Safa, Mhamad. "Reverberations and Post-War Trauma: The Sustained Aftermath of Aerial Strikes on Lebanon in 2006." *Sound Studies*, vol. 8, no. 1 (2022): 73–99.

Bibliography

Safa, Mhamad. "Collateral Listening: Towards an Acoustemology of Shockwaves." In *The Listening Biennial Reader*, vol. 2, edited by Rebecca Collins and Brandon LaBelle. Berlin: Errant Bodies Press, forthcoming.

Santos, Boaventura de Sousa. "A New Vision of Europe: Learning from the Global South." In *Demodiversity: Towards Post-Abyssal Democracies*, edited by Boaventura de Sousa Santos and José Manuel Mendes, 31–53. New York: Routledge, 2021.

Schäfers, Marlene. *Voices That Matter: Kurdish Women at the Limits of Representation in Contemporary Turkey*. Chicago: University of Chicago Press, 2023.

Scudder, Mary F. *Beyond Empathy and Inclusion: The Challenge of Listening in Democratic Deliberation*. Oxford: Oxford University Press, 2023.

Shah, Rajni. *Experiments in Listening*. Lanham, MD: Rowman & Littlefield, 2021.

Shiao-Yin, Kuik. *The Power of a People*. Singapore: Epigram Books, 2019.

Shipley, Sheila D. "Listening: A Concept Analysis." *Nursing Forum,* vol. 45, no. 2 (April–June 2010): 125–34.

Siisiäinen, Lauri. *Foucault and the Politics of Hearing*. London: Routledge, 2013.

Simpson, Leanne Betasamonsake, and Kite. "Discussion with Leanne Betasamonsake Simpson." *Ear, Wave, Event*, no. 7 (Spring 2023): 1–8.

Singh, Julietta. *No Archive Will Restore You*. Goleta, CA: 3Ecologies Books/Immediations, 2018.

Snyder, Gary. *The Practice of the Wild: Essays*. Berkeley: Counterpoint, 2020.

Sowards, Stacey K., and Valerie R. Renegar. "The Rhetorical Functions of Consciousness-Raising in Third Wave Feminism." *Communications Studies*, vol. 55, no. 4 (Winter 2004): 535–52.

Spahr, Juliana. *Everybody's Autonomy: Connective Reading and Collective Identity*. Tuscaloosa: University of Alabama Press, 2001.

Stauffer, Jill. *Ethical Loneliness: The Injustice of Not Being Heard*. New York: Columbia University Press, 2018.

Stavrides, Stavros. *Towards the City of Thresholds*. Brooklyn, NY: Common Notions, 2019.

Stengers, Isabelle. "We Are Divided." *e-flux journal,* no. 114 (December 2020): 1–5.

Sundar, Pavitra. *Listening with a Feminist Ear: Soundwork in Bombay Cinema*. Ann Arbor: University of Michigan Press, 2023.

Taylor, James S. *Poetic Knowledge: The Recovery of Education*. Albany, NY: State University of New York Press, 1998.

Teich, Michael. "AI Voice Cloning—and Its Misuse—has Opened a Pandora's Box of Legal Issues: Here's What to Know." August 9, 2023, *ipwatchdog*, accessed July 20, 2024. https://ipwatchdog.com/2023/08/09/ai-voice-cloning-misuse-opened-pando ras-box-legal-issues-heres-know/id=163859/#.

Toufic, Jalal. *The Withdrawal of Tradition Past a Surpassing Disaster*, 2009, accessed July 23, 2024. https://jalaltoufic.com/downloads Jalal_Toufic,_The_Withdrawal_of_ Tradition_Past_a_Surpassing_Disaster.pdf.

Tsing, Anna Lowenhaupt. *The Mushroom at the End of the World: On the Possibility of Life in Capitalist Ruins*. Princeton: Princeton University Press, 2015.

van der Kolk, Bessel. *The Body Keeps the Score: Mind, Brain and Body in the Transformation of Trauma*. London: Penguin Books, 2015.

van der Wal, Eeke. "Dragon NaturallySpeaking: Being Listened To and the Subservience of Speech." *Soapbox: Practices of Listening*, vol. 1, no. 1 (Fall 2018): 41–63.

Varela, Francisco. *Ethical Know-How: Action, Wisdom, and Cognition*. Redwood City, CA: Stanford University Press, 1999.

Vélez, David. "Listening with Plants: Contesting Coloniality in Sonic Art Collaboration with Vegetal Life." Paper presented at Soundings: Assemblies of Listenings and Voices across the Souths, Berlin, August 2022.

Villarosa, Linda. *Under the Skin: The Hidden Toll of Racism on Health in America*. New York: Anchor Books, 2022.

Vrbančić, Mario. *The Lacanian Thing: Psychoanalysis, Postmodern Culture, and Cinema*. Amherst, NY: Cambria Press, 2011.

Waks, Leonard. "Listening and Questioning: The Apophatic/Cataphatic Distinction Revisited." *Learning Inquiry*, vol. 1, no. 2 (August 2007): 153–61.

Watson, Christie. *The Language of Kindness: A Nurse's Story*. London: Vintage, 2018.

Weber, Andreas. *Enlivenment: Toward a Poetics for the Anthropocene*. Cambridge, MA: MIT Press, 2019.

Wilson, Shawn. *Research Is Ceremony: Indigenous Research Methods*. Halifax & Winnipeg: Fernwood, 2008.

Williams, Marcellus "Bear Heart," with Molly Larkin. *The Wind Is My Mother: The Life and Teachings of a Native American Shaman*. New York: Berkley Books, 1996.

Winnicott, D. W. *Playing and Reality*. London: Routledge, 2005.

Zechner, Manuela. *Commoning Care and Collective Power*. Vienna: transversal texts, 2021.

Zehr, Howard. *The Little Book of Restorative Justice*. New York: Good Books, 2015.

Index

Abbott, Tony 75
Aboriginal and Torres Strait Islander
    Peoples 75, 79
acoustic 27
    dimension 22
    harmony 173
    imaginary 200
    information 199
    niche 173
    politics 200
    of the soul 122
    voice 173
affectional reciprocity 87
affective component 84
affective neuroscience 93, 114–15
affective potencies 56, 58–9, 73, 86
Afrofuturism 138 n.27
Al-Atabeh 192
Amaro, Ramon
    The Black Technical Object 134–9, 157
Anzaldúa, Gloria 10, 39–42, 44–5, 47, 49
    *Borderlands/La Frontera: The New
        Mestiza* 46
    *This Bridge Called My Back: Writings by
        Radical Women of Color* 46
apophatic listening 161
architectures of listening 168
archives 157, 165
Arendt, Hannah
    *Eichmann in Jerusalem: A Report on the
        Banality of Evil* 208
    The Life of the Mind 207
artificial intelligence (AI) 135, 137, 139
art of bricolage 138–9, 157
art of listening 19, 19 n.8, 26, 187
art of noticing 12, 109 n.45, 169, 172, 204,
    208, 211
Aspire Mirror 135
Attali, Jacques
    Noise: The Political Economy of Music
        131–2, 134, 139, 167

auditory I 30, 37, 188–9
awakened dreams 40–1, 45
"the Awareness Body" 101

Bachelard, Gaston 40, 109, 110
Baker, Willa Blythe 11, 103, 106, 109, 117
    The Wakeful Body 100–2
Bear Heart. *See* Williams, Marcellus
    "Bear Heart"
Becker, Judith 11
    "Trancing" 120–2
being heard/be heard 2, 10, 52, 61–2, 70,
    72, 81, 84, 86, 133, 134, 200–3
Benjamin, Jessica 10, 38, 66, 72 n.48, 74,
    81, 83, 84
    Beyond Doer and Done To 67–9,
        69 n.41–2
Bennett, Jane 11, 112–15, 117, 124
    Influx and Efflux 111
Berardi, Franco "Bifo" 55–6, 58
Bhabha, Homi K. 72 n.48
Billimore, Yvonne 184
bioacoustic research 177 n.18
biological invention 205, 207
biomechanic 131
biophonic vitality 173–8
biophony (Krause) 173
biopoetics 197–9
    biopoetical (Weber) 198–9, 205, 207
Blaser, Mario 12–13, 181–2
bodily grief 101
bodily power (Federici) 11, 93–103, 106,
    110, 112, 113, 118–25
Body Weather 123–4, 124 n.83
Bohm, David
    On Dialogue 56 n.11
brown, adrienne maree 160–3
Brown, Wendy 190–1
Buolamwini, Joy 135
Bustamante, Ariel 175 n.14, 176
    The Listening Biennial 175

222   *Index*

Cadena, Marisol de la 12–13, 181–2
Calder, Gideon 140, 141, 158
care of the self 9, 16–21, 19 n.8, 24–6, 28, 34, 37–9, 46–9
caring communion 103–10
Center for Feminist Foreign Policy (CFFP) 11, 151
Center for Peace and Conflict Studies 11, 142, 144
Cha, Theresa Hak Kyung 10, 47, 49
   Dictée 42–5
chamber music 24, 50
choosing to listen 88
chronology 119, 120
chronopolitical 120
circle keepers 149
Citton, Yves 171, 194–5, 205
Cixous, Hélene 126, 126 n.84
Clément, Catherine 11, 119–21, 127
Clément. Gilles 205–7
Code, Lorraine 12–13, 179, 186, 193
cognitive consonance 171
coherent narrative 155
collateral listening 3 n.1
colonial medicine 98
communism of love 88
concept-tactics 145
conductivity 4–5, 16
conflict resolution 131, 149, 167
connatural knowledge 109, 112, 126
Connor, Steven 17, 20, 206
   "auditory I" 30
   "The Modern Auditory I" 188
consciousness-raising (groups) 2, 10, 49
   listening-into 39–48
Constitutional Convention 75
contaminated diversity 169
co-ownership of an inner world, listening-into 48–50
cosmopoetical technique 31–7, 39, 45, 49
Coulthard, Glen Sean
   Red Skin, White Masks 78–9
courage to listen, listening-into 39–48
crisis of sensing 199
critical listening positionality 3 n.1, 19
Cullinan, Cormac 170
culture of death 196–7

Dakota Pipeline Protests (2017) 117
Damasio, Antonio 103–4, 114
Dana, Deb 98
dance 63, 66, 97, 119, 121, 123–7
Daughtry, J. Martin
   Listening to War: Sound, Music, Trauma and Survival in Wartime Iraq 3 n.1
Davis, Megan 79–80
Decolonizing Architecture Art Research (DAAR) 191–4
Deep Democracy (Mindell) 11–12, 130, 146–8, 150, 161
deepest knowing 116
deep listening as healing (Baker) 11
deep medicine 11, 14, 117
delirium 11, 119–21
democratize democracy 180
demodiversity 180, 183, 190
dengbejs 71
de-politicization 141
de Quincey, Tess 123–4, 124 n.83
de Sousa Santos, Boaventura 179
differentiating Third 68
diplomatic arts 162, 164, 166
diplomatic force 141, 148
disturbed ecologies 169
divine memory (wakeful body) 102, 111
Dobson, Andrew 129, 140–2, 154, 158, 166, 167
Dragičević, Nina
   Auditory Poverty and Its Discontents 61–2

"the Earth Body" 101
Earth Community 170
ear-witnessing 3 n.1
eavesdropping 147
ecofeminism 186
ecological poetics 13
ecological thinking 169–70, 180–1, 186–7, 189, 191–2, 197–8, 208
ecologies of memory 147
ecology of attention 171, 182, 193, 194–5, 208
ecology of learning 189–95
ecosophical framework 195
écriture féminine 126 n.84

Index

Eichmann, Adolf
  thoughtlessness 208
Elfving, Taru 184
embodied action 114
encounter-based collaboration 169
energetics of ethics 113, 115
energetic theories 114
enlivenment economies 197
environmental audio 174
environmental self 31, 34
epistemological work of listening 179–89
epistemologies of the South 179–80
Ernst-Berendt, Joachim
  The Third Ear: On Listening to the World
    176–7, 176 n.16
ethical know-how (Varela) 91, 114–15,
    123, 209
ethics of life 201
ethics of listening 2, 6, 7, 10, 13, 19 n.8, 26,
    51, 54, 59, 61, 66, 73, 77, 151, 178
evidentiary knowledge making 154

Fanon, Frantz 40
Farinati, Lucia 10
  The Force of Listening 46–7
Fassin, Didier 201
Federici, Silvia 11, 96, 98–100, 102, 105,
    110, 116, 118, 120, 125, 127, 211
  Beyond the Periphery of the Skin 93–4
feelings of interdependency 166, 170
feeling-thinking 103–10, 116, 124
feel interdependency 163
felt-consciousness 122
felt sense 96, 98, 102, 103, 105, 109–10,
    123, 126, 166
feminist foreign policy 151–3
feminist policies 148–53, 166
feminist security 152
feminization of politics 151
first knowledge 32, 109, 109 n.45, 112, 118
Firth, Claudia 10
  The Force of Listening 46–7
Fiumara, Gemma Corradi 86, 187, 189
  *The Metaphoric Process: Connections
    between Language and Life* 57–8
  *The Other Side of Language: A Philosophy
    of Listening* 4
Follestad, Berit 150, 150 n.51

force of listening 10, 148
Foucault, Michel 9, 18–19, 25, 29, 30, 40, 94
  on inner voice engaged in work of
    liberation 39
  *Politics, Philosophy, Culture: Interviews
    and Other Writings of Michel
    Foucault* 19 n.8
Freeman, Damien 84
Freud, Sigmund 20
  theories of unconscious 20–1 n.9

Ghosh, Amitav
  The Nutmeg's Curse 180, 180 n.26–7, 193
the gift 32, 33, 146, 161, 178, 199
Gilman-Opalsky, Richard 87–8
Global North 179
Gobodo-Madikizela, Pumla 83
grammar of animacy (Kimmerer) 8, 181,
    203, 208, 211, 1698
gravitational sympathy 112
Green, Esmin 97
Griffin, Fred L. 37
Guattari, Félix
  Three Ecologies 195

Hanisch, Carol
  "The Personal Is Political" 47
Haraway, Donna 186
Harjo, Joy 116–18, 126
Hartman, Saidiya 12, 155, 157, 165
Haskell, David George 199–200
  Sounds Wild and Broken 173–4, 176
healing justice (Raffo) 11, 95–9, 102, 105,
    110, 111, 113, 116, 117, 123
heart listening (Mayo) 1, 74–85
Hećimović, Nizama 61
Heidegger, Martin 187
Hilal, Sandi 191
hip-hop 138–9, 157
holding-listening 110
Honneth, Axel 86–8
  The Struggle for Recognition 52
hooks, bell 88
Hunter, Nicola 84
hybrid languages 105

the I 27–30, 50
identity category 147

Index

impossible listening, listening-into 18–31, 45
indecision 206–7, 206 n.88
indecisiveness 206 n.88, 207
inner auditorium 17, 20, 30
inner life 2, 9–10, 13, 15–17, 20, 33–9, 42, 44, 47–50, 132, 153
inner listening 9, 16–17, 20, 23–5, 31, 33–4, 37, 94
inner voice 23, 25, 26, 29–30, 33–4, 37–41, 47–9, 91, 93–4, 103, 165
    art of listening and 19 n.8
    care of the self 9
    listening-into 18–31
    of reasoning self 17
    as self-destructive 20
    social recognition and 10
interconnectedness 92, 106, 109 n.45, 111–13, 115, 117–18, 123, 177, 189, 196, 198, 204
intercultural democracy 180
interdependency (feelings of) 5, 151, 162–4, 166, 170, 183
intergenerational practices 100, 105
intersubjectivity 7, 10, 53, 67–8, 71–4, 81
inter-voice 30
intra-voice 30
Irigaray, Luce 7, 10, 188
    The Way of Love 53–6, 56 n.11, 57–66, 68–9, 71–2, 74, 77, 80, 86

Jensen, Kyle 12, 149, 157
    Rhetorical Listening in Action 144–5, 147

Kagan, Paula N. 107–8
keeping up 120
Khodyreva, Anastasia (A) 13 n.23, 184, 186
kilam 70–1
Kimmerer, Robin Wall 199, 203
    Braiding Sweetgrass 177–8, 181
    "grammar of animacy" 8
King, Martin Luther Jr. 88
Koskinen, Camilla A-L 107–8
Krasny, Elke
    "On Care and Citizenship" 96–7
Krause, Bernie 198–9
    The Great Animal Orchestra 173

Laakkonen, Jaana 184
Lacan, Jacques 20, 23, 30, 33 n.30, 37, 188
    formulation of subjectivity 22, 25
    psychoanalysis 33 n.30
    theorizations of subjectivity 21
    the Thing 22–6, 28–9, 30, 32, 33, 36, 37, 39, 50, 126, 195
language
    affective potencies of 56
    of the body 92, 109
    mathematization of 56
    relational function 58
    and voice 55–6
Laub, Dori 85–6
Lazaro, German
    The Listening Biennial 175
Leigh, Simone 96, 97, 113
    The Waiting Room 96–8
Leira, Johanne Thingnes 7, 108
the life in things 211
liminality (liminal community) 2, 4–5, 59, 60, 62, 72
Lindström, Unni Ä. 107–8
Lispector, Clarice 10, 29, 31, 33–4, 40, 48, 49, 50
    Água Viva 23, 24, 26
listen in 29, 77, 91, 130, 210, 211
listening
    ability to foster connection 6
    agents 133
    binary thinking and 5
    characteristics of 4–6
    citizenry 168
    compared with poetry 6
    conductive listening 4
    as cosmopoetical, listening-into 31–9
    as diplomatic force 140–8
    as emergent strategy 160–5
    empowering and controlling 3
    enacting otherwise 5
    imaginary 15
    institutions 131
    metonymically 147
    mindset 145
    as obeyance 210
    possessive and distributive nature of 5
    as radically receptive 2
    and recognition 51–2

risk and responsibility 4
and sensitivity 7
Listening Academy, The 194
listening-across 13, 14, 169–208
  biophonic vitality 173–8
  epistemological work of listening 179–89
  self-organized study as ecology of
    learning 189–95
  sounded creations 173–8
  sounding a livable life 195–204
  will to listen 204–8
  worlds within a world 179–89
listening activism 80
listening-against 11–12, 14, 129–68
  feminist policies 148–53
  listening as diplomatic force 140–8
  listening as emergent strategy 160–5
  machine listening 131–9
  negative listening 153–60
  power of listening 165–8
  restorative circles 148–53
  techniques of surveillance 131–9
The Listening Biennial 184, 194
listening-into 14, 15–50
  consciousness-raising 39–48
  co-ownership of an inner world 48–50
  courage to listen 39–48
  impossible listening 18–31
  inner voicing 18–31
  listening as cosmopoetical 31–9
  lost voices 39–48
listening out 141–2
listening project 143
listening to 1–3, 6, 9, 48, 53–4, 88, 93, 94,
    98–9, 102–3, 105, 133, 140, 152–3,
    158, 164–5, 169–70, 173, 175, 187,
    209, 210
listening-toward 10, 14, 51–89
  behavior and 53
  heart listening 74–85
  love of the world 85–9
  others as transformative 52
  third listening 66–73
  third voice 66–73
  Uluru Statement 74–85
listening-with 11, 14, 91–127
  to be body for others 118–25
  bodily power 93–103

caring communion 103–10
dance 125–7
feeling-thinking 103–10
sympathy 110–17
therapeutic work 93–103
trans-figuring bodily power 118–25
The Listening Zones of NGOs 143 n.36
living mind 174
logos 9, 18–19, 24–6, 31, 33, 34, 38, 49, 94
Longmire, Warren C.
  "Odd Futures: How Hip Hop Defined
    Post-Modernism" 138
lost voices, listening-into 39–48, 117
love of the world 85–9
Lunz, Kristina 153
Lyotard, Jean-Francois 188

machine learning 134–7, 139
machine listening 11, 131–9
Macnamara, Jim 168
Marya, Rupa 11, 13, 98–9
Mayor (Mayo), Thomas 80, 89
  Finding the Heart of the Nation 76, 77, 81
Mbembe, Achille 196–7
the Me 27–9, 50
Mead, George
  concept of gestures 27–8
meditation (Buddhism) 11, 97, 100, 101,
    102, 106, 117, 123, 125, 177
mestiza consciousness 40, 41, 44–6, 49
metaphor 59, 86
metaphorization 58
methodological pessimism 155, 159
micropolitics 152–3
Mindell, Arnold 130, 146–7, 149
mindfulness 100–2, 125
mixed identity 39–40
Mlodinow, Leonard 114
monolithic 179
moral Third 68
more-than-human 3, 8, 93, 111, 113, 160,
    169, 182, 183, 193–4, 197–8, 204, 206
Moten, Fred 7–8, 57
music 28–30
  within 38
  chamber 24, 50
  in enactments of torture 3 n.1
  inner 25–6

myths and 32
social 31
without melody 30

Nancy, Jean-Luc 16, 25–6, 31
  on omnidimensionality of the self 34
narrative restraint 155, 157
narratives of creation 174, 176, 184, 200
natural anticapitalism 197
Navaro, Yael 12, 154–5, 158, 164
necropolitics (Mbembe) 164, 196–8
necropower 197
negative listening 12, 153–60, 165
negative methodology 12, 154–5, 164
negative others 20, 33
neoliberal ideology 56
new listening 54, 64, 73, 74, 80
nonetheless speaks 22, 37
nonviolent communication 150, 150 n.51
Noongar, David 77, 79
norms of intelligibility 201

object of collective consultation 163
ocularcentric paradigm 188
Oliveros, Pauline 121
  on deep listening 107
ontology of visibility 194–5
opening out 141
opening up 123, 141, 160
othering 51

Papaeti, Anna 3 n.1
  "On Music, Torture and
    Detention: Reflections on Issues of
    Research and Discipline" 3 n.1
paradigm of life 2, 8, 14, 58, 110, 204
Parliament of Organisms Democracy
  202, 203
Pasanen, Anu 184
passivity 208
Patel, Raj 11, 13, 98–9
peace-building 11, 131, 142–4, 148, 151,
  165, 209
Pearson, Noel 79–80
personal development 187
Petti, Alessandro 191
Philip, M. NourbeSe 12
  Zong! 155–60, 165

planetary curriculum 197, 204
planetary practices 169, 171, 187, 189, 201
pluriversality 182
poethics 8
poeticization 6, 24
poetic knowledge 32, 109, 109 n.45, 110
poetic language 56, 57, 71, 118
poetic uprising 58–9
poetry 8, 33, 57, 96, 102, 111, 116–17,
  126, 190
  compared with listening 6
  in context of meditation 106
  language 109, 110
  living 105
  semiocapitalism 56
policies of enlivenment 198
policies of life 13, 197, 205
political listening 159, 164, 166
political violence 2, 8, 12, 83, 117, 154–5,
  159, 164
politics of listening 12, 46
power of listening 46, 107, 131, 165–8
practices of domination 99
primary relationships 87
Provan, Anna 151
psychoanalytic listening 7, 17, 20–1, 37, 39,
  67, 69 n.41
psycho-social effects 78

Raffo, Susan 11, 69 n.42, 102, 105–6, 109,
  111–13, 116–17, 170
  Liberated to the Bone 94–7
raising consciousness 9–10
Rancière, Jacques 65, 132
Ratcliffe, Krista 12
  Rhetorical Listening in Action 144, 145,
    147, 149, 157
readiness for action 115, 118, 125
receptivity 9, 13, 17, 108, 163–4, 166, 183,
  204, 208, 210
recognition 10
  affirmative processes of 53
  cultural logics and languages 16
  and listening 51–2
  mutual 13
reflection 9, 30, 50, 55, 81, 106, 125, 130,
  135, 142, 167, 178, 195–6, 207–8
  critical 16

on inner voice 25
personal 8
private 20
on social ritual 60
Reik, Theodor
  psychoanalytic work 7
  the third ear 7, 35–7
re-politicization 140–2, 148, 149, 168
research-based practices 191
responsiveness 2, 6, 32, 62, 113, 115, 120,
  129, 140, 154, 167, 178, 192
restorative circles 148–53
restorative justice 11–12, 149
rhetorical art 144
rhetorical listeners 145
rhetorical listening 144, 145–6, 157, 159
rhetorical problems 12, 144, 145
rhetorical situations 148, 157
rhetorical strategies 145
rhythmic Third 68–9
Robinson, Dylan 3 n.1, 84

Safa, Mhamad 3 n.1
Sands, Bobby 201
Sanni Yakuma ritual 121
Schäfers, Marlene 70–2
Scudder, Mary F. 142
self-determination 10, 25, 33, 41, 45, 47, 52,
  79, 80, 91
self-organized study, as ecology of
  learning 189–95
self-reflection 15, 19, 25–6, 30, 170
semantic mayhem 156, 157, 160
sensitivity 2, 5–6, 48, 55, 69, 92, 110, 115,
  120, 123
  affective 133
  for bodily hurt and need 11
  care and 27
  critical 51
  ecological 185
  environmental 175
  and listening 7
  for past 93
  poetic 14
  for unstated hauntings 164
Shadow-Beast 45
Shah, Rajni 64–5
Shakespeare, William

Hamlet 206 n.88
sharing of speech 7, 54–6, 58–9, 62, 63, 65,
  69–72, 74
Sherbany, Anna 47
Shiao-Yin, Kuik 141
Simpson, Leanne Betasamonsake 133
Singh, Julietta 165
situatedness 94, 114–15, 127, 145, 146, 167
Ska 138
slow violence 11, 95, 102, 106
Snyder, Gary
  etiquette of freedom 205
  The Practice of the Wild 172, 174
social labor 71–4, 81, 85–6
social movements 8, 59, 80, 86, 151, 162
social recognition 10
Soja, Edward 72 n.48
somatic listening 8, 11, 26, 123
sonic trauma 3 n.1
sonorant family 173
Śoqo Pawlu 175
sounded creations 173–8
sounding a livable life 195–204
speaking-with 10, 54, 55, 57, 59–60, 63–4,
  66, 71–2, 77, 86, 88
spectral listening 184, 185–6
Spectral Listening Group 204
split subject 20, 21 n.9, 31
Stauffer, Jill
  Ethical Loneliness 74
Stavrides, Stavros 59–60
Stengers, Isabelle
  "We Are Divided" 162, 163, 166
structured disagreement 142
"the Subtle Body" 101
Sundar, Pavitra 153
sympathetic 106
sympathetic knowing 112, 115
sympathetic knowledge 109–10, 117
sympathy 110–17
sympathy (currents of) 11
synchronization 153
syncope (Clément) 119–22

Tanaka, Min (Body Weather) 123–4,
  124 n.83
Taylor, James S. 7, 32, 109, 109 n.45, 110
techniques of surveillance 131–9

Thami paxś 175
therapeutic work 93–103
the Thing (Lacan) 22–6, 28–9, 30, 32, 33,
    36, 37, 39, 50
thick relationality 14, 179, 183, 186, 203–5
the Third 66–7
    differentiating Third 68
    moral Third 68
    rhythmic Third 68–9
the third ear (Reik) 7, 35–7
third listening 10, 66–73, 74, 77, 86
thirdness 7, 10, 67–74, 72 n.48, 81, 85,
    206
third-sphere 72, 72 n.48
third thing 65, 72
third voice 66–73
to be body for others 118–25
to hear 16, 29, 38, 52, 71, 103, 158, 160,
    176, 200, 203
Toufic, Jalal
    "surpassing disaster" 43
trance experience 11
trance ritual 11, 120–1
transfigural 120, 123, 126
trans-figuring bodily power 118–25
Tree School (DAAR) 191–4
Truth and Reconciliation Commission
    (TRC) 81–3
Tsing, Anna Lowenhaupt 12, 169, 179,
    204
    The Mushroom at the End of the World
    109 n.45, 172, 206
Tutu, Desmond 82

Uluru Statement from the Heart 10, 74–85

Universal Declaration of Organisms'
    Rights 202

van der Wal, Eeke 136–7
Varela, Francisco 114–15
Villarosa, Linda
    Under the Skin 95
Vincent, Esther 211
vitalist politics 180, 180 n.27
vitalist position 13–14, 198, 205, 211
vocal ecologies 70, 71
voice
    cloning 133–5
    crisis of 56 n.11
    and language 55–6
Vrbančić, Mario 22
Vurdelja, Nina 184
Vygotsky, Lev 72 n.48

Waks, Leonard 161
"Water Is Life" (song) 117
way of feeling 92
Weber, Andreas 13, 14, 195, 196–8, 200
Weil, Simone 87, 171
Williams, Marcellus "Bear Heart" 9,
    31–3, 48
will to listen 204–8, 209–11
Winnicott, D. W. 38
worlds within a world 179–89
Wroldsen, Nina 150, 150 n.51

Yli-Annala, Kari 184

Zechner, Manuela 151–3
Zehr, Howard 150

www.ingramcontent.com/pod-product-compliance
Ingram Content Group UK Ltd.
Pitfield, Milton Keynes, MK11 3LW, UK
UKHW021938110625
459525UK00005BA/26